IDEAL CODE, REAL WORLD

Ideal Code, Real World

*A Rule-consequentialist
Theory of Morality*

BRAD HOOKER

CLARENDON PRESS · OXFORD

OXFORD

UNIVERSITY PRESS

Great Clarendon Street, Oxford OX2 6DP

Oxford University Press is a department of the University of Oxford
It furthers the University's objective of excellence in research, scholarship,
and education by publishing worldwide in

Oxford New York

Athens Auckland Bangkok Bogotá Buenos Aires Calcutta
Cape Town Chennai Dar es Salaam Delhi Florence Hong Kong Istanbul
Karachi Kuala Lumpur Madrid Melbourne Mexico City Mumbai
Nairobi Paris São Paulo Singapore Taipei Tokyo Toronto Warsaw

with associated companies in Berlin Ibadan

Oxford is a registered trade mark of Oxford University Press
in the UK and in certain other countries

Published in the United States
by Oxford University Press Inc., New York

British Library Cataloguing in Publication Data

Data available

Library of Congress Cataloging in Publication Data
Hooker, Brad, 1957–
Ideal code, real world: a rule-consequentialist theory of
morality / Brad Hooker
p. cm.
Includes bibliographical references and index.
1. Consequentialism (Ethics) 2. Rules (Philosophy) I. Title.
BJ1031 .H755 2000   171'.5—dc21   00–057113
ISBN 0-19-825069-X (hardcover : alk. paper)

1 3 5 7 9 10 8 6 4 2

Typeset by Invisible Ink
Printed in Great Britain
on acid-free paper by
Biddles Ltd.,
Guildford & King's Lynn

For my parents,
Henry and Alice Hooker

ACKNOWLEDGEMENTS

The generosity of many people are reflected in this book. For giving me helpful advice and encouragement time after time, I am deeply grateful to John Andrews, Robert Audi, Jamie Ball, Elaine Beadle, Tom Carson, Tim Chappell, John Cottingham, Garrett Cullity, Roger Crisp, Jonathan Dancy, Max de Gaynesford, Robert Frazier, Berys Gaut, James Griffin, John Heil, Keith Horton, Thomas Hurka, Hugh LaFollette, Andrew Leggett, David McNaughton, Dale E. Miller, Andrew Moore, Tim Mulgan, Mark Nelson, David Oderberg, Derek Parfit, Madison Powers, Michael Proudfoot, Eric Rakowski, Geoffrey Sayre-McCord, Michael Smith, Alan Thomas, Peter Vallentyne, and Jonathan Wolff.

Others who have given helpful comments on one part or another of the work in this book include Richard Brandt, David Brink, John Broome, Robert Card, Neil Cooper, Anthony Duff, Gerald Dworkin, Anthony Ellis, Alan Fuchs, Sam Fremantle, Ray Frey, Eve Garrard, Mark Greenberg, George Harris, Tsutomu Hoshino, Rosalind Hursthouse, Craig Ihara, Dale Jamieson, Noriaki Katagi, Paul Kelly, Dudley Knowles, Rahul Kumar, Iain Law, Margaret Little, Bob Lockie, Michael Lockwood, Penelope Mackie, Guy Marsh, Michael Martin (London), Michael Menlowe, Alan Miller, Eugene Mills, Phillip Montague, Christopher Morris, Adam Morton, Liam Murphy, Ingmar Persson, Gerald Postema, Peter Railton, Piers Rawling, Sophia Reibetanz, Jon Reynard, Howard Robinson, Gloria Rock, Tim Scanlon, William Shaw, John Skorupski, Peter Smith, Eldon Soifer, Timothy Sprigge, Martin Stone, Phillip Stratton-Lake, Makoto Suzuki, Richard Taylor, Bernard Williams, James Williams, and Nick Zangwill. There are probably other people my debts to whom should also have been listed. My apologies to them.

I received extremely helpful comments from anonymous reviewers for Oxford University Press, and from the copyeditor, Angela Blackburn.

A number of people have published pieces that criticize some of my earlier discussions of rule-consequentialism. I have learned a great deal from this work by Thomas Carson, Tim Mulgan, Richard Brandt, Philip Stratton-Lake, Berys Gaut, Alan Thomas, Phillip Montague, Dale E. Miller, Iain Law, and the teams of David McNaughton and Piers Rawling, and Philip Pettit and Michael Smith.

When I was a graduate student, R. M. Hare told me to read Richard Brandt's *A Theory of the Good and the Right*. I thought Brandt's rule-utilitarianism interesting but accepted the mainstream view that the theory could not survive the standard objections. Years later, Alan Fuchs advised me to reconsider whether Brandt's theory could survive these objections. That piece of advice led to this book.

My fascination with moral thought goes back much further—indeed as far back as I can remember. My parents, while acknowledging moral complexity, stressed morality's overwhelming importance. But they did not sugarcoat the message with the fib that being moral always pays. On the contrary, my parents openly acknowledged that moral projects are often trying. Raising a son fascinated by a subject at once so difficult and emotionally charged as moral philosophy served as a case in point.

Institutions helped fund my research. I thank Virginia Commonwealth University and the University of Reading for research leaves and grants. I also thank the National Endowment for the Humanities for a summer research grant in 1993, and the British Academy for funding for a research leave in 1996.

I have borrowed extensively from some of my published articles. I thank Oxford University Press, Edinburgh University Press, Blackwell Publishers, and the editors of *Mind, Proceedings of the Aristotelian Society, Utilitas, American Philosophical Quarterly, Analysis*, and *Pacific Philosophical Quarterly* for permission to use sentences, paragraphs, or whole sections from the following articles:

'Rule-consequentialism,' *Mind* 99 (1990), 67–77.

'Brink, Kagan, Utilitarianism and Self-sacrifice,' *Utilitas* 3 (1991), 263–73.

'Rule-consequentialism and Demandingness: A Reply to Carson,' *Mind* 100 (1991), 269–76.

'Is Rule-consequentialism a Rubber Duck?' *Analysis* 54 (1994), 92–7.

'Compromising with Convention,' *American Philosophical Quarterly* 31 (1994), 311–17.

'Rule-consequentialism, Incoherence, Fairness,' *Proceedings of the Aristotelian Society* 95 (1995), 19–35.

'Does Being Virtuous Constitute a Benefit to the Agent?' in R. Crisp, ed., *How Should One Live?* (Oxford: Clarendon Press, 1996), 141–55.

'Ross-Style Pluralism versus Rule-consequentialism,' *Mind* 106 (1996), 531–52.

'Rule-utilitarianism and Euthanasia,' in H. LaFollette, ed., *Ethics in Practice* (Oxford: Blackwell, 1997), 42–52.

'Reply to Stratton-Lake,' *Mind* 106 (1997), 759–60.

'Rule-consequentialism and Obligations to the Needy,' *Pacific Philosophical Quarterly* 79 (1998), 19–31.

'Rule-consequentialism,' in H. LaFollette (ed.), *The Blackwell Guide to Ethical Theory* (Oxford: Blackwell, 1999), 183–204.

'Impartiality, Predictability, and Indirect Consequentialism,' in R. Crisp and B. Hooker, eds., *Well-Being and Morality: Essays in Honour of James Griffin* (Oxford: Clarendon Press, 1999), 129–42.

'Reflective Equilibrium and Rule Consequentialism,' in B. Hooker, E. Mason, and D. Miller, eds., *Morality, Rules, and Consequences: A Critical Reader* (Edinburgh: Edinburgh University Press, 2000), 222–38.

CONTENTS

I
Introduction

1.1 RULE-CONSEQUENTIALISM

Shouldn't we try to live by the moral code whose communal acceptance would, as far as we can tell, have the best consequences? Isn't the code best suited for internalization by humanity the one we should try to follow? If the consequences of everyone's feeling morally free to do a given kind of act would be better than the consequences of everyone's not feeling free to do it, how can acts of this kind be wrong?

These questions picture morality as ideally a collective enterprise, a practice to be shared. A moral code, or at least the most basic moral code, should be internalized and followed by everyone, not just by you or by me or by any mere sub-group of the whole. As David Copp (1995: 112) holds, 'To subscribe to a moral code realistically, one must *desire* that it be the social moral code. That is, one must desire it to be socially enforced, culturally transmitted, and generally subscribed to as a moral code in one's society.'[1]

So, given that a moral code is for our collective internalization, what would an *ideal* code be like?

A number of different theories make moral permissibility turn on considerations about ideal codes.[2] This book focuses on just one such theory—rule-consequentialism. Rule-consequentialism evalu-

---

[1] Bernard Gert (1998: 9) writes, 'Anyone who takes the trouble to look at what is normally considered to be morality realizes that morality is best conceived as a guide to behaviour that rational persons put forward to govern the behaviour of others, whether or not they plan to follow that guide themselves.' Cf. discussion in Mackie 1977: 87, 152; 1985a: 178; and Blackburn 1998: 281.

[2] The term 'morally right' is systematically ambiguous as between 'morally required' and 'morally permissible'. Hence, I shall generally use the more useful terms 'morally required' or 'morally permissible' instead of 'morally right'. I assume what is morally required overall is also morally permissible overall. But what is permissible is not always required. Indeed, I shall usually use 'permissible' to mean 'permissible but not required'.

ates codes by their consequences. Rule-consequentialism holds that the code whose collective internalization has the best consequences is the ideal code. The collective internalization of a code amounts to the establishment of a shared conscience. Thus the theory *could* have come to be known as 'collective conscience consequentialism'. But the name that stuck was 'rule-consequentialism'. I shall stick with the name that stuck.

Some versions of rule-consequentialism claim an act is wrong if and only if forbidden by the code that would *actually* turn out to be ideal, even if no one could predict what the rules in this code would be. Other versions of the theory claim an act is wrong if and only if forbidden by the codes whose consequences have the greatest *expected* value.

By 'code with the greatest expected value', I mean, roughly, the code whose internalization could reasonably be expected to produce more aggregate value than could reasonably be expected to result from any other code. More exactly, the 'expected value' of a code is calculated as follows. Identify the possible outcomes of a code's internalization. Assess the value of each of these outcomes. For each possible outcome, assess the probability that that outcome would result from the code's internalization. Multiply the value (or disvalue) of each possible outcome by the probability of this possible outcome's coming about. Sum the products of the multiplication. This yields the expected value of the code.

I will illustrate with an example in which two codes are compared. The example is artificially simple in many ways. One way in which the example is artificial is that for each code there are only two possible outcomes. Another is that the values of the possible outcomes can be precisely quantified, and are known, as are the probabilities. Still, artificial simplicity has its uses. The example is set out in Table 1.1.

Normally, of course, there are many more than two possible outcomes of a code's internalization. We will normally lack precise estimates of the values and probabilities of possible outcomes. In fact, hardly ever is a 'calculation' of the expected value of a code going to have anything like mathematical precision. And yet we can judge that some codes are more promising than others without having to pretend to precision.

Making rough judgements about the expected values of code, we may find that there is more than one such code with unsurpassed

TABLE 1.1

	Value of possible outcome if it comes about	Probability of this possible outcome's coming about	Expected value of this possible outcome	Expected value for code
Code A {	10	.4	$10 \times .4 = 4$	$4 + 1.2 = 5.2$
	2	.6	$2 \times .6 = 1.2$	
Code B {	4	.8	$4 \times .8 = 3.2$	$3.2 + 1.8 = 5.0$
	9	.2	$9 \times .2 = 1.8$	

expected value. Rule-consequentialism needs to say which of these equally best codes should be followed. I shall argue later that, from the set of codes with unsurpassed expected value, the one we should follow is whichever is closest to the conventionally accepted code—that is, whatever is closest to the one already established in society.

Rule-consequentialism is not new.[3] Moreover, most contemporary moral philosophers classify it as 'tried and *un*true'. Although rule-consequentialism looked attractive to many philosophers in the 1950s and 60s, most contemporary philosophers think that the theory's appeal faded as objections to the theory multiplied.

I will show in this book that there is an attractive version of rule-consequentialism against which the usual objections will not work. Most discussions of rule-consequentialism never get beyond the usual objections. If I am right that there is an attractive version of the theory against which the usual objections will not work, then less common objections to the theory become very important. I discuss in this book many objections to rule-consequentialism. If the theory can plausibly answer all these objections, it has an enormous amount going for it.

[3] Berkeley 1712; Austin 1832; Urmson 1953; Harrison 1952/3; Brandt 1959, 1963, 1967, 1979, 1988, 1989, 1996; Hospers 1972; Harsanyi 1982, 1993; Barrow 1991: ch. 6; Haslett 1987, 1994: ch. 1, 2000; Attfield 1987: 103–12; Johnson 1991; Riley 1998, 2000; Shaw 1999.

1.2 METHODOLOGY

How should we assess moral theories?

(1) Moral theories must start from attractive general beliefs about morality.[4]

(2) Moral theories must be internally consistent.

(3) Moral theories must cohere with (i.e. economically systematize, or, if no system is available, at least endorse) the moral convictions we have after careful reflection.

(4) Moral theories should identify a fundamental principle that both (a) explains why our more specific considered moral convictions are correct and (b) justifies them from an impartial point of view.

(5) Moral theories should help us deal with moral questions about which we are not confident, or do not agree.

These five criteria would, I hope, seem commonsensical to most people. This is not to say that all these criteria are uncontentious in contemporary moral philosophy. Criteria (1) and (2) seem particularly unproblematic, but in the rest of this section I explain why I listed these criteria. Criteria (3), (4), and (5) are much more controversial among philosophers than (1) and (2) are. I defend (3), (4), and (5) in later sections.

I listed (1) because, even if a moral theory fulfilled perfectly the other four criteria, this theory would presumably be suspect if it offered a seemingly alien account of right and wrong. Certainly, if there were two rival theories that did equally well in terms of the other four criteria, but only one of these theories offered an account that starts from familiar and attractive ideas about morality, this theory would seem markedly superior.

Rule-consequentialism does offer an account of morality that taps into and develops familiar general beliefs about morality. I opened this book by invoking the general idea that we should try to live by the moral code whose communal acceptance would, as far as we can tell, have the best overall consequences, impartially considered. When wondering about the morality of some conduct, we ask,

---

[4] I am grateful to Dale Miller for discussion of this point.

'What would the consequences be if everyone felt free to do that?'
There is no denying the familiar appeal of this question. And there
is no denying that rule-consequentialism is a natural interpretation
of the question.

Note that the question is, 'What would the consequences be if
everyone *felt free* to do that?' This is not same as the question, 'What
would the consequences be if everyone *did* that?' Suppose I plan to
make all of my book purchases at the store on the corner of
Lexington and Fifth. If everyone did the very same thing, the consequences would be bad. At first, the store would be overrun. Then
all its competitors would be driven out of business. The store would
then have a monopoly. Its owners would gain but everyone else
would lose. What this illustrates is that choosing an act or line of
conduct can be morally permissible even when everyone's choosing
the same thing would have bad results. It is absurd to hold that, if
everyone's doing some kind of act would have bad consequences,
that kind of act must be morally wrong.

So return to the thought that an act is wrong if everyone's feeling
free to do it would have bad consequences. Everyone's feeling free to
buy their books at the shop on Lexington and Fifth would not have
bad consequences, because most people will not want to exercise this
freedom. Most people will prefer to buy their books closer to where
they live or work, or from a variety of different merchants.

As I have indicated, rule-consequentialism taps into and develops
the thought that an act is wrong if everyone's feeling free to do it
would have bad consequences—and this is a thought with familiar
appeal. However, we could *not* claim that rule-consequentialism is
the only theory to tap into and develop familiar and intuitively
attractive general ideas about morality. On the contrary, all rule-
consequentialism's leading rivals do this.

One of rule-consequentialism's rivals is act-utilitarianism. Act-
utilitarianism holds that an act is permissible if and only if no other
act open to the agent at the time had greater (actual or expected)
utility, utility being understood as aggregate well-being for sentient
creatures. Act-utilitarianism can be seen as emerging from the
initially appealing idea that a morally right act is one that impartially promotes what ultimately matters, namely, the well-being of sentient beings.

One of the most influential proponents of this view was Henry
Sidgwick. He pointed to 'the self-evident principle that the good of

any one individual is of no more importance, from the point of view (if I may say so) of the Universe, than the good of any other' (1907: 382). He went on: '[A]s a rational being I am bound to aim at good generally,—so far as it is attainable by my efforts,—not merely at a particular part of it.' (See also Brink 1989: 236.)

Another leading argument for act-utilitarianism is J. J. C. Smart's. Smart (1973: 7) represents act-utilitarianism as appealing to 'generalized benevolence—that is, the disposition to seek happiness, or at any rate, in some sense or other, good consequences, for all mankind, or perhaps for all sentient beings'. The dictates of any alternative view will at least sometimes prescribe 'avoidable' misery, or at least missed opportunities for benefit (Smart 1973: 5–6).

I shall later discuss this theory in considerable detail. The point I am making now, however, is merely that act-utilitarianism starts from intuitively appealing beliefs.

So does Hobbesian contractianism. This is the view that morality is a system of co-operative conventions for our mutual advantage.[5] Everyone is better off if everyone eschews attacking one another, stealing, breaking promises, and lying than if everyone engages in such forms of behaviour at will. While on a particular occasion a person might benefit from attacking others, or from stealing, etc., each person benefits more from everyone's accepting such restrictions than he or she would benefit if no one accepted them.

Any single individual would be better off being allowed to do whatever he or she wanted, given that everyone else would still have to abide by those restrictions.[6] But others will not agree to a rule

---

[5] Plato *Protagoras, Republic*; 369–72; Hobbes 1651, ch. 13; Buchanan 1975; Harman 1975, 1977, 1978; Gauthier 1986; Kavka 1986: pt. 1; Hampton 1986; and the discussions in Vallentyne 1991b. Cf. Toulmin 1950: 137; Strawson 1961: 1–17. For writers who seem more interested in explaining the evolution of (all or part of) extant moral views in terms of mutually beneficial conventions than in limiting morality to these conventions, see Hume 1740: bk. III, pt. ii; Warnock 1971: esp. pp. 16, 26, 72–3, 77, 149–50; Mackie 1977: ch. 5, 1978, 1982a; Ullmann-Margalit 1977; Axelrod 1984.

[6] As Hart (1961: 85) wrote, '[O]bligations and duties are thought of as characteristically involving sacrifice or renunciations, and the standing possibility of conflict between obligation or duty and interest is, in all societies, among the truisms of both the lawyer and the moralist.' Mackie (1977: 106), following Hobbes and Warnock, identifies 'narrow morality' as 'a system of a particular sort of constraints on conduct—ones whose central task is to protect the interests of persons other than the agent and which present themselves to an agent as checks on his natural inclinations or spontaneous tendencies to act'. Cf. Scanlon's conception of narrow morality as 'what we owe each other' (1998: 6, 171–7, 270–71).

exempting one person from restrictions that everyone else has to follow. Such an exemption for one person would obviously be unfair.

Yet, on a contractarian view, there are no moral reasons except the ones identified in a social contract. On the contractarian view, moral reasons do not pre-exist and limit what can appropriately be decided upon by the contractors. Thus, from a contractarian point of view, unfairness cannot be the reason everyone else would refuse to accept a contract exempting one person from the contract's restrictions.

The reason others would not accept such an exemption is, rather, that it reduces the protection they receive. Better to be protected against absolutely everyone than to have to worry about one person who feels free to be a murderer, thief, promise-breaker, liar, and so on.

Hobbesian contractarianism draws on an extremely appealing idea—that morality is a system of mutually beneficial co-operation. Reciprocity does seem to be a central moral idea, and it can be used to explain much of morality.

But it does not seem to be able to explain all of morality. As the standard joke has it, Hobbesian contractarianism *contracts* morality beyond plausibility. For there are some groups who cannot reciprocate whatever restraint we exercise toward them. Most of us believe that inflicting pain on lower animals to entertain ourselves is morally wrong, although there is no prospect of their internalizing moral norms. Since I shall have much more to say about this example later, let me switch to another one. People who live centuries after we do will not be able to reciprocate toward us the sacrifices we make for them. Yet we should not do things we know will probably later harm them (e.g. disposing of toxic waste in such a way that it will begin to leak out after a hundred years).

And what about the severely handicapped alive already? At least some of these human beings can't reciprocate the benefits we give them, and yet it would clearly be wrong to ignore their welfare. Another example of a group towards whom we have certain duties but who cannot benefit us in return may be the starving in the poorest countries. In short, the idea that morality is founded on mutual advantage seems inconsistent with the common assumption that one of morality's primary roles is to protect the weak and vulnerable from the strong.

Another kind of social contract theory starts from the idea of social agreement not for the sake of reciprocal advantage, but as expressing respect for the value of rational creatures. T. M. Scanlon, for example, writes,

The contractualist ideal of acting in accord with principles that others (similarly motivated) could not reasonably reject is meant to characterize the relation with others the value and appeal of which underlies our reasons to do what morality requires. This relation, much less personal than friendship, might be called a relation of mutual recognition. Standing in this relation to others is appealing in itself—worth seeking for its own sake. (1998: 162; see also 155, 181, 268)

Scanlonian contractualism develops from the idea that morality—or at least the central part of morality, which is concerned with what we owe each other—is identified with principles that could not be reasonably rejected by anyone seeking reasonable agreement on a moral code. I shall have much more to say later about Scanlon's influential and impressive theory.

Let me mention here just one more theory, and even more briefly than the previous one. An approach often called 'virtue ethics' grows from the thought that right and wrong actions can be understood only in terms of choices that a fully virtuous person would make.[7] Virtue ethics suggests that we thus take the nature of and rationale for the virtues as the primary focal points for our moral philosophy.

All the moral theories mentioned above (and others besides) arise from and develop more or less compelling general ideas about morality.[8] The conclusion to draw from this is simple. The fact that a theory arises from and develops attractive general ideas about morality is hardly enough to show that it is superior to all its rivals.

Now let me briefly explain why I mentioned that a moral theory must be internally consistent—that is, criterion (2). Rule-consequentialism is frequently accused of failing on this criterion. So I want to call attention to the point that a moral theory had better not be guilty of internal inconsistency (and therefore of incoherence).

In due course, I shall explain why rule-consequentialism is intern-

---

[7] Those who are widely thought to be leading advocates include Aristotle *Nicomachean Ethics*; Anscombe 1958; Foot 1978; MacIntyre 1981; Trianosky 1990; Slote 1992; Hursthouse 1999.

[8] I do not mean to suggest that each of the theories I have mentioned are necessarily incompatible with every other one mentioned, including rule-consequentialism. Certainly, some forms of contractualism are compatible with rule-consequentialism, as are some forms of virtue ethics, in that they require the same acts.

ally consistent. Just as rule-consequentialism is not the only theory to arise from attractive general ideas about morality, it is not the only moral theory to be internally consistent. Hence the importance of *further* criteria for evaluating moral theories. I shall later explain why I think rule-consequentialism fulfils criteria (3), (4), and (5) impressively well. But first I need to defend these as criteria.

1.3 COHERENCE BETWEEN MORAL THEORIES AND OUR CONSIDERED CONVICTIONS

Criterion (3) seeks a moral theory whose implications are coherent with the moral convictions we share and have confidence in, including our convictions about general moral principles. In John Rawls's words,

The test is . . . how well the view as a whole meshes with and articulates our more firm considered convictions, at all levels of generality, after due examination, once all adjustments and revisions that seem compelling have been made. A doctrine that meets this criterion is the doctrine that, so far as we can now ascertain, is the most reasonable for us. (1980: 534)[9]

Following Rawls, I used to think that we may never reach perfect reflective equilibrium between our theory and our considered convictions. I now think this thought is premised on too narrow a conception of what counts as a moral theory.

Moral theories standardly try to specify intuitively plausible universal and general principles from which the truth of our less general convictions can be derived. Must we choose a theory made up of some such principles? But what if no set of universal and general principles coheres with our considered convictions?

Let us use the term 'moral theory' broadly enough so that we can refer to the *particularist* 'theory' that there are true informative

---

[9] Rawls has been by far the most influential *modern* exponent of this methodology (see his 1951; 1971: 19–21, 46–51; 1974/5: sect. 2; 1980: 584; also see Aristotle *Nicomachean Ethics* bk. 8). Rawls has also been one of the two or three most influential nonconsequentialists of the twentieth century. Thus, perhaps the methodology is more closely associated with non-consequentialists than with consequentialists. But many consequentialists have endorsed the methodology, most notably Sidgwick (1907). For recent endorsements by consequentialists, see Kagan 1989: 11–5; Brink 1989: 103–4, 250–2; Hurka 1993: 4–5.

particular moral propositions but no true informative general ones.[10] Particularists can think the only convictions we would have after careful consideration would be about particular cases. Particularists who do think this could also think their theory coheres with all these convictions, in the sense that it endorses them.

I realize that to take '*x* coheres with *y*' to mean only '*x* endorses *y*' is far less than most writers mean by 'coherence'.[11] Unlike many of these writers, I am not taking coherence to require that every proposition of a coherent theory be explained, or even entailed, by all the rest. For to do that seems to me condemn deeply pluralist moral theories as incoherent. True, most of these pluralist theories must be inadequate. (For they conflict with one another and, at most, only one of them can be correct.) But the problem with pluralist theories is not that they are incoherent, at least as the word 'incoherent' is used in ordinary language.[12]

So let us say that a moral theory 'coheres' with our considered moral convictions if the theory specifies general principles entailing the truth of these convictions, or if at least it endorses these convictions without appeal to general principles. Likewise, let us use the term 'reflective equilibrium' very broadly so that a theory stands in reflective equilibrium with our convictions even if the theory merely endorses our convictions.

Given these wide readings of 'moral theory', 'cohere', and 'reflective equilibrium', we *must* be able to reach perfect coherence or reflective equilibrium between our theory and our considered convictions. This would be achieved by a long list of principles that, taken together, endorse all and only the moral judgements in which we have most confidence. If particularists are right that we cannot find such principles, then, at the limit, even particularists' completely unprincipled theory could count as standing in reflective equilibrium with our considered convictions.[13] Thus, the question is not

---

[10] Particularism can admit that there are true *un*informative general principles such as that the moral wrongness of acts never counts morally in favour of doing them.

[11] For some accounts of coherence, see Bradley 1914: 202–3; Blanshard 1939: ii. 265–6; Sellars 1973; Lehrer 1974; Dancy 1985: ch. 8; Sayre-McCord 1986, 1996.

[12] Unlike me, Sayre-McCord takes it to be a necessary condition of coherence that 'the principles of the theory must either justify or be justified by other principles of the theory' (1986: 171). And he argues that coherence 'requires that theories be effectively monistic at the level of first principles' (172). Like me, however, he attacks (in the rest of that article) the idea that our moral theory must have such features.

whether there is a theory that coheres with our convictions. Rather, the question is which theory best coheres with our convictions.

Although common, the attempt to find a theory that coheres with our considered convictions can seem too conservative. This methodology starts with our moral convictions. The methodology allows, indeed presumes, that our convictions may need some revision if they are to be made consistent with one another and with the best principles we can find. Nevertheless, the methodology is likely to preserve systematic or central defects in our moral sensibility. Hence Richard Brandt's complaint:

Various facts about the genesis of our moral beliefs militate against mere appeal to intuitions in ethics. Our normative beliefs are strongly affected by the particular cultural tradition which nurtured us, and would be different if we had been in a learning situation with different parents, teachers, or peers. . . . What we should aim to do is step outside our own tradition somehow, see it from the outside, and evaluate it, separating what is only the vestige of a possibly once useful moral tradition from what is justifiable at present. The method of intuitions [the method of testing theories against our convictions] in principle prohibits our doing this. It is only an internal test of coherence, what may be no more than a reshuffling of moral prejudices. (1979: 21–2)[14]

Such criticism has considerable force. But there are some powerful replies to it.

Note first that we cannot evaluate our evaluative beliefs, or anything else, *from a completely non-evaluative point of view*. If we take up a point of view stripped of all evaluative conviction, we have no basis for evaluation (Williams 1985: 110; Gaut 1993: 33, 34; R. Dworkin 1996).

But why not just turn our back on all moral evaluation and embrace moral scepticism? Rather than trying to make good sense of our moral convictions, moral scepticism claims they are all mistaken, or at least that we do not have sufficient justification for holding them. But moral scepticism occupies a vulnerable position. For if we *can* make good sense of our moral convictions—that is, if we can show how they fit one another and fit with other things we

---

[13] However, particularism stands in reflective equilibrium with our considered convictions *only if* the contents of our considered convictions never take the shape of general principles.

[14] See also Hare 1975; Brandt 1996: 5 and ch. 6. But Brandt had earlier and influentially endorsed the methodology he here attacks. See his 1967: sect. 2.

believe—then moral scepticism is unjustified (Sayre-McCord 1996: 179).

Another difficulty for moral scepticism is that some moral claims seem overwhelmingly compelling. Indeed, we may wonder how anyone who *really* understood them could sincerely deny them.

Imagine a case in which, after some negotiation, two people freely and with full information agree to a morally innocent contract, the terms of which are beneficial to both of them. Like many contracts, this one requires one of the parties to benefit the other now in return for benefits from the other later. Suppose one party fulfils his side of the contract at considerable personal expense. Now the other party, having got what she wanted from the contract, refuses to uphold her side of it. To serve her own ends, she simply cheats the other person. One would have to be morally blind not to see that this is wrong.

There are many other examples. Suppose bored soldiers entertain themselves by torturing their prisoners. This is obviously wicked.

These brief remarks about moral scepticism draw on the difficulty of *sincerely* rejecting the moral judgements in which we have the most confidence. This difficulty should also be salient when we turn to the evaluation of moral theories.

We should evaluate rival moral theories in terms of their ability to cohere with the convictions in which we have the most confidence after due reflection. How a moral view would look from the perspective of evaluative beliefs in which we have little or no confidence could not matter as much to us as whether the moral view is consistent with the moral beliefs in which we have the most confidence after due reflection. As Frank Jackson (1998: 135) writes, '[W]e must start from somewhere in current folk morality, otherwise we start from somewhere *unintuitive*, and that can hardly be a good place to start.'

If we are to start somewhere intuitive as opposed to unintuitive, we shall have to start with beliefs that come with *independent credibility*, by which I mean beliefs that seem correct even before we consider how they fit with our other beliefs. W. D. Ross focused on what he called self-evident propositions. A self-evident proposition is 'evident without any need of proof, or of evidence beyond itself'.[15] In

---

[15] Ross 1930: 29. See also Plato, *Republic*; Aristotle *Nicomachean Ethics*, bk. 1, chs. 3–4; Butler 1726; Clarke 1728; Price 1787; Reid 1788; Sidgwick 1907: 338–42, 379–83; Moore 1903: chs. 1 and 6; Prichard 1912; Carritt 1930; 1947; Broad 1930;

Ross's terminology, it is part of the definition of self-evidence that self-evident propositions must be true, though we could be mistaken about which propositions have self-evidence (Audi 1996: 107–8, 131). I believe clarity is served by talking instead in terms of independent credibility. Like a self-evident proposition, an independently credible one is 'evident without any need of proof, or of evidence beyond itself'. Unlike a self-evident proposition, an independently credible one might turn out to be mistaken (Timmons 1999: 232).

A belief can seem correct to us independently of how (or whether) it fits with our other beliefs, and yet this belief may not be compelling on first look (Ross, 1930: 29; Audi 1996: 112–13). We may have to think very carefully before we start thinking that a belief is independently credible. Furthermore, independently credible beliefs need not be certain, or beyond all challenge or revision (Ewing 1947: ch. 8; 1951: 58–63; Audi 1996: 107–8, 131; Scanlon 1998: 70).

Of course, moral beliefs can draw support from their relation to other moral beliefs. For example, if two different moral beliefs are each non-inferentially credible, and one *explains* the other, this adds to the credibility of both these beliefs.[16] For example, one initially credible belief is that behaving in some way is wrong if the consequences would be bad if everyone felt free to behave in that way. Another is that being a 'free rider' on the sacrifices (or contributions or restraint) of others is wrong. The first belief seems to explain the second, and this lends further credibility to each of these beliefs.

In short, we search for a coherent set of moral beliefs and are willing to make many revisions so as to reach coherence. But we should start with moral beliefs that are attractive in their own right, that is, independently of how they mesh with our other moral beliefs.[17]

While coherence is a good thing, and can supply some justification for beliefs, doesn't coherence have its limits? Consider, for example, the following passage from Jonathan Dancy (1985: 122):

Ewing 1947; Nagel 1986: ch. 8, 1997: ch. 6; McNaughton 1988; Thomson 1990: 12–20; Dancy 1993; Ebertz 1993; Audi 1996: 106–14; R. Dworkin 1996; Griffin 1996: 13, 52, 125; Crisp 2000a: 116–19. Timmons 1999: ch. 5.

[16] Crisp (2000a: 120) is excellent on this; the example in my text is not his. See also Brink 1989: ch. 5, esp. p. 103.

[17] Sencerz 1986; Holmgren 1987; DePaul 1987, 1993; Ebertz 1993; Audi 1996.

We might try . . . distinguishing between two sorts of security that beliefs can have, antecedent and subsequent. *Antecedent security* is security which a belief brings with it, which it has prior to any consideration of how well it fits with others or of the coherence of the set [of beliefs]. We could hold that sensory beliefs have a degree of antecedent security in being prima facie reliable or justified; there will be greater degrees of antecedent security up to infallibility. *Subsequent security* is security which a belief acquires as a result of its contribution to the coherence of the set. All justified beliefs, on a coherence account, have a degree of subsequent security.

But is the coherence theory correct that a *necessary* condition of a belief's being justified is that it contributes to the coherence of the agent's overall set of beliefs? Apparently not, since a belief can persistently seem justified even though it conflicts painfully with our other beliefs. Likewise, coherence does not seem to be a *sufficient* condition for full justification.[18] In any event, coherence is certainly not a sufficient condition for truth (Sayre-McCord 1996: 171, 177–8). Admittedly, coherentism is a resourceful approach. Furthermore, non-coherentist approaches run into the problem that anything we can recognize as an improvement in our present beliefs must find something in our present beliefs to recommend it. Nevertheless, a great deal of moral theorizing rightly consists in the attempt to find principles consistent with certain firm convictions, the ones that seem credible even before we consider what could support them or what they entail.

Noncognitivists in ethics believe that moral convictions are not really beliefs but instead sentiments or commitments.[19] Some other philosophers (such as Mackie 1977: ch. 1) accept that moral convictions are beliefs, but think these beliefs are never literally true. Yet most contemporary moral philosophers—no matter what their views on the metaphysics, epistemology, and language of morals— apply the same reflective-equilibrium methodology in normative ethics.[20] In the case of noncognitivists, the search is for a reflective equilibrium between the moral *attitudes* at different levels of generality. At least some of these attitudes are held on a non-inferential

[18] See Griffin 1996: 8–12; Blackburn 1996: 95–6; Scanlon 1998: 70–1, 382 n. 61; Crisp 2000a: 119–20. For arguments running the other direction, see Brink 1989: ch. 5; Sayre-McCord 1996.

[19] Ayer 1936: ch. 6; Stevenson 1944; Hare 1952, 1963, 1981; Smart 1973: 4–5; Blackburn 1984: ch. 6, 1993, 1998; Gibbard 1990.

[20] A point noted by Williams (1985: 94), Nelson (1991: 116–7), and Griffin (1996: 3, 9). See also Pettit 1997: 103–12.

basis. In according weight to the non-inferentially based attitudes, but then searching for a coherent set, noncognitivist ethicists look very like cognitivist ethicists.[21]

In this book, I shall remain neutral about whether moral views can be literally true and about the ontological status of moral properties.[22] Hence I normally avoid referring to moral *beliefs* and *intuitions* but instead use the more neutral term *convictions*. And even when I refer to moral beliefs and intuitions, I mean these in a metaethically neutral way. I do not mean to be begging any questions in metaphysics, epistemology, and the philosophy of language. Such metaethical neutrality is possible because the vast majority of moral philosophers, whether they accept that any moral convictions can be literally true beliefs, share the same methodology in normative ethics—the search for reflective equilibrium.

A distinction often made in this area is that between 'narrow' reflective equilibrium and 'wide' reflective equilibrium (Rawls 1971: 49; 1974/5: 7–8; Daniels 1979, 1980, 1985). Narrow equilibrium is obtained when we find a set of principles that economically systematizes our considered moral convictions. Wide reflective equilibrium is narrow reflective equilibrium *plus* consistency with 'background conditions'. These background conditions are composed of theories of personal identity, human flourishing, rationality, and everything else. For a moral theory to be in wide reflective equilibrium requires narrow reflective equilibrium plus consistency with the best theories of personal identity, human flourishing, rationality, and so on.[23]

---

[21] I admit that some noncognitivists such as Ayer (1936: ch. 6), Smart (1973: 4–9), Mackie (1977: ch. 1), and Peter Singer (e.g. in his 1993) have sometimes taken delight in the way they took their theory to eschew appeal to contemporary moral views. And certainly some other philosophers allege that noncognitivist views threaten much more of our ordinary moral reasoning than some noncognitivists admit. (This line of argument can be found in Sturgeon 1986; R. Dworkin 1996; and Nagel 1997: ch. 6.) So perhaps I should instead say that, *if* noncognitivism is as unthreatening as Blackburn (1998: 74, 307) and Gibbard (1990) claim it is, then the noncognitivist way of framing the reflective equilibrium methodology matters little in practice.

[22] Scanlon (1998: 59) comments on the contest between 'belief' (i.e. cognitivist) and 'special-attitude' (i.e. noncognitivist) interpretations of judgements about reasons for action. He writes, '[F]or most purposes, including mine in this book, the choice between them turns out to make very little difference, as long as there are standards of correctness for attitudes of the relevant sort.'

[23] On the relation between moral theory and theories of personal identity, see Rawls 1971: 185–9; 1974/5: 15–20; Parfit 1984: 331–9. On the relation between moral theory and theories of rationality, cf. Scheffler 1982: ch. 4, 1985; Gauthier 1986: 1; Griffin 1986 141–3, 146–7, 153–5, 173–5.

I have already defended the search for narrow equilibrium. But many moral philosophers say that narrow reflective equilibrium is hardly enough.[24] They think we should search for wide reflective equilibrium.

Of course, rule-consequentialism should be consistent with other things we believe (or ought to believe), including the background conditions. But it is. And so are its main rivals.[25] Hence, thinking about these background conditions will not be much help when we are trying to decide which of the best versions of the main moral theories is the best theory.

1.4 MORAL CONVICTIONS WE SHARE

Reflective equilibrium starts with moral beliefs about which we confidently agree. What are these?

Most of us confidently agree morality can require us to help others, even if we have no special connection to them. Suppose that, with no cost to yourself, you could save thousands of innocent people from some horrible fate. Perhaps, in order to warn them of an approaching danger, all you have to do is push a nearby button. If you do not warn them, they will suffer and die. If you do warn them, they will escape the approaching danger. Obviously, when you can save many innocent people at *no* cost to yourself or to others, morality requires you to save them.[26]

Morality does not stop there. Helping the needy can be morally required, even if it does involve self-sacrifice. People who are not in need ought to be prepared to make some self-sacrifice to help those who are. Yet morality does not require you to be *constantly* making *huge* self-sacrifices for the sake of other people to whom you have no special connection. So much altruism is admirable, even saintly. But most of us believe that stopping short of sainthood is morally permissible.

Most of us also believe that we owe more altruism to certain

---

[24] D. Miller 2000 presses this objection against me.

[25] I discuss this more fully in Hooker 2000c: sect. 5.

[26] I have encountered denials of this claim. But I cannot believe such denials could have been the product of careful reflection.

people than to others. Other things being roughly equal, your allocation of your own resources should favour your own parent, or child, or friend, or those to whom you have a debt of gratitude over those who do not have any special relationship with you. If you could give a painkiller either to your own child or to a stranger suffering the same amount or even a little more, you should give it to your child.

Sometimes other things aren't even roughly equal. You may have already promised the painkiller to the stranger. Or your parent or child may have waged war on you. Or you may be making decisions while occupying a professional role that demands absolute impartiality.

For example, a nurse deciding whom to give the remaining medicine to is not morally or legally allowed to give her own friends or family special consideration. The same is true of a judge making decisions in court, a policewoman making decisions on duty, and a civil servant awarding government contracts. This sort of role-based obligation to ignore personal relationships arises from the fact that the agent in that role is allocating resources (money, services, whatever) which do not belong to that agent.[27]

Nevertheless, most of us believe that, with respect to *your own* resources and absent special circumstances, your reasoning about what to do *should* give greater weight to the welfare of those who stand in special relationships to you.

We also share confident beliefs about the moral impermissibility of certain kinds of act. Morality prohibits physically attacking innocent people or their property. It also prohibits taking the property of others, lying, breaking one's promises, and so on.

To be sure, there may be exceptional cases in which normally prohibited acts become permissible. Treating people in ways that are normally prohibited may be permissible, for example, when they have given their informed consent. In certain competitive sports, all parties agree to being physically attacked by their opponents—but only within certain rules. Such physical attacks are morally permissible because the players have consented to play a game where whose rules allow certain kinds of physical attack. Likewise, presumably doctors are allowed to cut into people only because they are in as

---

[27] This point I borrow from Cottingham 1998: 11.

good a position as possible now to know what will best promote a person's health and only when they have the person's consent.

In addition, treating people in normally impermissible ways may be justified when necessary to protect innocent third parties. If someone is attempting to kill or injure an innocent person without that person's informed consent, physical force can justifiably be used to thwart the attacker (or to prevent the attacker from escaping and so being able to attack again). Violence used in self-defence can also of course be justified. And protection of the innocent is the normal justification for violence by the army and police.

Likewise, we find commonsense moral views about promising building in protections for the innocent. Promises exert no moral force if they are promises to infringe the moral rights of others (Sidgwick 1907: 305, 308; Thomson 1990: 313–16; McNaughton and Rawling 2000). Promises exert no moral force if they were obtained by fraud or threatens to infringe someone's (e.g. the promisor's) rights.[28] In addition, when a promisee no longer wants the promise kept, the promisee can release the promisor from keeping it. But a promise does have moral force as long as (a) the promisor was not tricked into making it, (b) she was not coerced into making it by a threat to infringe someone's (e.g. her) moral rights, and (c) the promise was not a promise to infringe the moral rights of others. It is a further question when the force of a promise outweighs competing considerations.

More generally, we must acknowledge that there are disputes about which kinds of acts are morally prohibited or required. And there are disputes about what exception clauses are needed in moral norms. But these acknowledgements should not blind us to the fact

---

[28] See Sidgwick 1907: 305–6; Fried 1981, ch. 7; Thomson 1990: 311; Scanlon 1998: 326. A more general view is that actions done 'under compulsion or owing to ignorance' are involuntary (Aristotle *Nicomachean Ethics*, 1109b35–1110a1) and that a promise has no moral force unless it is voluntary. But, as Thomson rightly stresses, my ignorance at the time I made a promise to you undermines the moral force of the promise only if you misled or withheld information from me. As for promises made in response to threats to infringe the promisor's or someone else's moral rights, Scanlon (1998: 325) offers an intriguing explanation of why, even though the keeping of the extorted promise is not owed to the promisee, failing to keep it can dishonour the promisor. Perhaps it is worth adding that, even if you contracted to be someone's slave without being tricked or bullied into the deal, the contract would not be binding since its implementation would infringe your inalienable right not to be a slave.

that there is wide agreement that certain kinds of act are morally prohibited, at least in normal circumstances.

1.5 WHY LOOK FOR A UNIFYING ACCOUNT?

I have mentioned beliefs about what we are morally required to do *for* others and beliefs about what morality forbids us to do *to* others. As I indicated, these are the moral beliefs about which most of us are confident and agree. But we lack confidence and agreement about what (if anything) ties these beliefs together, and about whether there is anything other than their own immediate authority that can be offered in support of them. This is hardly an ideal situation. And so, in Frank Jackson's words,

> Although . . . we should seek the best way of constructing a coherent theory out of folk morality, respecting as much as possible those parts that we find most appealing, to form mature folk morality, it may well be that one part or other of the network is fundamental in the sense that our search for mature folk morality will go best if we seek to derive the whole story starting at that part. The history of ethical theory is full of attempts to identify, out of the mass of moral opinions we find initially appealing, a relatively small number of fundamental insights from which all of what we find (or will or would find) most plausible under critical reflection . . . can be derived. (1998: 134)

Many serious philosophers, however, believe that morality just does consist of a considerable plurality of principles and values, even at the most fundamental level.[29] Consider the theory that the basic, fundamental principles of morality are reflected in the convictions I listed in the previous section. For example, this account claims we have duties not to physically harm others except when necessary to defend innocent people from physical harm. It claims we have duties not to take or harm the possessions of others, and duties not to lie, or to break our promises. It also claims we have

---

[29] Broad 1930: 283–4; Ross 1930: ch. 2; Carritt 1947: 12; Berlin 1969: esp. Introduction and Essay 3; Davidson 1969: 105–6; Urmson 1975; Feinberg 1978; Nagel 1979; Hampshire 1992; Williams 1979, 1985: 93–119, 185–7; 1988; Rachels 1993: 114–16, 120–38, 180–93; Gaut 1993, 1999, 2001; Frazier 1995; McNaughton 1996; Stratton-Lake 1997; Montague 2000; Thomas 2000. For an influential discussion of this sort of pluralism, see Rawls 1971: sect. 7.

duties to give special weight in our decisions about the allocation of our own resources to the interests of those to whom we have special connections. And it claims we have a duty to help others more generally (up to some level of self-sacrifice). The account might add duties to be grateful to those who have gone out of their way to benefit us, and to make reparation to those whom we have wronged.[30]

No one would deny that some of these duties are *normally* stronger than others are. There is, however, a debate among advocates of this kind of moral pluralism about whether some of these duties are absolutely always overriding. I shall comment upon that debate later. The important point I want to make here is that, whatever the internal disputes among philosophers proclaiming a fairly long list of moral first principles, these philosophers would all say that we have no reason to assume there must be some one first principle from which our general duties derive.

I agree we should not assume this. As W. D. Ross (1930: 23) wrote, 'Loyalty to the facts [to the moral beliefs in which we have most confidence] is worth more than a symmetrical architectonic or a hastily reached simplicity.' And our confident moral convictions certainly give us no guarantee that there is a single first principle. On the contrary, the sort of moral pluralism described above may well turn out to be the best moral theory.

But just as we must not assume that a theory with many first principles is *not* the best theory, we must not assume it *is* the best theory. Some other theory might be just as good at matching our intuitions, but go further in finding some more basic principle that ties together and explains our various general moral duties in terms of something simpler. Ross (1930: 23) admitted that a theory with one basic principle could conceivably be better than his theory. Likewise, E. F. Carritt (1947: 11) wrote:

This, in fact, has been one of the chief objects of moral philosophers: to discover some other character or relation common to all the acts we ought to do which is the reason why we ought to do them. It is conceivable there might be some such common ground.[31]

Like Ross, Carritt thought that in fact there is no such common

---

[30] Such additions, plus a duty to promote justice and a duty of self-improvement, would make this list much like Ross's (1930: 21).

[31] See also McNaughton 1996: 440, Audi 1996: 117–18, and Pettit 1997: 115–17.

ground. But the important point here is the acknowledgement that a deeper principle, or common ground, would be desirable—or at least is typically desired. Joseph (1931: 67) noted that if no theory supplies a plausible deeper principle, then 'our obligations will be an unconnected heap'. And of this, Joseph observed, 'That conclusion is disconcerting to philosophy, which attempts to bring a diversity of facts under some unity of principle.' Likewise, Raphael (1994: 55) wrote that the kind of moral pluralism outlined above

does not meet the needs of a philosophical theory, which should try to show connections and tie things up in a coherent system. To look for unity where none exists would, of course, be foolish; if the diversity of moral rules were intractable, it would be pointless to go on searching for some way of tying them up together. But the moral rules of ordinary life are not obviously all different from each other.[32]

Suppose we find a theory with one first principle that explains all the general duties on the moral pluralist's list. Such a theory would have everything the pluralist's theory has—*plus something extra*. The comparison is illustrated in Table 1.2.

The something extra, the deeper underlying principle, would be an interesting discovery. If other things are equal as between moral pluralism and the theory with the deeper principle, then the theory with the deeper principle contains information that moral pluralism does not. By finding a deeper principle from which all our general duties can be derived, this theory would contain a deep connectedness omitted by moral pluralism. The theory with the deeper principle would be able to explain more on the basis of fewer assumptions. In these senses, the theory with the deeper principle is *more informative and integrated*.

Part of what pushes us to ask what, if anything, ties together and explains our various general moral principles is brute curiosity. In other words, many of us would want to know what, if anything, explains and ties together these moral principles, even if the knowledge would have no effect on our practice.[33] Some kinds of

---

[32] Compare Brink 1989: 250–2: 'Coherentism makes justification a matter of relations among beliefs; other things being equal, the more interconnections and mutual support among beliefs, the better justified those beliefs are. Coherentism, therefore, favors unified moral theories over nonunified or fragmented moral theories.' See also Holmgren 1989: 55, and especially Sidgwick 1907: 101–2.

[33] A point eloquently made by Eric Rakowski (1991: 369).

TABLE I.2

Moral pluralism	Some other theory
Implications for particular cases	Implications for particular cases
General duties (e.g.)	General duties (e.g.)
Non-maleficence	Non-maleficence
Trustworthiness	Trustworthiness
Beneficence	Beneficence
Loyalty	Loyalty
Gratitude and reparation	Gratitude and reparation
There is *no deeper principle* underlying general duties listed above	There *is* a deeper principle underlying general duties listed above. It is . . .

knowledge are valuable in their own right. So, other things being at least roughly equal, a theory that specifies an underlying rationale for our various general principles is better than one that does not. This is part of the idea expressed in my criterion (4), at the beginning of section 1.2.

While finding out what ties together and explains our general moral principles would be intellectually satisfying even if it had no important effects on our practice, presumably it would have some important effects on our practice. In particular, an account of what explains these principles could help us deal with moral questions about which we are now uncertain or disagree (e.g., euthanasia, embryo research, surrogacy, business ethics, capital punishment). Not only *might* such an account help resolve unsettled moral matters, it *should* do so (at least sometimes). For we turn to moral theory not merely to enlarge our understanding but to guide our practice (Scheffler 1992: 47, 51). A moral theory that did not help with unsettled moral questions would thus let us down.

Why not just shrug our shoulders and give up on unsettled moral questions? This question is understandable given the frustrations some moral questions visit on us. But a policy of giving up on unsettled moral questions is unsustainable. Many unsettled moral questions just will not let us turn our backs on them. And we cannot satisfactorily settle them by non-rational means. Given what is at stake, we would be mistaken to abandon the search for a useful moral theory containing as much system as is consistent with the moral convictions we have after careful reflection.[34]

1.6 WHY SEEK A FUNDAMENTALLY IMPARTIAL THEORY?

Even if we seek a deeper justification (unifying explanation) for our moral convictions, why seek an *impartial* justification? To answer that question, we must first ask what impartiality is.

Impartiality in Application of Rules

There is a minimal sense of impartiality according to which impartiality requires merely that the considerations be applied impartially, that is, in an unbiased way. Bernard Gert defines 'impartial' as follows: 'A is impartial in respect R with regard to group G if and only if A's actions in respect R are not influenced by which members of G benefit or are harmed by these actions.' (1998: 132). The 'in respect R with regard to group G' here typically cashes out as 'in applying certain rules to group G'. So an umpire might like or admire some players more than others and yet still impartially apply the rules in a game among them. The umpire is *impartial in this respect* towards the players, though not *impartial in all respects* towards them.

Gert (1998: 133) proceeds to claim that impartiality in general does not require consistency. If the umpires choose to change the rules of a baseball game regularly at five-minute intervals to keep themselves entertained, this is not a failure of impartiality, according to Gert, since the umpires are not making these changes in order to advantage or disadvantage some players rather than others. Gert (1998: 135) goes on to admit that the particular kind of impartiality that is required by morality demands consistency. But I myself cannot understand how impartiality as such could require merely a lack of bias in applying rules but not also require consistency in applying

---

[34] And to quote the close of Derek Parfit's 1984 book (p. 454), 'Non-Religious Ethics is at a very early stage. . . . Since we cannot know how Ethics will develop, it is not irrational to have high hopes.'

them. Clearly, to apply rules impartially is (at least to aim) to follow them. And if you do not follow them consistently, you do not fully follow them.

Compare H. L. A. Hart's masterly discussion of justice in the application of law:

[T]he relevant resemblances and differences between individuals, to which the person who administers the law must attend, are determined by the law itself. . . . Indeed, it might be said that to apply a law justly to different cases is simply to take seriously the assertion that what is to be applied is the same general rule, without prejudice, interest, *or caprice*. (Hart, 1961: 156–7, italics added)

Certainly, the most common cause of refusals to be guided by relevant moral distinctions or reasons is bias towards some of the affected parties. But, as Gert and Hart note, it is not the only source. It is one thing to refuse to be guided by relevant moral distinctions because of one's bias towards some potential beneficiaries. It is another thing to refuse to be guided by relevant moral distinctions because of caprice. Both are morally unjustified. To apply rules impartially is to apply them in a consistent and unbiased manner to everyone who falls into the categories specified in the rules.[35]

Impartiality in Scope

In addition to the impartial application of rules or reasons, there is the related idea that moral reasons and rules are impartial in their scope.

Warnock (1971: 149) wrote,

[I]t is part of the concept . . . of morality that no person is simply to be excluded from moral consideration, and furthermore . . . that if he is to be considered differently from some other person, the difference made must be justified by some morally relevant ground of distinction.

But this remark might spark an immediate objection to the idea that moral reasons are impartial in their scope. The objection is that moral reasons apply only to those in relevantly similar circumstances. Thus, a moral reason to help the needy applies *only* to those

---

[35] On the unfairness of moral arbitrariness, see Rawls 1971: 5; Scanlon 1998: 212, 216, 219.

who can help the needy, and a reason to pay special attention to the welfare of one's friends applies *only* to those who have friends.

Yet the thought that moral reasons and rules are universal in scope is compatible with the thought that the same moral reasons apply only to those in relevantly similar circumstances—as long as 'relevantly similar circumstances' are defined without reference to particular persons, places, or times. In short, moral reasons must apply to all cases that have exactly the same universal features (properties).[36] The claim might be made, for example, that it is true *of every single person* that, when she can help the needy at small or moderate cost to herself, there is a moral reason for her to do so. Likewise, it is true *of every single person* that he has a moral reason to focus on the welfare of his friends, if he has any.

Impartiality in Justification

To show that moral convictions entail the unbiased, consistent, and universal application of rules and reasons to everyone in relevantly similar circumstances is not yet to provide impartial *justification* for various moral convictions. Impartiality in the application and scope of rules is one thing; impartial justification of rules is another. Impartiality in the application and scope of rules obviously takes these rules as givens. Impartial justification of rules does not start by taking these as givens. Impartial justification of rules argues *to* them, not *from* them.

Thomas E. Hill, Jr., wrote,

All the impartiality thesis says is that, if and when one raises questions regarding fundamental moral standards, the court of appeal that one addresses is a court in which no particular individual, group, or country has special standing. Before that court, declaring 'I like it', 'It serves my country', and the like, is not decisive; principles must be defensible to anyone looking at the matter apart from his or her special attachments, *from a larger, human perspective.* (1987: 132, italics added. See also Gerwith 1988.)

---

[36] That moral principles and reasons must apply universally is now known as the principle of universalizability. For discussions, see Hare 1952: ch. 11, 1963: chs. 2, 3, 6, 7, 1981, chs. 1, 2, 4–6, 1996: 192–4; Mackie 1977: ch. 4, 1985a; Pettit 1987, 1997: 119–21, 134–6. On keeping moral principles from containing finely crafted sets of universal properties meant to pick out particular individuals or groups, i.e. 'rigged definite descriptions', see Rawls 1971: 131; Hare 1981: 41; Scanlon 1998: 210–11.

What does it mean to look at things 'from a larger, human perspective'? Indeed, why the limit to 'human'? Remember the reference above to Sidgwick's 'point of view . . . of the Universe'. This comes in for its share of criticism. Gert (1998: 132), for example, writes, 'There has also been talk about moral impartiality as involving a God's eye view, or the point of view of the universe, or some other profound-sounding but useless and misleading characterization.' (See also Williams 1982.)

Despite such criticism, the most obvious conception of impartiality remains one holding the well-being of each to have equal importance in the sense that benefits or harms to one individual matter exactly the same as do the same size benefits or harms to any other individual. This is the familiar utilitarian conception of impartiality. But it is not the only, nor indeed Hill's own, conception of impartiality.

A non-utilitarian conception of impartiality made popular by John Rawls (1971) models impartiality on the idea of a social contract. Here, principles are impartially justified only if they could get the uncoerced consent of each person. Further conditions are often added to ensure that no one individual or group can trick or bully others into agreeing to some particular arrangement. Rawls famously argued that this model of impartiality would end up prescribing, first, that everyone should have equal opportunities and certain liberties and, second, that otherwise the basic structure of society should be arranged so as to maximize the resources for the worst-off group, no matter what the cost to those better off.

Rawls has often been criticized for giving the interests of the worst off absolute ('lexical') priority over the interests of the better off. It is one thing to think that the worst off should be given some priority over the better off. It is another thing to think that a tiny benefit to the worst off is more important morally than a huge benefit to the better off. Indeed, the view that even a tiny benefit to the worst off is more important morally than a huge benefit to the better off is implausible.[37] But what is very plausible is the view that the worst off should have *some* degree of priority in our thinking. As I

---

[37] There are many discussions of whether equality, fairness, justice, or equality always overrides considerations of aggregate well-being. Most of these focus on the question of whether those considerations are always overriding in the direct assessment of acts, but some instead consider the question of whether they are always overriding in the assessment of rules. See Broad 1916: 389; Hart 1961: 161; Lyons 1965:

shall explain later, this view seems to animate certain widely shared judgements about cases.

However, even the view that the worst off should have *some* degree of priority is open to serious challenge. For we might worry whether this priority conflicts with strict impartiality. If we are giving priority to the worst off, then in some sense we are not being purely impartial. If we are giving priority to the worst off, we are not giving the well-being of any better-off individual as much weight as we are the well-being of the worse-off individual.

On the other hand, while giving priority to the worst off, we might very well be considering the matter apart from our own special attachments. Giving priority to the worst off, if this is entirely independent of any special attachments we have, *may* qualify as being impartial. I shall return to this.

The idea that the moral point of view is impartial, in at least one of these senses, has widely been taken as axiomatic. This is hardly surprising. In the first place, the idea that the moral point of view is impartial bears some testimony to the historical association of morality with belief in an impartially benevolent god, a god described as loving all 'his' children equally. Secondly, the idea that the moral point of view is impartial bears testimony to the role morality plays in interpersonal justification. How could morality play this role if it weren't impartial? Suppose I do something against your interests. How could my appeal to the moral point of view appease you unless the moral point of view is impartial?[38]

Yet there are powerful arguments against the idea that moral justification must be fundamentally impartial. One such argument is as follows: to construe the moral point of view as the point of view of impartiality will make morality constantly severely demanding. But we are more strongly committed to the idea that morality is not constantly severely demanding than we are to any construal of morality that conflicts with this idea. So we should not construe morality as wholly impartial.[39]

171–7; Feinberg 1978: 116; Scanlon 1978: sect. 2; Scheffler 1982: 31–2, 74, 77–8; Skorupski 1992; Hampshire 1992: 140; Blackburn 1998: 114.

[38] Atheists who think that one of the essential roles of morality is to provide a mechanism for resolving moral conflict may think this helps explain why theists associate morality with the idea of an impartially benevolent god.

[39] See Scheffler 1992: chs. 6, 7 (esp. pp. 102–7, 124, 127); Nagel 1991: 15, 25, 30, 40; and R. Miller 1992: ch. 10.

One of the most prominent impartialist moral theories is act-utilitarianism. This theory is impartialist in that it counts benefits or harms to any one person for neither more nor less than the same size benefits or harms to anyone else. As I shall discuss much more fully later, a comfortably off agent *is* required by act-utilitarianism (and indeed by most versions of the broader theory, act-consequentialism) to repeatedly make enormous personal sacrifices for the sake of needy people with whom that agent has no special connection.[40] But to reject act-utilitarianism is not necessarily to reject impartialism. There may be some other impartial theory that, while attractive and plausible, is not so demanding.

I have been focusing on the objection that impartialism requires you to be strictly impartial as between yourself and each other person. Another objection is that impartialism requires you to be strictly impartial as between all others, no matter how some of them may be connected to you. An obvious problem with such a requirement is that certain immensely valuable goods are constituted in part by a special concern for specific other people—that is, constituted in part by partiality. Friendship, for example, is partly constituted by the special concern the friends have for one another.[41] But, again, impartialism may be able to embrace this point. It had better be able to do so.

Any moral theory will be terribly counterintuitive if it requires you to make every decision on the basis of an equal concern for everyone. To be plausible, a moral theory must leave room for some considerable degree of bias (a) towards yourself and (b) towards your family, friends, benefactors, etc. Indeed, we might hope to find a theory that, on the one hand, offers an impartial perspective for selecting moral rules and, on the other hand, selects rules that allow partiality towards ourselves, and require partiality towards those to whom we have special connections.[42]

---

[40] P. Singer 1972a and 1993: ch. 8; cf. Kagan 1989: chs. 1–2, 5–10. And, for an argument that Hare's important version of impartialism commits him to an extremely demanding morality, see Carson 1993: sect. II.

[41] So Scanlon (1998: 219) writes, '[A] principle requiring strict neutrality between friends and strangers would be unacceptable simply because it would be incompatible with the attitudes and values of friendship.' Fletcher writes, 'Loyalty is a form of partiality' (1996: 184), and, 'In the realm of loyalty, inequality reigns: Outsiders cannot claim equal treatment with those who are the objects of loyal attachment' (1993: 7).

[42] For particularly helpful discussions of the distinction between being impartial at the level where moral rules are evaluated and being impartial throughout daily life,

Despite the fact that the moral point of view was for quite some time identified with the impartial perspective, I know of no knock-down argument for concluding that morality *is* fundamentally impartial. That a theory is impartial would not be enough to make us accept it if it had severely counterintuitive implications. My main point in this section is that a theory that is fundamentally impartial in its justification of moral permissions and requirements and that has intuitively plausible implications seems more attractive than one with equally plausible implications but without this fundamental impartiality. Other things being roughly equal, fundamental impartiality seems a decisive advantage in a moral theory (Pettit 1997: 150).

1.7 A PRELIMINARY PICTURE

Does rule-consequentialism accord with the convictions we share about moral permissibility and requirement? Rule-consequentialism selects rules on the basis of expected value, impartially calculated. Thus the theory is clearly impartial at the level of rule selection. As I shall argue later, the impartial assessment of rules will favour rules that (a) allow partiality, within limits, towards self and (b) require partiality, within limits, towards family, friends, etc. This partiality towards self and loved ones will then be allowed to guide a great number of people's day to day decisions (not all, of course).[43] Therefore, while rule-consequentialism is purely impartial at the

---

see Hill 1987; Baron 1991; Powers 1993; Barry 1995: chs. 8, 9; and Scanlon 1998: 203–4, 205, 219, 224, 225, 397 n. 36.

[43] Sidgwick (1907: 432) writes, 'Bentham's dictum [every man to count for one, nobody for more than one] must be understood merely as making the conception of the ultimate end precise—laying down that one person's happiness is to be counted for as much as another's (supposed equal in degree)—not as directly prescribing the *rules of conduct* by which this end will be best attained' (italics added). Haslett (2000: n. 9) is especially clear about this: '[E]veryone's interests are to be taken as equally important—that is, given equal consideration—not for determining *what act to perform*, but for determining *what code of morality is most justified*. . . . [T]hat code which is most justified certainly will not require that, in all cases, we give everyone's interests equal consideration for determining what *act* to perform. This code will permit us, in many cases, to give the interest of our own children priority over the interests of other children, and to give the interests of decent people priority over the interests of, say, serial killers.' See also the references in Ch. 6 n. 20.

foundational level where a code is selected, the code thus selected makes demands on action that are moderate and intuitively plausible. Rule-consequentialism is fundamentally impartial, but not implausibly demanding.

Rule-consequentialism also accords with common moral beliefs about what we are *prohibited* from doing to others. As I observed, most of us believe morality prohibits physically attacking innocent people, taking or harming the possessions of others, breaking our promises, telling lies, and so on. Rule-consequentialism endorses prohibitions on these kinds of act, since on the whole the consequences, considered impartially, will be far better if such prohibitions are widely accepted. (In Chapter 6, I argue that rule-consequentialism's implications concerning prohibitions and special duties are plausible.)

But, as I have also suggested, coherence with our convictions about particular cases and general principles is not enough to take us all the way to rule-consequentialism. As I indicated, we would also like—which is not to say we will find—a moral theory that meets other criteria. But if the whole comprised of our convictions together with these criteria does support rule-consequentialism, then the picture we get is set out in Diagram 1.1.

1.8 OBJECTIONS TO BE ADDRESSED

Despite its success in providing an impartial underpinning for our settled moral beliefs about prohibitions and permissions, rule-consequentialism has regularly been misunderstood and dismissed. In the next chapter, I will explain the theory in greater detail. Later chapters say more about the theory's attractions and its advantages over its rivals, as well as about why the standard objections to the theory are mistaken. Rule-consequentialism has been accused of being too mechanical, of collapsing into act-consequentialism, of being internally inconsistent, of potentially leading to disaster, of being unable to account for the moral importance of whether others are doing as they ought, and of being paralysingly indeterminate. I will try to answer all these objections and more. Then I will try to illustrate rule-consequentialism's ability to help with questions in applied ethics.

| Convictions about general duties and particular cases + Criteria for assessing a moral theory: (1) It must start from attractive general beliefs about morality (2) It must be internally consistent (3) It must cohere with our considered convictions (4) It should tie together our various principles and provide impartial justification for them (5) It should help us deal with unresolved moral questions. | → | Rule-consequentialism (consisting of) ――――――――――― Principle for selecting rules + The principle that acts are morally permissible if and only if allowed by the rules thus selected |

DIAGRAM 1.1

2

What Are the Rules to Promote?

2.1 A PICTURE OF RULE-CONSEQUENTIALISM

There are many versions of rule-consequentialism. The version I favour is as follows:

> RULE-CONSEQUENTIALISM. An act is wrong if and only if it is forbidden by the code of rules whose internalization by the overwhelming majority of everyone everywhere in each new generation[1] has maximum expected value in terms of well-being (with some priority for the worst off). The calculation of a code's expected value includes all costs of getting the code internalized. If in terms of expected value two or more codes are better than the rest but equal to one another, the one closest to conventional morality determines what acts are wrong.

Picture the theory like this:

TABLE 2.1. Rule-consequentialism

Wrongness determined either (1) by the code whose internalization by the overwhelming majority in each new generation has the greatest expected value or (2) if two or more codes are equally best, by the one closest to conventional morality.	*Conditions:* The people by whom rules are to be internalized (a) are the overwhelming majority in each new generation and (b) are beings with *cognitive* and *affective* limitations.	*Thus, rules* (i) whose *publicity* would have good consequences and (ii) whose internalization costs would be cost-effective.

---

[1] Assume that new generations are not changed genetically. If genetic engineering alters human genetic makeup, the codes that are best will probably be different.

I will explain this picture, piece by piece. Some pieces I will explain in this chapter. Others I will not reach until the next chapter.

2.2 RULES ARE NOT TO BE VALUED IN TERMS OF NUMBERS OF ACTS

Before I explain what is in the picture, let me mention what is not in the picture. The version of rule-consequentialism in which I am interested evaluates rules *only* in terms of how much aggregate well-being (with some priority for the worst off) results from the internalization of these rules. It does not hold that rules should be evaluated in terms of how many acts of kindness, justice, promise-keeping, and loyalty, for example, result from the internalization of the code. Nor does it hold that rules are to be evaluated in terms of how few acts of unkindness, injustice, promise-breaking, and disloyalty result. The version of rule-consequentialism in which I am interested posits well-being (with some priority for the worse off) as the primary thing with intrinsic value. It does not posit intrinsic moral value or disvalue for any kind of act.

Note that I was careful to leave room for the idea that rule-consequentialism might hold that some acts themselves play a constitutive role in a life valuable for the person who lives it.[2] For example, if friendship and achievement are two components of well-being, and if certain acts are constitutive of friendship or achievement, then these acts can play a constitutive role in well-being. Perhaps rule-consequentialism needs to allow that acts can have intrinsic non-moral value in this way.

Consider a version of rule-consequentialism that went much further by positing positive and negative intrinsic *moral* values for different kinds of act. Such a version would hold that the positive and negative statuses of different kinds of act are beyond explanation. Admittedly, versions of rule-consequentialism positing that certain kinds of act have intrinsic moral disvalue can 'explain' why

---

[2] Some philosophers would prefer to call such a theory teleology, rather than consequentialism. Consequentialism is said to be the kind of teleological theory that accords no intrinsic value to acts themselves—that is, no value apart from their (causal, as opposed to conceptual) consequences. See Scheffler 1982: 1 n., 2 n.; Brink 1989: 9–10, 215–16, and esp. 237; cf. Broome 1991b: ch. 1.

killing, wounding, robbing, promise-breaking, and so on are wrong. They are wrong because of their intrinsic disvalue, according to these versions of rule-consequentialism. Likewise, versions of rule-consequentialism attributing intrinsic moral value to certain kinds of act can 'explain' why doing them is morally right. They are right because of their intrinsic moral value, according to these versions of rule-consequentialism.

But better will be versions of rule-consequentialism that can equally well explain why acts are wrong (or right) *without* positing intrinsic moral goodness or badness as properties of acts. For, other things being equal, a theory that does not posit intrinsic goodness or badness as properties of acts makes fewer assumptions. And if a theory making fewer assumptions can explain just as much as a theory making more assumptions, the theory making fewer assumptions is better.

There is another reason not to posit that acts can have intrinsic value or intrinsic disvalue. Some central cases of morally required actions do not plausibly have the requisite kind of value. For example, if promise keeping has intrinsic positive value, then there would be value simply in making promises so that we can keep them and thereby increase the amount of promise-keeping.[3] This implication is crazy, so crazy as to drain the assumption from which it comes of any plausibility.

What is far from crazy is the idea that certain virtues have value in and of themselves, in addition to the value of the consequences they normally produce. Do the dispositions to generosity, honesty, loyalty, and the like have intrinsic value? Are they valuable necessarily rather than contingently? Here is a test case, slightly adapted from W. D. Ross (1930: 134–5). Compare two imaginary worlds. In one, there is a certain amount of aggregate well-being, but people are highly vicious. In the other world, people are thoroughly virtuous, but this world has far fewer natural resources. Suppose that, because of the fewer natural resources, the world with virtuous people has only the same level of aggregate well-being as the other world. So our choice is between two worlds with the same level of

---

[3] Here I am drawing on remarks by Brandt (1963: n. 2); and by Griffin (1992: 122–5). I take it that Hardin (1988: 63) takes much the same view when he writes that the value from promising '*comes from* the contribution promising makes to our actual conditions, not from any a priori rightness above such value'.

well-being but one with virtuous people and the other with vicious people. The world with virtuous people seems clearly better. This case seems to suggest that virtue is not only instrumentally but also intrinsically valuable.

Actually, we need to go carefully here. There are other possible explanations of our ranking the virtuous world higher.

For one thing, we might be assuming we are being asked which world to bring into existence, on the supposition that we ourselves won't exist in either. We understandably feel more sympathy for the virtuous people than for the vicious ones. This makes us 'on their side', and thus inclined to rank their world higher.

Second, we might be outraged by the cosmic injustice of the vicious people being as well off as the virtuous. So our sense of justice immediately puts us on the side of the virtuous as against the vicious.

Third, we might be imagining that we are being asked in which of these worlds we ourselves would prefer to live. In this case, we have the difficulty of getting our minds around the stipulation that we would not be happier in the virtuous possible world than in the vicious one. If we are being asked to imagine possible worlds such that we would not be happier in the virtuous one than in the vicious one, are these not *very distant* possible worlds? If so, our intuitions about them may be unreliable. In particular, the explanation of our preferring the virtuous world may be that we simply fail to take to heart that we would not be happier there.

These alternative possible explanations of our reaction to Ross's example should make us pause before accepting Ross's conclusion that virtue is intrinsically valuable. Furthermore, Ross's conclusion may have implications we cannot accept. If virtue is intrinsically valuable, then presumably it is not always less important than other intrinsic values. But in that case, a loss in terms of other values could be outweighed by a gain in virtue. This threatens to imply that a world in which bad things occur to sentient beings, but where people respond virtuously to these bad things is better than a world without the bad and thus without those opportunities to respond virtuously. That is a familiar reply to the Christians' problem of explaining how there could be an all-powerful, perfectly benevolent god who creates or allows suffering and other evil.

We might be able to believe that virtue is intrinsically valuable without believing that this gives Christians a good answer to their problem. For in order for there to be opportunities for virtue, it is not necessary for bad things *really* to happen, but only for agents to *think* bad things can happen. You can exercise the virtue of kindness if you react to what you reasonably believe is my (actual or potential) suffering by trying to help me. So an all-powerful benevolent god could, while avoiding actually injecting suffering into the world, stage opportunities for people to exercise virtues.

Despite my worries about Ross's example and about his conclusion that virtue has intrinsic value, I do tentatively accept his conclusion. Does this entail abandoning rule-consequentialism? I think not. I think rule-consequentialists can agree that virtue per se is not only instrumentally but also intrinsically valuable.

For as Tom Hurka (2000: ch. 2) argues, to think virtue not only instrumentally but also intrinsically valuable is not to supply a criterion for what constitutes virtue. Nor is it to think virtue can stand alone, unconnected to other intrinsically valuable things. On the contrary, there are various ways of maintaining that what makes something a virtue is its connection with other intrinsically valuable things. Hurka's own account holds that virtue is constituted by loving the good and hating the bad.[4] On his account, virtue is thus conceptually parasitic on other values. But he holds, mainly because of the sort of example from Ross I have just outlined, that virtue is nevertheless intrinsically valuable.

Perhaps rule-consequentialism can make a similar move. Thus rule-consequentialism might hold:

(a) that, apart from virtue, well-being and perhaps some property of its distribution are the only other intrinsically valuable things;

(b) that prospective moral codes should be evaluated in terms of the effects their widespread internalization would have on aggregate well-being, and perhaps some property of its distribution;

(c) that what makes some dispositions virtues is that these dispositions are essential parts of accepting the rules prescribed by the code with the greatest expected value;

---

[4] To loving the good and hating the bad, Hurka adds recursive principles about loving the loving of the good, hating the loving of the bad, loving the hating of the bad, and hating the hating of the good.

(d) and that people's having these prescribed dispositions is not only instrumentally but also intrinsically valuable.

On this form of rule-consequentialism, the virtues per se have intrinsic value, but rule-consequentialism tells us what makes something a virtue.[5]

2.3 WELL-BEING

Since the version of rule-consequentialism under consideration here evaluates rules in terms of well-being, we need to ask what exactly well-being is. Some philosophical theories about well-being point to subjective features of us. These theories hold that we benefit to the extent that we get pleasure or enjoyment, or to the extent that our desires are fulfilled. Other theories hold that there are certain objective goods whose contribution to our well-being is not exhausted by the extent to which they bring us pleasure or enjoyment or fulfil our desires.

All utilitarians have held that pleasure and the absence of pain are at least a large part of well-being. Indeed, utilitarianism is often said to maintain that pleasure and the absence of pain are the *only* things that matter in themselves. Philosophers call this view hedonism. It is normally taken to be the view of the classic utilitarians Jeremy Bentham (1789), J. S. Mill (1861), and Henry Sidgwick (1907).[6]

This view has run into enormous difficulties. First of all, there

---

[5] I explore the relationship between rule-consequentialism and contingency at greater length in my 2000c.

[6] However, in Sidgwick's case, equality seems to have independent weight as a tie breaker (Sidgwick 1907: 417). Moreover, Fred Rosen (1998: esp. 140–3) argues that Bentham and Mill conceived of maximizing utility as favouring equality, even over aggregate utility. The security of expectations about the rewards of economic activity, for Bentham, outweighed the importance of economic equality—mainly because of the economic advantages of incentives to work. (In a forthcoming edition of Bentham's writings edited by Philip Schofield, we find Bentham stating: 'Equality in property is destructive of the very principle of subsistence; it cuts up society by its roots. Nobody would labour if no one were secure of the fruits of his labour.') Still, according to Rosen (141 n. 31), Bentham, if no issue of security arose, 'would choose 100 units of welfare equally distributed between two groups over 110 units unequally distributed, where the majority receives more at the expense of the minority'. See also Kelly 1990. But let me delay questions about equality and distribution until later.

seems to be no distinctive feel that all pleasures have in common, nor any that all pains have in common (Brandt 1979: 35–42; Parfit 1984: 493; Griffin 1986: 8). Compare the pleasure of watching *King Lear* with the pleasure of satisfying an intense desire for sugar.

With this difficulty in mind, hedonism is usually modified to the equation of a person's pleasure with features of his experience that both (a) he likes or prefers and (b) are *introspectively discernible* by him.[7] On this view, something cannot affect your well-being unless there is an effect on how your life seems *from the inside*. This view has implausible implications.

Compare two lives I might have. In both of these alternatives, all the following are true: (a) I believe my 'friends' like me. (b) I believe that I have successfully completed my main aims. (c) I believe I am in control of my own life (at least to the extent people normally are). And (d) I believe I have true beliefs about other important facts. Now, in one of the lives we are comparing, all these beliefs are correct. In the other life, they are false. Suppose that, in the life in which the beliefs are false, I never find out that my 'friends' don't like me, that I fail in my main aims, that someone else is manipulating my life in a way I cannot see, and that I am deluded about other important facts. Now suppose this deluded life is a little more pleasant. This is the one and only introspectively discernible difference between the lives. So, according to the view that the sole component of well-being is the introspectively discernible quality of one's mental states, this is life in which I have greater well-being. But, looked at objectively, this seems not to be the better life (Smart 1973: 20–1; Nozick 1974: 42–5; 1989: ch. 10; Glover 1984: 92–113; Griffin 1986: 9).

Notice that we are comparing lives that are close in terms of pleasure. I do not mean to deny that *sometimes* the truth would hurt so much, be so debilitating, that the person would be better off not knowing it. A deluded life full of pleasant mental states might well be superior to an undeluded life going from one torture chamber to another. To reject the hedonistic theory of the good, we need only contend that there can be occasions on which knowing the truth makes someone better off without making her or him happier. We do not need to, and should not, contend that knowing the truth *always* makes a person better off overall.

In the face of objections such as the one about the slightly more

---

[7] I borrow the helpful term 'introspectively discernible' from Parfit 1984: 494.

pleasant life that involves massive delusion, most philosophers have abandoned the hedonistic theory of well-being.[8] Perhaps more common during the second half of the twentieth century has been the view that well-being is constituted by the fulfilment of people's desires, even if these desires are for things other than pleasure. Many people, even when fully informed and thinking carefully, persistently want for themselves things in addition to pleasure. They want, for example, to know important truths, to achieve valuable goals, to have close friendships, to live autonomously (by which I mean, in broad accordance with their own choices rather than always in accordance with someone else's) (Glover 1984: 95–6, 100–1, 107–8, 112–13; Griffin 1986: pt. 1; Crisp 1997: chs. 2, 3). The pleasure these things can bring is of course important. Still, human beings can care about these things in themselves, in addition to whatever pleasure they bring.

There are objections to the view that human well-being is constituted by the fulfilment of people's desires. Some of our desires seem to be about things too unconnected with us for them to play a direct role in determining our good. Consider an example of Derek Parfit's (1984: 494). You meet a stranger on the train and she tells you of her life-threatening illness. You form a strong desire that she should recover fully from her illness. She does recover, but you never find out. Now, does the fulfilment of your strong desire that she should recover make her recovery good *for you*, even if you never find out about her recovery nor indeed see or hear from her again? The question is whether the bare fulfilment of your desire that she should recover constitutes a benefit to you. Naturally, the fulfilment of such a desire would *instrumentally* benefit you if it brought you pleasure or peace of mind. But this is not to say that the bare fulfilment of your desire that the stranger should recover constitutes a benefit to you. Rather, if you get pleasure or peace of mind from the fulfilment of this desire, this *pleasure* or *peace of mind* constitutes a benefit to you (since you doubtless also desire pleasure and peace of mind for yourself).

The view that the fulfilment of your desires itself constitutes a benefit to you—if this view is to be at all plausible—will have to limit the desires in question. The only desires the fulfilment of which

---

[8] Though compromises between hedonism and its critics are explored in Sumner 1996, 2000.

constitutes a benefit to you are your desires for states of affairs that have to do with your life in some way. We might say that the states of affairs that have to do with your life in this way are ones in which you are an essential constituent, in the sense that your existing at time *t* is a logically necessary condition of the state of affair's obtaining at *t* (Overvold 1980; 1982). Examples of desires for states of affairs in which you *are* an essential constituent are your desires that *you* paint beautiful pictures, that *you* have true friends, that *you* know the truth about the origin of the universe, and that *you* bring the wicked to justice. Examples of desires for states of affairs in which you are *not* an essential constituent are your desires that the stranger on the train recover from her illness, that the innocent go free, that humanity survive forever.

Richard Brandt (1979: 330) and Gregory Kavka (1986: 41) objected that this makes irrelevant to one's own good such desires as the desire for posthumous fame. More generally, if personal success is part of one's well-being, and if personal success requires that certain states of affairs obtain after one's death, then we need to amend Overvold's criterion. We might hold that a state of affairs one desires is part of one's well-being if and only if the state of affairs logically could not exist without one's existing at *some time or other*, though not necessarily at the same time that the state of affairs exists.[9] On this criterion, some desires about events after your death could be relevant to your well-being. Still, the state of affairs in which the stranger from the train recovers is not.

There seem to be reasons for further restrictions on the desires directly relevant to personal good. Think how bizarre desires can be. When we encounter particularly bizarre ones, we might begin to wonder whether the desired things would benefit the agent simply because these things are desired. Would my desiring to count all the blades of grass in the lawns in my neighbourhood make my count-ing them good for me (Rawls 1971: 432; cf. Parfit 1984: 500; Crisp 1997: 56)? Whatever *pleasure* I get from the activity would be good for me. But it seems that the *desire-fulfilment as such* is worthless in this case. Intuitively, the fulfilment of my desires constitutes a bene-fit to me only if these desires are for the right things. Indeed, some things seem to be desired because they are perceived as valuable, not

---

[9] I am grateful to Tom Carson for suggesting this formulation to me, although I do not mean to suggest that he endorsed all its implications.

valuable merely because desired or pleasant (Brink 1989: 64, 225, 230–1; Crisp 1997: 57–62; Scanlon 1998: 124–33).

Views holding that something benefits a person if and only if it increases the person's pleasure or desire-fulfilment are in a sense 'subjectivist' theories of personal good. For these theories make something's status as a benefit depend always on the person's subjective mental states. In contrast, 'objective list' theories claim that the contributions to personal good made by such things as important knowledge, important achievement, friendship, and autonomy are not exhausted by the extent to which these things bring people pleasure or fulfil their desires.[10] These things can constitute benefits beyond the pleasure they involve and even when they don't involve pleasure. Likewise, they can constitute benefits even when they are not the objects of desire. These 'list' theories will typically add that pleasure is, of course, an objective good. List theories also typically hold that delusion, failure, friendlessness, servitude, and pain constitute objective harms.

There are also mixed views. One mixed view holds that your getting pleasure from—or at least desiring—some state of affairs is a necessary but not sufficient condition of its being beneficial to you. On this view, for something to benefit you it must not only appeal to you but also be an objectively good source of pleasure.[11] From the point of view of list theorists, that mixed view is mistaken to claim that a state of affairs can constitute a benefit to you only if you endorse it. For example, some achievement in your life might constitute at least a small benefit to you, might have contributed at least some small meaning to your life, even if you never cared about it. From the point of view of list theorists, the mixed view is also mistaken to claim that getting pleasure from something is not a sufficient condition of its constituting at least some small benefit to you.

Many people reject the list theory because they think it has outrageously paternalistic implications: they see looming the horror of people imposing 'the good life' on others. However, the list theory identifies autonomy as one of the prudential values. It might even go

---

[10] See Finnis 1980, 1983; Parfit 1984: Appendix I; Hurka 1993: chs. 7–10; Brink 1989: 221–36; Scanlon 1993; Griffin 1996: ch. 2; Crisp 1990, 1997: ch. 3; Bailey 1997: 7; Gert 1998: 92–4; Arneson 1999a. The chapters from Hurka 1993 present a compelling account of how to rank different kinds of knowledge and achievements.
[11] Compare Wolf 1997: 211; Frankena 1973: 91; Nozick 1981: 611, 1989: 168; Parfit 1984: 502; Trianosky 1988: 3–4; Scanlon 1998: 124–5.

so far as to give overriding importance to autonomy. Therefore, the list theory itself might prohibit what we intuitively think of as objectionable paternalism.[12]

Furthermore, even if autonomy were not one of the things on the list, paternalism would be in the offing only if *morality* requires or permits forcing things on people that they do not want. But morality might not require or permit this. For example, there may be a good moral rule telling us to keep our nose out of others' business (except in certain fairly obvious cases, like when they are drunk).

Whenever possible, in this book I will be neutral about which of the leading theories of well-being is best. When thinking about what acts are morally right, we can normally remain neutral as between the leading theories of well-being because, despite their disagreements over principle, that is, their disagreements about what *constitutes* well-being, in practice there is wide agreement among the main theories of well-being. This is because what gives people pleasure or enjoyment is normally also what satisfies their desires and involves the things that could plausibly be listed as objective goods. So in most situations we do not need to decide among these theories of personal good (Smart 1973: 26).

But sometimes we do need to decide. Suppose the ruling elite believed that quantity of pleasure is all that matters. They might believe (to take a familiar leaf from some futuristic novels) that aggregate pleasure would be maximized by deceiving the masses and even by giving the masses drugs that induce contentment but drain ambition and curiosity. In this case, the ruling elite might feel justified in establishing such practices.

Or suppose the ruling elite believed that the fulfilment of desire is all that matters. Again, the ruling elite might feel justified in manipulating the formation and development of desires such that these are easily satisfied. Or consider the case of starving people whose desires for anything beyond the most basic necessities are reduced by prolonged deprivation (Sen 1973: 15–18). These people's reduced desires might then be *completely* fulfilled. But really these people would not be flourishing.

Admittedly, wisdom might recommend that, to some extent, our desires should be modified so that there is some reasonable hope of

---

[12] This point is made in many places, e.g. Finnis 1983: 50; Griffin 1986: 71; Hurka, 1993: 151–6.

fulfilling them. But this shaping of our desires can be pushed too far, either in the name of maximizing pleasure or in the name of maximizing desire-fulfilment. A life could be maximally pleasurable, or have maximum desire-fulfilment, and still be shallow. This would be the case if the life were devoid of friendship, achievement, knowledge, and autonomy. While pleasure and success in one's aims are certainly important parts of well-being, these other things are important in their own right.

So, to come clean, I think the most plausible form of rule-consequentialism will involve some modest form of objective list account of well-being. Such an account will recognize the central role of autonomy. Equally, it will recognize the importance of differences in people's aptitudes, capacities, and inclinations. Still, there is more to life than pleasure, and the bare fact that some state of affairs is desired does not make it valuable.

2.4 WELL-BEING VERSUS EQUALITY

The most familiar versions of rule-consequentialism evaluate rules in terms of nothing but how much aggregate well-being they produce. Let me refer to any version of rule-consequentialism that evaluates rules solely in terms of aggregate well-being as *rule-utilitarianism*. Non-utilitarian versions of rule-consequentialism say the consequences that matter are not limited to net effects on overall well-being. Most prominently, some versions of rule-consequentialism say that what matters is not only how much well-being results but also how it is distributed.[13] Diagram 2.1 is a way of picturing the area.

Which version of rule-consequentialism is best? The problem

---

[13] The use of 'consequentialism' and 'utilitarianism' so that consequentialism allows for a concern for distribution in a way that utilitarianism does not is very common. For some examples, see Mackie 1977: 129, 149; Scanlon 1978: esp. sect. 2; Scheffler 1982: 26–34, 70–9; Sen and Williams 1982: 3–4f; Parfit 1984: 26; Griffin 1986: 151–2; 1992: 126, 1996: 165. Examples of writers who include distributive considerations *within* utilitarianism are Brandt 1959: 404, 426, 429–31; Rescher 1966: 25; Raphael 1994: 47; Skorupski 1995: 54; and arguably Bentham (see Rosen 1998: 139–43) and Mill 1861. For writers who want to mix concern for aggregate well-being and concern for distributive matters, see not only those listed above but also Sidgwick 1907: 417; and Broad 1930: 283.

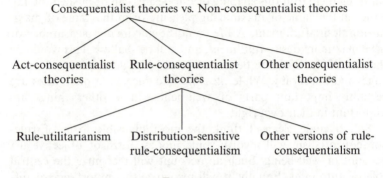

DIAGRAM 2.1

with rule-*utilitarianism* is that it is ultimately insensitive to the distribution of well-being. For the sake of illustration, imagine a society with only two groups in it. One group—let us call it group A—has 10,000 people in it. The other group—group B—has 100,000 in it. Of course, this is a highly simplified example, but this is what makes it useful for bringing out certain ideas. So consider a code of rules whose internalization would leave each member of group A very badly off and each member of group B very well off (see Table 2.2).

TABLE 2.2. First Code

	Units of well-being per person	per group	Total well-being for both groups
10,000 people in group A	1	10,000	
100,000 people in group B	10	1,000,000	
			1,010,000

Remember that utilitarianism (as I am using the term) is concerned with aggregate well-being, not with how equally well-being is distributed. Thus, if no alternative to the above code would provide greater net aggregate well-being, *utilitarians* would endorse this code.

Yet suppose that, from the point of view of utility, the next best code would be one with the results set out in Table 2.3. The second code results in greater equality of well-being, but less well-being in total.

In a moment, I will consider objections to the view that the sec-

TABLE 2.3. Second Code

	Units of well-being		Total well-being for both groups
	per person	pergroup	
10,000 people in group A	8	80,000	
100,000 people in group B	9	900,000	
			980,000

ond code must be better than the first. But before I do that, there is the prior question of what is attractive about the second code. The obvious answer might be that the second code contains greater equality of well-being. But the obvious answer might not be right.

To use Derek Parfit's excellent example, suppose that equality between people who are blind and people who can see could be achieved only by blinding those who could see. Such 'levelling down' would be outrageous (Parfit 1997; Gert 1998: 255; Arneson 1999b: 232–3). Anyone attracted to egalitarianism will see the point of benefiting the worse off even when this costs the better off. But careful reflection on equality suggests that a cost to the better off can be justified *only if* it benefits the worse off. The lesson is that what is important is not equality of well-being per se, but rather improvements in the well-being of the worst off. This idea has come to be called the principle of according *priority to the worst off*, or the principle of *prioritarianism* (Parfit 1997; Arneson 1999b).

Return now to our comparison of the first and second codes above. There is more equality with the second code. And the worse off are a lot better off with the second code than with the first. Parfit's work has shown us that what matters is not really equality of well-being as such but rather improvements in the well-being of the worst off. So I conclude that what makes the second code more attractive than the first is that any plausible version of the principle of giving priority to the worst off will favour the second code.

2.5 FAIRNESS, JUSTICE, DESERT

I used to think that rule-consequentialism should evaluate codes of rules in terms of aggregate well-being *and fairness*, though I was openly unsure how to characterize fairness.

On further investigation, I am not surprised I was unsure about how to characterize fairness. As Shelley Kagan (1998: 54) writes, '[T]he notion of fairness is somewhat amorphous and seems to pick out different features in different contexts. Often, indeed, to say of something that it is unfair is to say nothing more than that it is illegitimate or unjustified.' Similarly, Bernard Gert (1998: 195) observes, '"fair" is now often used as a synonym for "morally acceptable"'.[14] In this all-inclusive sense of 'fair', to say rules have to be fair is just to say that the rules have to be sensitive to all the morally relevant distinctions, as Kagan immediately goes on to remark. But this broad sense of 'fairness' invokes rather than supplies those distinctions.

Aristotle (*Nicomachean Ethics* 1130b18–20) observed that there is a broad sense of 'justice' that subsumes all the virtues having to do with the treatment of others. This sense of 'justice' refers to whatever virtue (in our dealings with others) favours overall (Sidgwick 1907: 393). This is very close to the all-inclusive meaning of 'fairness' above.

That the terms 'fairness' and 'justice' have this meaning in common is not surprising since 'justice is often used to mean fairness' (Shaw 1999: 211). Hence the magnetism of the phrase, 'Justice as fairness.'[15]

The range of meanings for 'justice' and 'fairness' is enormous. We have already seen that they can be all-inclusive moral concepts. At the other end of the range, there is a sense of 'justice' and of 'fairness' that equates to one of the minimal senses of impartiality. In this minimal sense, justice and fairness, like impartiality, preclude bias or inconsistency in the application or interpretation of rules. This is called *formal justice*. Thus John Rawls (1971: 58–9) wrote,

[The] impartial and consistent administration of laws and institutions, whatever their substantive principles, we may call formal justice. If we think of justice as always expressing a kind of equality, then formal justice

---

[14] Gert rejects this broad use of the term 'fair' and immediately goes on to claim that 'in its basic sense, fairness is playing by the rules. To enlarge the concept by applying it to the making of the rules is to invite confusion.' (Gert 1998: 195) He denies that social practices can themselves be fair or unfair. I cannot accept this limitation on the concept. It is a further question whether fairness in the terms of a social practice is a foundational value, or instead one entirely derived from the value of aggregate well-being.

[15] A phrase whose currency testifies to the impact of Rawls 1958.

requires that in their administration laws and institutions should apply equally (that is, in the same way) to those belonging to the classes defined by them. . . . Formal justice is adherence to principle, or as some have said, obedience to system.

However, just as rules can be impartially applied without being impartially justifiable, they can be fairly or justly applied without being fair or just. As Sidgwick (1907: 267) wrote, '[L]aws may be equally executed and yet unjust: for example, we should consider a law unjust which compelled only red-haired men to serve in the army, even thought it were applied with the strictest impartiality to all red-haired men.'

While we cannot assume that fairly applied rules are fair (or just), we also cannot assume they are not. Frederick Schauer (1991: 136–7) argues that rule-based decision-making does 'not further the aim of treating like case alike and unalike cases differently', since rule-based decision-making can focus on morally irrelevant features and thereby treat differently cases that are actually relevantly similar. But if the rules are fair ones, then they will draw attention to, rather than overlook, relevant similarities.

What are the relevant similarities? Plato proposed that justice is 'rendering to each his due' (*Republic* Bk. 1). And Aristotle remarked, 'all men agree that what is just in distribution must be according to merit in some sense, though they do not all specify the same sort of merit' (*Nicomachean Ethics* 1131a 25–8). I call attention to these remarks because I believe that, if we read the terms 'due' and 'merit' as 'desert', we have the common view of the matter. On this view, for a rule to be morally fair it must render to each what she deserves (cf. Kagan 1998: 58).

But just as there are wide senses of 'just' and 'fair', there is a wide sense of 'desert'. So the claim that people should get what they deserve can be heard as the tautology that people should be treated as the balance of relevant moral reasons require. Here again we see a moral concept being used so broadly as to require for its application an account of all other moral reasons. If fair rules are defined as the ones that give people what they deserve, and what people deserve is to be treated as the balance of relevant moral reasons require, we have made little progress. The question is what the relevant moral reasons are.

However, I think 'desert' is normally used for a narrower class of considerations. If I am less well off than you are because I played games while you worked, then there hardly seems a good moral reason for me to be given part of what you earned. If in a competitive economy you successfully strove to be productive and I didn't bother, you deserve greater rewards. Similarly, if you are kind and trustworthy, and I am selfish and dishonest, you deserve a better life than I deserve.[16]

Sometimes there is a criterion for a just and fair outcome that is entirely independent of any procedure for reaching this outcome. But, in some kinds of case, there is no criterion for a fair outcome that is independent of a procedure for reaching this outcome (Rawls 1971: 85–6). In some cases, what people deserve is whatever the fairly conducted procedure produces. For example, in games of chance or competitions of skill, there is no criterion for a fair outcome except what is produced by the procedure, fairly conducted. These cases are known as cases of 'pure procedural fairness'.

Now to account for procedural fairness, we must take into account not only benefits and harms but also *probabilities* of and *opportunities* for benefits. If, in a game of luck, neither of us deserves better odds, then the game is fair if and only if we each have an equal probability of success. If, in a competition, neither of us deserves more opportunities than others do, then the competition is fair only if we indeed have equal opportunities. In the context of the present discussion, we would get off track if we paused here to investigate whether anyone ever does deserve better odds in games of luck or greater opportunities in competitions of skill.

In virtually any human activity, some people are better at it than others. If you are better at some activity than I am, then you deserve that no one should say that you are not better at it. Whether your superiority is something anyone wants to comment upon is another thing. For various reasons, everyone—including you—might prefer your superiority in the activity not to be mentioned.

Of course, in many contexts we do want people to notice that we are better at some activity than others. And, in many contexts, desirable consequences will flow from the establishment of explicit

---

[16] For classic discussions of desert, see Feinberg 1970, 1974; and the writings collected together in Pojman and McLeod 1999. Attempts to fold desert into consequentialism can be found in Feldman 1997: pt. III; see also the discussions in Kagan 1999; Arneson 1999b.

rewards for demonstrated superiority in certain activities. Who wants randomly selected people running our government, or playing on our city's team, or the drawings of randomly selected people exhibited in the museums? Competition is obviously desirable in many contexts.

Many people believe that, where there are fair economic competitions, the winners deserve their rewards. Suppose the person who owns the cornfield announces in advance of the harvest that, in addition to a basic per day salary, whichever two workers gather the most corn will get a 25 per cent bonus each. If everyone has an equal opportunity to enter this competition and if the competition is run fairly, then the two who are most productive deserve their greater spoils.

Commonsense morality also holds that those who are kind and trustworthy should do better than those who are selfish or untrustworthy. Unfortunately, often the winners of economic competitions are neither kind nor trustworthy. As Richard Arneson (1999b: 241) writes,

a competitive market responds to supply and demand, not fine-grained or for that matter coarse-grained estimations of different individuals' degrees of deservingness and responsibility. If we imagine institutions that would do better to bring about distribution of the good in accordance with people's true deservingness, but at significant cost of priority-weighted aggregate well-being, would we then be inclined to scrap the competitive market in order to institute a tolerably adequate moral meritocracy?

In any event, a common view is that to evaluate codes of rules in terms of fairness or justice is to evaluate them in terms of whether differences in the benefits (including probabilities of and opportunities for them) that individuals get correspond to differences in the individuals' desert.

This line of thinking often seems irresistible. When a kind and honest person dies of cancer in the prime of his life, this is a terrible loss not only to him but also to his family and friends. Meanwhile, many selfish and untrustworthy people enjoy long lives and unearned riches. Who could fail to be struck by such injustice?

Indeed, once we have noticed the tight conceptual connections between justice, fairness, and desert, we might also begin linking the concept of moral rights to these other concepts. A familiar line of thought is that, just as *justice* and *fairness* call for people to get what they deserve, people have a moral *right* to whatever benefits they deserve.[17]

But this may be a thought too far. Did the person cut down by cancer in the prime of his life have a moral right to a life of average length? Against whom could he have such a right?

Suppose that in the end we think there is something confused about the claim that a person has a moral right to a life of average length. But even if in this case there is no moral right that has been infringed, there is still injustice. When there is injustice for which no human is responsible, perhaps we have to call it 'cosmic injustice'. If we accept that there is this category of injustice and if we think injustice always involves the infringement of rights, we have to believe that there are rights against the cosmos. Alternatively, we could give up the idea that injustice always involves the infringement of rights.

I certainly agree that there is terrible injustice when the good die young or the wicked prosper. I also believe that at least some of these injustices are ones for which no one is responsible. But I cannot accept that there are rights against the cosmos, so I must deny that injustice always involves the infringement of rights. To deny this is not to think injustice any less awful.

Since injustice and unfairness are so awful, perhaps any proposed rules should be evaluated in terms of whether they serve justice and fairness—that is, leave people with what they deserve. To be more specific, perhaps any rules should be evaluated in terms of whether their internalization would end up rewarding only the deserving. There is the further consideration of proportionality—that is, that equals are treated equally and unequals unequally (Aristotle, *Nicomachean Ethics* 1131a20–4). Combining the ideas of desert and proportionality, we could propose that rule-consequentialism evaluate rules either wholly or partly in terms of whether they reward people *in proportion with their desert*. If rule-consequentialism did this, it would accord desert a foundational role in the theory.

Desert, justice, and fairness seem so important that this way of

---

[17] J. S. Mill (1861: ch. 5, para. 15) claimed, 'Justice implies something which it is not only right to do, and wrong not to do, but which some individual person can claim from us as his moral right.' See also Broome's account of fairness (1991b: 194–6). Broome argues that you and I are treated fairly if the respective *duties owed to us* are satisfied in proportion to their respective strengths.

constructing rule-consequentialism is difficult to resist.[18] Yet, rule-consequentialism should *not* start by helping itself to the assumption that some people deserve more than others. Rule-consequentialism does not need to assume this, because rule-consequentialism can explain why certain rules that encourage some kinds of activity and discourage others are highly desirable (cf. Kagan 1998: 55; Arneson 1999b: 238–9).

In this book, I will say only a little about punishment. Again, the rule-consequentialist rationale for rules is that their internalization has high expected value. This will be true of rules not only about how people should treat those who behave well but also about how people should react when others break the rules. If there is net value in people's internalizing a rule, there is typically net value in reinforcing conformity with that rule. So rule-consequentialism will have no trouble explaining why someone guilty of breaking its rules should be put in a more or less uncomfortable position, 'if not by law, by the opinion of his fellow creatures; if not by opinion, by the reproaches of his own conscience' (Mill 1861: ch. 5, para. 14).

Likewise, someone who has fully internalized and complied with the code should be rewarded by the combination of noninterference from the law, a good reputation in society, and a clear conscience. In addition, rules that reward those who produce what others want serve to establish further incentives. The establishment of appropriate incentives yields greater aggregate well-being than would result were there no such incentives.[19]

So rule-consequentialism can explain why rules should punish certain kinds of behaviour and reward other kinds. And it can do this without presupposing that certain kinds of behaviour inherently *deserve* to be rewarded. A moral theory is better off *explaining* why certain distinctions are morally important than simply *assuming* they are.

Return to the supposed connection between desert and fairness. If what is fair is determined by what people deserve, and if rule-consequentialism should not be formulated as evaluating rules even

---

[18] Hence the enormous appeal of views like those found in Feldman 1997 and Kagan 1999.

[19] People have different levels of ability and different appetites for work as opposed to leisure. For these reasons, I assume any system of economic incentives will result in at least some economic inequality.

partly in terms of desert, then it should not be formulated as evaluating codes even partly in terms of fairness.

2.6 FAIRNESS, CONTRACTS, AND PROPORTION

So far, I have discussed fairness as the unbiased application of rules, and fair or just rules as ones that allot to individuals what they deserve. But neither of these things is what I had in mind when I proposed in earlier publications that rules should be evaluated in terms of fairness as well as aggregate well-being. In those publications, I had simply taken for granted that the appropriate rules were to be fairly applied. And I had assumed that the appropriate rules would determine the principles of desert, rather than take desert as the ground of the rules. But I also assumed that, for the purposes of evaluating rules, there must be some relevant consideration other than aggregate well-being.

Consider again the case of the person who owns the cornfield and announces before the harvest that, in addition to the per day salary, the two workers who pick the most corn will get a bonus. Suppose the promise was for a 50 per cent bonus, on top of the basic per day salary. Now suppose the second most productive cornpicker picks 1,000 ears of corn and the third picks 999. Is it fair that, when the difference in their performance is so small, the second best cornpicker gets a far bigger reward than the third best cornpicker?

Consider another case. Suppose the owner of the cornfield offers only a 5 per cent bonus, beyond basic per day salary, to each of the two most productive cornpickers. And suppose the two best are really far quicker and thus more productive than all the others. So imagine that the second best picks 1,000 ears and the third best picks only 500. Is it fair that, when the difference in their performance is so large, the difference in their reward is small?

I think most people would think that if the parties were competing according to one set of reasonably fair rules—and so making decisions on the basis of one set of reasonable expectations—then fairness requires that those rules and expectations be upheld. It is striking that the *first* rule of substantive justice mentioned by Sidgwick (1907: 269) is that one should do what one has contracted to do. Moral fairness requires that a contract is binding provided all of the following.[20] (a) The contract was entered into by sane people. (b) The contract was not the result of one party's withholding information to which the other party was entitled. (c) The contract was not the result of one party's threatening to infringe someone's moral rights. (d) The contract does not itself require one or more parties to infringe moral rights (this is why, for example, contracts to commit murder or robbery are not binding). None of (a) through (d) undermine the contract which we are imagining the owner of the field made with the workers.

Contracts can of course be changed by mutual consent. But in our example there was no such change. And it is not fair for one party to a deal to change the terms of the deal unilaterally, especially after others have made decisions based on expectations created by this party.

Over the last four decades, much has been made of the principle of fair play (Hart 1955; Rawls 1971: sect. 18). But Nozick (1974: 93–5) showed that, even if you have benefited from a communal practice, and even if the benefit you received was greater than your fair share of sustaining the practice would have cost you, you may not be morally obligated to contribute to the practice. What matters is whether you *knew*, when you accepted the benefits, that you would be expected by others to contribute to the practice. If you did know, then others will take your having accepted those benefits as your having implicitly agreed to do your part in return. As Kagan (1998: 143) observes,

the more we move in the direction of requiring that benefits first be freely and knowingly accepted, the more plausible it becomes to view the agent as having made an implicit *promise* to obey the rules governing the practice. Thus, even if there is a sound version of the principle of fair play, despite initial appearances it may not actually point to a normative factor distinct from that of promising.

Earlier we saw that fairness requires the (consistent and impartial) following of appropriate rules. Now we have to add the idea

---

[20] The claims here echo my earlier remarks about promising. Again, see Sidgwick 1907: 305–11; Hart 1961: 192–3; Fried 1981: esp. ch. 7; Thomson 1990: ch. 12; Scanlon 1998: ch. 7. One difference between a promise and a contract seems to me to be that the insane can make a morally forceful promise but not an enforceable contract. Another is that promises need not involve 'consideration', i.e. exchange.

that what is fair really depends not so much on what individuals *would* have agreed to, but rather what they *actually* did agree to.

However, not all agreements are binding. For example, if I get you to agree to something by threatening to torture you, or by threatening to torture someone else, any promise you make to prevent me from carrying out this threat is not morally binding. What this shows is that to explain fully the concept of fairness we must appeal to the concept of a morally binding promise. And to explain the concept of a morally binding promise, we must appeal to the idea of a promise that was *not* made in response to a threat to infringe someone's moral rights. The concept of fairness turns out to depend on the concept of moral rights after all.

And what generates moral rights? We cannot at this point refer back to fairness, since that would be circular. One extremely plausible suggestion is that a set of moral rights is justified if their communal acceptance maximizes expected utility (Mill 1861: ch. 5; Sumner 1987). Again, perhaps we need to add a weighting so that the well-being of the worst off gets priority. I shall come back to this in a moment.

First, I want to acknowledge that many would feel some regret about the result for the cornpicker who performs far better but gets only a slightly bigger payment. Similarly, many would feel some regret about the result for the cornpicker who performs only slightly less well but gets a far smaller payment. Although proportionality is not always important, proportionality between reward and productivity in producing what others want does seem important in establishing general economic incentives.

Our conception of fairness is infused both with the idea of proportionality and with the idea that agreements between sane people should be honoured (given that the agreement was not extracted by fraud or by the threat to infringe moral rights, and given that the agreement does not itself require one or more parties to it to infringe moral rights). Since sane people can agree not to divide benefits in proportion to productivity, fairness sometimes gets into a fight with itself. Rule-utilitarianism can explain the importance of keeping your side of a deal once other parties to the deal have done their side. It can also explain the general advantages of proportional rewards. Making reward proportional to productivity seems justified in terms of creating incentives. The backbone of a system of incentives is the expectation that agreements will be honoured. So where agreements create a system of non-proportional rewards, the pressure to honour the agreements seems greater than the pressure to make rewards proportional. All this seems correct both from the point of view of rule-utilitarianism and from the point of view of our moral intuitions. My references to fairness in earlier publications were caused partly by a worry that a code of rules whose internalization would maximize aggregate well-being might leave well-being distributed in an unacceptably unequal way. However, I thought that inequality is bad only if it is unfair (Broome 1991b: 199). I continue with questions about distribution in the next section. But first let me mention that another part of my reason for referring to fairness in earlier publications was that I thought building fairness into rule-consequentialism could help the theory answer some of the concerns about fairness that Lyons expressed in his 1965 discussion of rule-utilitarianism (Lyons 1965). I shall come back to these problems when I discuss compromising with convention.

2.7 PRIORITY TO THE WELL-BEING OF THE WORST OFF

In the example I gave earlier, a form of rule-consequentialism could favour the second code over the first, not in the name of fairness, nor in the name of simple equality, but in the name of priority for the worst off. A possible objection to giving priority to the well-being of the worst off when we are evaluating possible moral codes is that this priority will militate against rules calling for the productive to get more than the lazy. The greater the priority towards the worst off, the greater this objection.

Let us look more closely at the question of economic incentives. It seems difficult to deny Nagel's claim:

Going by contemporary evidence, the advantages of a significant private sector in the economy . . . are enormous, as measured by productivity, innovation, variety and growth. The productive advantages of competitive market economies are due to the familiar acquisitive motives of individual.[21]

To be sure, working hard can make people feel good about themselves, give them a sense of accomplishment, or bring them some

[21] Nagel 1991: 91. See also pp. 122–3, 127–8.

other internal rewards. For some people in some jobs, the prospect of such rewards is sufficient to elicit hard work, year in and year out. But for very many people and jobs, this is not the case. It now seems unrealistic to hope that the main productive elements of the economy could be driven *efficiently* by anything other than the desire for material rewards for self and special others (Nagel 1991: 121, 127; Brandt 1996: 205–6).

But in fact there is no incompatibility between, on the one hand, thinking that, when we judge a code, we should take a special interest in the well-being of the worst off, and, on the other hand, thinking that economic incentives are justified. This was one of the lessons from Rawls (1971: sects. 11, 12, 42). A reasonable degree of priority to the worst off will not nowadays obscure the overwhelming long-term benefits of providing incentives for work.

Aggregate well-being combined with some priority for the worst off can be expressed as a *weighted sum of well-being*. This brings the priority toward the worst off into the calculation of the sum of well-being. The well-being of the worst off gets extra weight in this calculation. Look again at a comparison of codes (Tables 2.4, 2.5). The first code would produce more well-being if well-being is calculated strictly impartially: 1,010,000 > 980,000. But we earlier thought the second code more appealing because of its being so much better for the worst off while only a little worse for the better off. This sort of reasoning comes through in the idea of a weighted sum of well-being. If our calculation of total good gives twice the weight to well-being of each of the worst off as it does to the well-

TABLE 2.4. First Code

	Units of well-being per person	per group	Total well-being for both groups
10,000 people in group A	1	10,000	
100,000 people in group B	10	1,000,000	
			Impartially calculated: 1,010,000 Weighted with worst off × 2 and others × 1: 1,020,000

TABLE 2.5. Second Code

	Units of well-being		Total well-being
	per person	per group	for both groups
10,000 people in group A	8	80,000	
100,000 people in group B	9	900,000	
			Impartially calculated: 980,000 Weighted with worst off × 2 and others × 1: 1,060,000

being of each of the better off, then calculation comes out favouring the more equal distribution: 1,060,000 > 1,020,000.

The weighted sum approach illustrates the undesirability of levelling down. Compare Table 2.5 with Table 2.6. The second code (Table 2.5) is better than the third code (Table 2.6). Indeed, this will be true no matter how much priority is given the worst off, since the worst off are no better off with the strict equality resulting from the third code than they are with the slightly less equal results of the second code. The weighted sum approach accords with the idea that one result cannot be better than another unless there is at least one individual who gains. (See Parfit 1984: 359–64 for qualifications.)

TABLE 2.6. Third Code

	Units of well-being		Total well-being
	per person	per group	for both groups
10,000 people in group A	8	80,000	
100,000 people in group B	8	800,000	
			Impartially calculated: 880,000 Weighted with worst off × 2 and others × 1: 960,000

There are obviously advantages in formulating rule-consequentialism in terms of a weighted sum of well-being instead of in terms
of impartially calculated aggregate well-being weighed against some
priority for the worst off. For one thing, 'weighted sum of well-
being' is a more economical phrase than 'impartially calculated
aggregate well-being weighed against some priority for the worst
off'. On the other hand, 'impartially calculated aggregate well-being
weighed against some priority for the worst off' is less technical and
opaque than 'weighted sum of well-being'.

But I think more important than either of those considerations is
the fact that the term 'weighted sum' suggests a degree of precision
that is normally unavailable.

There are at least two reasons such precision is normally unavailable. First, virtually never can we *precisely* quantify levels of
individual well-being. This not at all to say that we can never compare the size of benefits and harms to different individuals, or the
extent to which different individuals are flourishing. We can compare these things, and do it every day. But our judgements about the
size of benefits and harms are normally rough, and do not really
admit of mathematical precision. Second, there must be some false
precision in any decision about the number by which the well-being
of the worst off should be multiplied in the calculation of the
weighted sum. In short, normally we can but make *rough* comparisons of the benefits and harms to different individuals, and we can
reasonably accord only a *rough* priority to the worst off.

I myself employed artificial precision in my example of how a
rule-consequentialist assessment of rules can prioritize the well-
being of the worst off. Let me now eschew such artificiality when
illustrating how a rule-consequentialist can take equality to be less
important than aggregate well-being, even when levelling down is
not in play. Suppose rule-consequentialists are choosing among
various possible rules about the distribution of a new technology (an
as yet unowned technology). Suppose none of the distributions
under consideration would make anyone worse off. Suppose also
that the better off would benefit far more from getting their hands
on this technology than the worst off would. A rule which results in
the better off getting the technology rather than the worst off getting it would significantly increase aggregate well-being but also
increase inequality somewhat. Here the gain in aggregate well-being
may be more important.

The example I have provided suggests we can make some generalizations about how, in the assessment of alternative possible codes of rules, a prioritarian rule-consequentialist should balance aggregate well-being against priority for the worst off. Big increases in aggregate well-being are more important than small increases in the well-being of the worst off. Big increases in the well-being of the worst off are more important than small increases in aggregate well-being.

However, such generalizations leave many cases undecided. Indeed, there is a large gray area where increasing aggregate well-being does not seem clearly more important, nor clearly less important, than increasing the well-being of the worst off. Furthermore, where exactly the borders of this gray area are is not clear.

2.8 UTILITARIAN IMPARTIALITY VERSUS PRIORITY TO THE WORST OFF

What I am calling rule-utilitarianism is the view that an act is morally permissible if and only if it is allowed by the set of rules whose internalization would have the highest expected (or actual) utility.[22] This view calculates utility impartially and refuses to give any priority to the well-being of the worst off. For a strict utilitarian, there is no need to weigh utility against equality.

By evaluating rules in terms of two considerations (well-being and priority for the worst off) instead of one (well-being), prioritarian rule-consequentialism involves complications and vagueness additional to those found in rule-utilitarianism itself. Rule-utilitarianism certainly has the advantage *if*, while eschewing the additional complications and vagueness, it can account for our considered convictions just as well as prioritarian rule-consequentialism can.

In two respects, rule-utilitarianism seems markedly simpler and more straightforward than prioritarian rule-consequentialism.

First of all, rule-utilitarianism is a welfarist doctrine, in the sense that at the foundational level it takes nothing as valuable expect the welfare of individuals. Usually, utilitarians limit this to the welfare of sentient individuals.

---

[22] Cf. Brandt 1959: ch. 16; Frankena 1973: ch. 3; Scanlon 1978.

Second—and to my mind more compelling—is the point that utilitarianism can be seen as the most natural understanding of fundamental impartiality. Utilitarianism straightforwardly develops the idea that everyone counts equally from the moral point of view.[23] Utilitarians can understandably allege that any criterion giving priority to the worst off is partial towards the worst off, and thus not impartial. My earlier discussion of weighted sums makes very clear the sense in which priority for the worst off attaches more moral importance to the well-being of the worst off than it does to the well-being of any better off individual.

In reply, prioritarian rule-consequentialists can but assert that their theory incorporates a recognizable impartiality. They might say that impartiality should be understood as demanding the *equal consideration of interests*, and that this bears interpretations other than the utilitarian one. Thus T. M. Scanlon (1978: sect. 2) wrote:

'Equal consideration' could, for example, be held to mean that in any justification by appeal to consequences we must give priority to those individual interests that are 'most urgent'. To neglect such interests in order to serve instead less urgent interests even of a greater number of people would, on this interpretation, violate 'equality of consideration'.

Likewise, John Skorupski (1996: 208) wrote that Rawls's version of priority toward the worst off

favours the worst off, in that it attaches an ethical priority to improvements in their well-being. But it can also be said to count everybody for one, nobody for more than one in this sense: it is indifferent to which concrete individual is under consideration. It takes account of no property of the individual other than his or her comparative well-being.

Consider parents who give priority to whichever of their children is worst off. These parents might think of themselves as nevertheless impartial. They might point out that they are not partial towards any particular child of theirs, but rather give priority to whichever one is worst off. In many cases, which one is worst off changes over time. In these cases, the parents might give priority first to one child of theirs, and then to another, and then switch again.

This more capacious interpretation of impartiality runs into the following problem.

---

[23] Singer 1993: 12–25; Harsanyi 1976: 13–14, 19–20, 45–6, 65–7; Hare 1984, pp. 106–12; Kymlicka 1990: 30–9; Bailey 1997: 10–12.

Some people hold in Nietzschean fashion that the priority should be not towards the worst off but rather towards the most accomplished and powerful. On this view, the interests of the worst off and indeed of people who are living only average lives should be sacrificed whenever this would help the great artists, writers, and generals to ascend even higher pinnacles. Those who hold this view might claim that it is an impartial view. They might point out that they are not partial towards any particular individual, but rather give priority to whichever one can achieve most. And which one can achieve most changes as people's powers develop or deteriorate.

This Nietzschean view goes beyond the obvious truth that one person's greater achievement can have more impartial value than another person's lesser achievement, even if the greater achievement was made by someone already better off in every way than the person who made the lesser achievement. The greater achievement can constitute a larger benefit to the already better-off person than the lesser achievement does to the less well-off person (though, for reasons outlined in Hurka 1993: ch. 12, this need not always be so). The Nietzschean view, however, holds that what matters are only the heights reached by the highest achievers. So, on this view, a small additional achievement by someone already at the summit is more important than a huge achievement by someone else that falls short of the summit.[24]

Take an even more familiar form of elitism. Some people want even greater amounts going to the richest royalty, movie stars, singers, and athletes. This is in effect the view that the very richest should get richer, even at the cost to the rest of us.

Now, admittedly, the principle 'Maximize the heights of achievement reached by humanity even if only a very few can reach it' might be a principle some people could prescribe universally. Likewise, the principle 'Maximize the heights of luxury, even if only a very few get it' is one that some people might be able to prescribe universally. But even if such elitist principles are universalizable, they certainly are *not* impartial.[25]

---

[24] This view focuses first on achievements that go beyond what anyone has ever done before. So, in considering it, we can ignore cases where someone's further achievements, since they are additional to but lesser than her earlier ones, drive down the average quality of her work.

[25] Hare argued (1981) that universalizability in fact generates what I am calling full impartiality. He would argue that the elitist principles under discussion, since they

The fact that elitist views are not impartial presents a clear problem for the priority for the worst off. If various forms of priority for those at the top is a rejection of impartiality, then how can priority for those at the bottom be impartial?

I cannot but think that the point about impartiality favours rule-utilitarianism over any form of rule-consequentialism that gives priority to some over others. So I think the point favours rule-utilitarianism over a form of rule-consequentialism that gives priority to the worst off. But I do not think this point necessarily decisive. For maybe the concept of impartiality can be stretched enough so as to accept as impartial a rule-consequentialism that gives priority to the worst off.

What could be decisive is whether rule-utilitarianism can account for our considered convictions as well as that form of prioritarian rule-consequentialism. Any rule-consequentialist theory that takes equality or fairness or justice to be, along with well-being, part of the maximand starts with certain assumptions about moral value. Rule-utilitarianism has no *moral* values in its maximand. But rule-utilitarians often say their theory has the resources to condemn the distributions that seem unjustifiably inegalitarian. If their theory can explain this rather than simply assuming it, that is an advantage their theory has over prioritarian rule-consequentialism.

But imagine a society in which a majority strongly prefers that a minority be 'kept in its place', that is, be kept much worse off. The collective internalization of rules oppressing this minority could maximize overall utility. To be sure, the cost to each member of the minority would be greater than the benefit to each member of the majority. Nevertheless, if there were enough more in the majority than in the minority, the greater number in the majority might offset, in purely aggregative utilitarian terms, the greater harm per person in the minority.

However, as John Harsanyi and Ronald Dworkin have argued, utilitarians who found their theory on the idea that everyone counts equally can insist that 'external preferences'—that is, preferences about how others' lives go—should not be counted in the assessment

---

are not impartial, are not really universalizable. I sidestep this debate here. My point is that the elitist principles are manifestly not impartial, whether or not they are universalizable.

of utility.[26] If external preferences do not count, then utilitarian assessment of rules would not count anyone's preferences that others be 'kept in their place' or the like. When utilitarians refuse to count external preferences, they pre-empt most of the examples intended to show that rule-utilitarianism can endorse oppression.

Now imagine a situation in which enormous inequality would maximize utility even though satisfaction of external preferences is not counted as part of utility. Another rule-utilitarian reply is that this situation is not realistic. In other words, the reply is that, in realistic circumstances, utility will be maximized *only* by rules that reward people more or less equally.[27] If rules benefit some far more than others without any obvious rationale, sooner or later the results will be alienation, resentment, and unrest.

Finally, an extremely important point is that material goods have diminishing marginal utility. Normally, the more food or bicycles or clothes or money you have, the less you will benefit from gaining an additional unit. This may not be true in the exceptional case where you are finishing off your collection or reaching some threshold of holdings. But it is nevertheless true normally.

Because material goods have diminishing marginal utility, the transfer of some of these goods from people who have a lot to people who have a little is *likely* to increase aggregate utility. If I have three winter coats and you have none though we live in the same cold climate, then the reduction in my well-being likely to result from my losing one of my coats is less than the increase in your well-being likely to result from your getting the coat.

The diminishing marginal utility of material resources gives utilitarians presumptive reason to favour egalitarian distributions of material goods. Those rule-utilitarians who think very egalitarian distributions of wealth are best have been particularly impressed by the diminishing marginal utility of material goods (Brandt 1979: 312–19; 1996: 206–21; Shaw 1993; 1999: 236–44). But all rule-utilitarians think that the phenomenon is important.

On the other hand, the diminishing marginal utility of material goods provides a utilitarian reason to equalize material goods only if people derive the same amounts of benefit from the same sets of

---

[26] Harsanyi 1982: 56; R. Dworkin 1985: 363; Kymlicka 1990: 36–7. For a broader discussion of illegitimate preferences, see Vallentyne 1991a.

[27] Brandt 1979: 306–26; Johnson 1991: 17–19, 64–6; Shaw 1999: 236–7.

material goods.[28] If I have disabilities and you do not, then I might well get less benefit from a stock of material goods than you get from the very same stock. Now suppose you and I have exactly equal stocks of material goods. Because you are in effect a more efficient converter of material goods into personal benefit, utility will be increased here if material goods are transferred from me to you. This will create inequality between us not only in material goods but also in levels of well-being.

However, there unquestionably is *rough* equality among people in terms of the benefits they derive from consumption of material goods. Where they are manifestly very unequal is in their abilities to flourish in a competitive economy.

Why have a competitive economy? Well, one good thing about a free market is precisely the freedom in it.[29] We are free to trade goods and services with one another however we want. Such freedom obviously has extrinsic value for many people. It may even have intrinsic value, in that it is a kind of autonomy.

Utilitarians have typically eschewed that sort of argument for free markets. Instead, they have noted another sort of argument that likewise accepts economic inequality as the foreseen by-product of an arrangement that utilitarianism endorses. This arrangement is the provision of economic incentives. As I indicated, this arrangement will predictably result in economic inequality.

So utilitarians have to trade off the diminishing marginal utility of material goods against the need for economic incentives. The conflict between these considerations will not, however, embarrass them. After all, the trade off between these considerations does seem the right focus for serious thinking about production and distribution.

These considerations seem to me to add up to a powerful case in favour of rule-utilitarianism over a distribution-sensitive (e.g. prioritarian) rule-consequentialism. Most weighty, to my mind, is the

---

[28] As John Broome (1991b: 176–7) points out.

[29] Rawls (1971: 272) wrote that a 'significant advantage of a market system' is that people 'have a free choice of careers and occupations. There is no reason at all for the forced and central direction of labor. Indeed, in the absence of some differences in earnings as these arise in a competitive scheme, it is hard to see how, under ordinary circumstances anyway, certain aspects of a command society inconsistent with liberty can be avoided.' Nozick's (1974: 163) quip was, 'The socialist society would have to forbid capitalist acts between consenting adults.'

point that the most plausible version of distribution-sensitive rule-consequentialism gives priority to the worst off, which can seem a departure from impartiality.

And yet there do seem to be real—not merely fanciful—cases in which offensively inegalitarian rules would or did maximize aggregate well-being.[30] I am driven by this point to conclude, albeit without much confidence, that on balance a purely utilitarian assessment of rules is inferior to prioritarian rule-consequentialism.

This is an issue on which deep disagreements about moral principle matter less in practice than differences about relevant empirical questions. Suppose Dick believes rules should be evaluated solely in terms of aggregate utility, and Dorothy believes rules should be evaluated in terms of aggregate utility with some priority for the worst off. Both Dick and Dorothy believe material goods have diminishing marginal utility. So both see some reason to favour systems that result in more equal distributions of material goods. But the need for incentives for hard work and innovation gives them utilitarian reasons to favour differential economic rewards. A system of economic incentives has the foreseen result of economic inequality.

How much economic inequality can they countenance? This will depend partly on their moral principles for evaluating codes, but also partly on their views about the consequences of one level of incentives versus another. Dick may think that very large incentives are not needed to elicit hard work and innovation. Dorothy may believe that large incentives are needed for these purposes. So Dick may endorse a system of rules that will foreseeably result in a more equal distribution than the system Dorothy endorses. Yet Dorothy was the one whose basic principles accorded priority to the worst off.

Again, I myself am tentative about the superiority of prioritarian rule-consequentialism over distribution-*in*sensitive rule-utilitarianism. And, again, the difference between these views may matter little in practice. I therefore propose to ignore the difference from now on, except where it is relevant. Thus when I refer to the 'expected value' of a code's consequences, I usually leave open whether this value is to be simply aggregate well-being, or aggregate well-being plus some priority for the worst off.

---

[30] Kymlicka 1990: 28.

2.9 WHOSE WELL-BEING COUNTS?
RULE-CONSEQUENTIALISM VERSUS
CONTRACTUALISM

Contractualism and rule-consequentialism share many attractions. They both involve a 'generalization test'. In other words, they both ask, 'What if everyone felt free to do what you propose to do?'[31] For rule-consequentialists, this question asks about the expected value of the internalization of rules that would leave everyone feeling free to do the kind of act. For contractualism, the question, 'What if everyone felt free to do what you propose to do?' asks whether anyone could reasonably reject rules leaving everyone feeling free to do the kind of act. Other attractions that contractualism and rule-consequentialism share are as follows. Both theories generate principles that agree with commonsense moral convictions that killing, stealing, promise-breaking, and the like are wrong, even when they would bring about somewhat more good. And both theories offer a fruitful way of addressing many moral problem areas. So contractualism and rule-consequentialism are somewhat similar in their forms of reasoning, very similar in the principles they arrive at, and similar in their offer of help with problem areas.

Yet contractualism's account of who has moral standing seems intuitively inferior to consequentialism's.

Animals (or at least many of them) count morally, in the sense that their welfare has direct moral importance. To make this point, we need not take a stand on moral questions about using animals to test drugs or as a source of food and clothing. Let us focus on a minimally controversial thesis about moral duties toward animals: severely torturing higher animals for the sake of very mild amusement for humans is morally wrong.[32]

What sense can contractualists make of the idea that morality imposes at least some constraints on how we treat animals? Kant, from whom much modern contractualism derives, claimed that 'our duties to animals are merely indirect duties towards humanity. [F]or

---

[31] Influential discussions of the generalization test published in this century include Broad 1916; Harrod 1936; Harrison 1952/3; Stout 1954; M. Singer 1955, 1961; Strang 1960; Hare 1963, 1981; Lyons 1965; Mackie 1977: ch. 4, 1985a; Regan 1980: ch. 6; and much of the contemporary discussion of Kant's categorical imperative.

[32] See Nozick's seminal discussion (1974: 35–42, esp. p. 36).

he who is cruel to animals becomes hard also in his dealings with men' (1989: 210).

There are two objections to Kant's view.

In the first place, we may doubt Kant's empirical claim about the connection between cruelty towards animals and cruelty towards humans. Plenty of people are quite indifferent to animal suffering but impressively altruistic toward human beings (and some people are the reverse).

More important is the second objection to Kant. This is the objection that, even if Kant is right to think cruelty to animals tends to lead to cruelty to humans, this does not exhaust our reasons not to be cruel to animals. For the sake of argument, imagine we had conclusive proof that treating animals cruelly did not in fact lead to cruelty towards fellow humans. Still, we would think it wrong to torture animals for our mild amusement. The reason here would have to derive from *their* suffering. It could not derive from negative indirect effects on how humans treat other humans, since by hypothesis there are no such effects on humans. I think this shows that the moral reason for not torturing animals for our mild amusement comes at least partly from their suffering, independently of effects on how we treat other humans.

Consider Peter Carruthers's contractualist arguments.[33] Carruthers contends, along much the same lines I have taken, that Kantian contractualism accords no direct moral weight to animals (1992: ch. 5). He then offers the Kantian addendum that people's indifference to animal suffering can manifest cruelty that is morally objectionable because of its connection to cruelty to humans. As he writes, 'Contracting rational agents should agree to try to develop a ready sympathy for one another's suffering, and sympathy for animal suffering is . . . merely a side-effect of this general attitude' (1992: 154).

Carruthers then offers a two-level account:

Since right action requires that you act for the sake of the animal, it is then easy to see how one might slip into believing that the animal itself has moral standing. But this would be to miss the point that there may be a variety of different levels to moral thinking. On the one hand there is the level of thought that manifests our settled moral dispositions and attitudes (this is where sympathy for animal suffering belongs), but on the other hand there

---

[33] Carruthers also has some non-contractualist arguments against according animals direct moral weight. I focus on his contractualist arguments.

is the level of theoretical reflection upon those dispositions and attitudes, asking how they may be justifiable by an acceptable moral theory. It is at this level that we come to realize, as contractualists, that animals are without moral standing. (1992: 157)

Carruthers admits intuition might seem to go against him on the question of animals' moral standing (1992: 158). But he claims that intuitions should yield here to theory—i.e. that our commonsense commitment to the moral standing of animals should be surrendered in the face of contractualism's superiority to other moral theories. Moreover, Carruthers wants us to surrender not only our beliefs about animals' moral standing, but also some of our beliefs about what sort of behaviour towards animals is morally permissible. Some societies may anthropomorphize animals less than other societies do. Carruthers writes:

In such a society a dog may be slowly strangled to death because this is believed to make the meat taste better, while it never occurs to the people involved that there is any connection between what they are doing and their attitudes to human beings—indeed, there may in fact be no such connection. While such an action performed by someone in our society would manifest cruelty, when done by them it may not (1992: 162).

And on his view, since (1) animals have no *direct* moral importance and (2) the slow strangulation of the dog may have no connection with cruelty *towards humans*, there may thus be nothing morally objectionable about it. But this conclusion is outrageously counter-intuitive. In fact, it seems nothing less than a *reductio ad absurdum* of any view committed to it.

Contractualists might claim that *our own strong concern for animals* impels us to ensure that any social contract protect them (cf. Gauthier 1986: 17, 268, 285; Scanlon 1998: 221–2). But such a claim would again miss the point. For intuitively we believe the reason animals matter morally is not that we care about them, or that the value in our lives will be greater if we stand in a certain relation to animals. As Bentham said, the reason they matter is that they can suffer. Intuitively, the overall good matters morally; animal welfare is at least some part of the overall good; and this does not depend on our happening to care about animals.

I agree with Carruthers that Scanlon's version of contractualism is the most plausible on offer. Carruthers thinks he is drawing the conclusions to which Scanlon's contractualism is committed. In

Scanlon's early formulation of his theory, he stated that his contractualism implies that 'morality applies to a being if the notion of justification to a being of that kind makes sense' (Scanlon 1982: 113). But justification *to* a rabbit, or a dog, or even a whale, manifestly does not make sense. So contractualism would leave animals outside the circle of moral consideration (here Carruthers and I agree about the implications of contractualism). Yet these animals do matter morally, and so contractualism is in trouble (here Carruthers and I disagree).[34]

Scanlon implicitly acknowledged that the moral status of animals might be a problem for contractualism. He pointed out that we could think of animals as having trustees rejecting or agreeing to proposed rules on their behalf (Scanlon 1982: 113). But Scanlon's recourse to the device of trusteeship is ad hoc, unmotivated on purely contractualist grounds.[35] And indeed, in his recent book Scanlon seems to be distancing himself from the idea that we should think of animals as having trustees in contractualist negotiations (1998: 184).

Scanlon now favours making a distinction between broad and narrow senses of morality (1998: 6, 171–8, 342–9). He suggests that contractualism is an account of only narrow morality. This is to admit that there is more to morality than contractualism describes. Scanlon goes on to propose that, while animals fall outside the scope of narrow morality's (i.e. contractualism's) protection, there are good reasons coming from *broad* morality to alleviate animal pain (1998: 181). Scanlon is here abandoning his earlier idea that whether something falls within the scope of morality's protection depends upon whether the thing is such that justification to it makes sense. He effectively acknowledges now that whether or not animals are able to reason, discuss, or bargain with us about rules, they have moral standing—*simply* because they can suffer.

I accept that contractualism can accommodate animals either by bringing in trustees or by delimiting itself as an account of only part of morality. But, as I indicated, the recourse to trusteeship seems ad hoc. And the distinction between narrow and broad morality seems

---

[34] For related criticism of Gauthier's Hobbesian contractualism, see Kavka 1993. But for attempts to show that Rawlsian contractualism can ascribe moral weight to the well-being of animals, see VanDeveer 1979; Elliot 1984; B. Singer 1988.

[35] Having made this claim in Hooker 1995, I then discovered Carruthers had made virtually the same criticism first (Carruthers 1992: 100).

to me one we should accept only if we have to. If another moral theory both is as good in other respects as contractualism is, and gets by without dividing up morality into a narrow part and a broad part, then so much the worse for contractualism. In fact, this seems to me just what rule-consequentialism accomplishes.

Construing animals' capacity to suffer as the reason they have moral standing is natural for rule-consequentialism, but difficult for contractualism. Thus, consequentialism seems superior on the question of who has moral standing. If other things are roughly equal between these theories, and I believe they are, then on balance rule-consequentialism has the upper hand.

2.10 VALUE IN THE NATURAL ENVIRONMENT

Many people believe that diversity and beauty in the natural environment are valuable *in themselves*—i.e. beyond whatever benefits they could bring to humans or animals now or in the future. Such non-instrumental environmental goods are even more difficult for contractualists than are animals. In contrast, rule-consequentialism can easily accommodate non-instrumental environmental goods. Rule-consequentialism can be formulated so as to evaluate rules in terms of not only the weighted well-being of sentient beings, but also these environmental goods.[36] In this case, rule-consequentialism can judge one set of rules better than another simply because widespread internalization of the first set would have greater expected value in terms of these non-instrumental goods than would widespread internalization of the second.

Rule-consequentialists who think environmental goods are valuable in themselves will be faced with the question of whether, in the ranking of alternative sets of rules, such goods are sometimes more important than the overall well-being of present and future sentient beings. I guess we can also ask whether environmental goods can outweigh the importance of improving things for the worst off. I cannot answer such questions.

Indeed, I myself am in two minds about whether the natural envi-

---

[36] Here I am indebted to helpful suggestions from Rae Langton and Tim Scanlon.

ronment matters beyond its present or future effects on sentient beings. The environment obviously has enormous effects on the well-being of sentient beings. Diversity and beauty in the natural environment have enormous instrumental value. For this reason alone, virtually everyone now agrees that many forms of environmental protection are very important. But there is no consensus on the view that the natural environment is important beyond the effects on present or future sentient beings.

So I will henceforth omit reference to the natural environment. But let me reassure those who are more confident than I that the natural environment is important beyond the effects on present or future sentient beings. I think everything I argue in the rest of this book could be recast so as to accommodate the view that rules should be evaluated in terms of not only (weighted?) well-being, but also environmental values.

3
Questions of Formulation

While our picture of rule-consequentialism is becoming clearer, it is not yet in sharp focus. If we attend to further questions about its formulation, we can more exactly define its shape.

3.1 REASONABLY EXPECTED, RATHER THAN ACTUAL, CONSEQUENCES

I formulated rule-consequentialism above in terms of the expected value of rules, not in terms of the *consequences that actually would result*.[1] I have done this because moral permissibility (and rightness and wrongness) should not be tied to facts that are too difficult (indeed, effectively impossible) to find out. No one can be blamed for failing to know just which rules are the ones whose internalization by the overwhelming majority actually would produce the best consequences. And if no one can be blamed for failing to know which rules actually would produce the best consequences, no one can be blamed for failing to comply with these rules. Thus, a plausible account of moral *blameworthiness* will not tie it to the rules that actually would produce the best consequences.

Some people insist on a distinction between wrongness and blameworthiness. They think that wrongness depends on the real facts of the situation, not on how the agent sees the situation. On this view, the wrongness might depend particularly on how things really would work out on various alternatives, not on how the agent expects they would work out. But it seems ridiculous to blame agents for what they couldn't reasonably expect. So blame should be appor-

---

[1] In my first papers on rule-consequentialism, I formulated the theory in terms of actual consequences rather than expected ones (1990: 67 and 1991a: 269, 1991b: 270). My change of mind was caused by Griffin 1992: 130–1; and Mulgan 1994b. Discussion with John Skorupski has heavily influenced my current formulation.

tioned depending on what the agent actually expected, or maybe on what the agent could reasonably have expected. But to distance wrongness so far from blame seems counterintuitive. Most of us believe that moral blameworthiness is very closely linked to moral wrongness. We might even be tempted to say that the acts of fully responsible agents are morally blameworthy if and only if morally wrong.[2] I add the qualification 'of fully responsible agents' so as to capture the idea that an act can be wrong without being blameworthy if part of the cause of the act is either some blameless motivational problem or some blameless informational deficit.

As an example of the sort of motivational problem I have in mind, suppose that you never drink alcohol, because you know it makes you mean and aggressive. However, at a party your apparently nonalcoholic drink has been secretly spiked, and so you get angry and punch someone. Here the punch was wrong, but arguably not really blameworthy, given that you had no reason to suspect that your drink had been spiked and thus had short-circuited your normal moral inhibitions on aggression.

Examples of agents' acting under informational deficits are even more familiar. Suppose you act under false beliefs about the circumstances. Walking down the street, you come upon one person apparently beating up another, and you try to stop this by hitting the attacker. Suppose the situation you happened upon was actually only street theatre, and so the apparent assault you saw was only play-acting. Your injuring the actor was arguably wrong, but in the circumstances not blameworthy.

In that sort of case, you knew the relevant rules: 'Avoid hurting innocent people', and 'If you can at little risk to yourself help innocent people who are being attacked, then do so.' What you did not know (and, let us suppose, did not have adequate reason to expect) was that the circumstances were such as to make relevant the first rule rather than the second. Because of your blameless ignorance about the actual situation, your breaking the rule 'Avoid hurting the

[2] For a careful attempt to explain the connection of wrongness to blameworthiness, see Gibbard 1990: 41–8. Gibbard acknowledges he is taking over and modifying Mill's famous proposal, in para. 14 of ch. 5 of *Utilitarianism*, about the connection between wrongness and optimal sanctions (i.e. the sanctions there *ought* to be). See also Copp 1995: 25–6 and ch. 5, esp. pp. 88–96. For an attack on the thesis that wrongness is to be connected to norms about blame, see Crisp 1997: 127–32.

innocent' was entirely unintentional. So your act was wrong but blameless.

What to say about such cases seems to me unclear. I could imagine holding to the view that when people do what is morally reasonable *given* their reasonable beliefs about the situations they are in, what they do cannot be morally wrong, however unfortunate it is.

But suppose I instead admit the little 'breathing room' between 'wrong' and 'blameworthy' that I outlined earlier. Still, it might seem that I have not gone far enough. Indeed, it might be claimed that rule-consequentialism would sharply distinguish the question of whether an act is wrong from the question of its blameworthiness. Someone might say that we should formulate rule-consequentialism as follows:

ACTUAL RESULT RULE-CONSEQUENTIALISM

An act is wrong if and only if it is forbidden by the code of rules whose internalization by the overwhelming majority *actually* would result in the best consequences. But agents should not be blamed for failing to follow the best rules when such failure results from legitimate ignorance, including legitimate ignorance of what the best rules are.

Contrast actual result rule-consequentialism with my earlier formulation of rule-consequentialism in terms of *reasonable expectations*. My formulation in terms of reasonable expectations is much less *epistemically* demanding than actual result rule-consequentialism. For my earlier formulation does not require us to find and follow the rules that *actually would* result in the best consequences.[3] To avoid acting wrongly, we need only find and follow the code that could reasonably be expected to have better consequences than any other code we can identify. Or, if two or more codes are equally best, we need only find which of these is closest to conventional morality.

I find actual result rule-consequentialism inferior to my earlier formulation of rule-consequentialism. For to tie wrongness to the rules that actually would result in the best consequences introduces too wide a gap between wrongness and blameworthiness. Quite possibly, there are many rules that actually would result in the best consequences, and yet could not reasonably be expected to produce

---

[3] On problems that more epistemically demanding 'objectivist' versions of consequentialism get into with the 'ought' implies 'can' principle, see Howard-Snyder 1997.

better consequences than identifiable alternatives. And if these rules could not reasonably be expected to produce better consequences than identifiable alternatives, then agents cannot be blamed for failing to follow them. So a plausible account of moral *blameworthiness* will not tie it to the rules that actually would produce the best consequences.

I think the same is true for a plausible account of *wrongness*. It seems pointless to identify wrongness with failing to follow rules that agents cannot be blamed for failing to follow.[4] If the concept of wrongness wanders too far away from blameworthiness, most (if not all) of the importance of wrongness seems lost. To retain its importance, wrongness has to stick fairly close to blameworthiness. Thus, wrongness, like blameworthiness, needs to be explained in terms of rules reasonably expected to be best, not rules that actually would be best.

I recognize that some may not share this view. They might think actual result rule-consequentialism is superior to my own version of rule-consequentialism. But their disagreement with me about this should not preclude their finding this book interesting. For they can gloss the version of rule-consequentialism I am developing here as an account merely of blameworthiness.

3.2 COMPLIANCE VERSUS ACCEPTANCE

Different forms of rule-consequentialism disagree about the conditions under which rules are to be evaluated. For instance, one version of rule-consequentialism is formulated in terms of the rules the *compliance with which* has the greatest expected value. Another version is formulated in terms of rules the *acceptance of which* has the greatest expected value.[5]

Cutting across the distinction between compliance and acceptance versions of rule-consequentialism is another distinction. This is the distinction between formulations of the theory in terms of

---

[4] Cf. Sorensen 1996.
[5] For an early emphasis on the importance of considering the *acceptance* of rules and not merely *compliance* with them, see Brandt 1963: 120–5. This has been prominent in Brandt's work ever since.

universal compliance or acceptance, and formulations in terms of *general* (i.e. something less than universal) compliance or acceptance. This distinction I shall not discuss until the next section. I put off that discussion so that in the present section I can concentrate on the compliance/acceptance distinction.

When we ask whether rule-consequentialism be formulated in terms of compliance or in terms of acceptance, our first thought might be that compliance with the right rules is the first priority. But compliance is not the only thing of importance. We also care about people's having *moral concerns*. So we had better consider the costs of securing not only compliance but also adequate moral motivation. From a rule-consequentialist point of view, 'moral motivation' means acceptance of the right rules. And 'acceptance of the right rules' incorporates not just the disposition to comply with these rules. Acceptance of rules also involves the disposition to encourage others to comply with them, dispositions to form favourable attitudes toward others who comply with them, dispositions to feel guilt or shame when one breaks them and to condemn and resent others' breaking them, all of which dispositions and attitudes being supported by a belief that they are justified.[6]

The focus on *acceptance* of rules, that is, on dispositions not only to behave in certain ways but also to feel in certain ways, is crucial. For the acceptance of a rule—or perhaps at this point it would be better to say the *internalization* of a rule—can have consequences over and above compliance with the rule.[7]

One way this can happen is that a given level of internalization of the rules does not result in that level of compliance with them. Why might internalization of rules fail to produce perfect compliance? People make mistakes, give in to temptation, and so on. This sort of thing is very familiar from the law. If we need people to drive no faster than 30 m.p.h. through some area, the speed limit should perhaps be set at 25.

---

[6] Brandt 1967: sect. 8 [1992: 120–1], 1979: 164–76, and 1996: 67, 69, 145, 156, 201, 266–8, 289; Blackburn 1998: 59, 62, 67–8; Scanlon 1998: 276, 334. For an especially detailed discussion, see Copp 1995: 82, 84–93.

[7] On this, see Sidgwick 1907: 405–6, 413; Lyons 1965, 140; Williams 1973: 119–20, 122, 129–30; Adams 1976: esp. p. 470; Blackburn 1985: 21 n. 12; Scanlon 1998: 203–4; Kagan 1998: 227–34. And see Kagan's (2000: 139) comment, '[O]nce embedded, rules can have an impact on results that is independent of their impact on acts: it might be, say, that merely thinking about a set of rules reassures people, and so contributes to happiness.'

I myself believe that rule-consequentialism should take into account many differences between internalization and compliance (on which more in a moment) but not this one. It seems to me counterintuitive that what is morally right depends on rules designed on the assumption that we will regularly fail to comply with them. If the point of setting a rule one place rather than another is that our actions will miss their target to some degree, then a human tendency to make mistakes is shifting the line between the morally allowed and the morally forbidden.

There are other differences between internalization and compliance that seem much more important to me. Suppose you accept a rule prescribing that you retaliate against attackers. Suppose also that you are totally transparent, in the sense that people can see exactly what your dispositions are. So everyone knows about your disposition to retaliate, and therefore *never* attacks you. Thus, your accepting that rule is so successful at deterring attack that you *never* have an opportunity to comply with the rule. Your accepting the rule thus obviously has important consequences that simply cannot come from your acting on the rule, since in fact you never do.[8]

Let us turn now to other examples. Scanlon (1998: 203) writes,

As agents, if we know that we must stand ready to perform actions of a certain kind should they be required, or that we cannot count on being able to perform acts of another kind should we want to, because they are forbidden, these things have important effects on our planning and on the organization of our lives whether or not any occasions of the relevant sort ever actually present themselves. If, for example, I lived in a desert area and were obligated to provide food for strangers in need who came by my house, then I would have to take account of this possibility in my shopping and consumption, whether or not anyone ever asked me for this kind of help.

Such examples illustrate what Harsanyi dubbed 'expectation effects'—the assurance and incentive effects of public awareness that

---

[8] For a seminal article about the importance of distinguishing between the consequences of making credible threats and the consequences of carrying them out, see Kavka 1978. Someone might object that, because you never annihilate anyone, you do in fact comply with the rule. This objection is confused. The rule is, 'If anyone attacks you, annihilate him or her.' That is a rule with which you never have an opportunity to comply. Not to annihilate anyone is to comply with a different rule, namely, '*Only* if someone attacks you, annihilate him or her.' But that rule is not the one in play in my example. I am not suggesting that one of these rules is better than the other, or than other possible rules. All I am arguing at this point is that a rule can have consequences apart from acts of compliance with it.

certain rules will be followed.[9] In the deterrence example, the behaviour of others is guided by their confident expectation about what you would do if attacked. The effect on their behaviour comes from their expectation about what you would do, not from anything you actually have done.

Many rules have extremely important expectation effects. This point is not necessarily lost on those who focus exclusively on the consequences of compliance with rules. The consequences of compliance with a rule would of course include the effects *on* people's expectations. The consequences of compliance with a rule would also include the myriad knock-on effects *of* these expectations. Some philosophers thus think the existence of expectation effects presents no reason to frame consequentialism in terms of acceptance rather than compliance.

But whether or not everyone's *complying* with a certain rule would maximize net good overall, we should consider the wider costs and benefits of rule *internalization*. Getting one rule internalized might involve greater costs than getting another internalized. As Brandt writes,

Obviously the basic motivations cannot be very numerous, since they have to be instituted by a process of conditioning, or some such device (e.g. the use of prestigious persons as models). Again, the complexity of the conduct enjoined or banned is limited by the intellectual capacities of the average person. What these rules may require is limited by the strain of self-interest in everyone, and the specific desires and aversions bound to develop in nearly everyone, including some degree of benevolence; and they are also limited by the fact that these other desires are prior in the sense that the basic motivations can be acquired by conditioning only by building essentially on them.[10]

So one objection to a code might be that it is so complicated or calls for so much self-sacrifice that too much of society's resources would have to be devoted to getting it widely internalized. The internalization costs would be too high for the code to be optimal.

---

[9] Harsanyi 1977, 1982: 58–60, 1993: 116–18. See also Brandt 1979: 275–7, 1992: 142, 144, 149, 153, 1996: 126, 144; C. Johnson 1991: esp. chs. 3, 4, 9. Again, I myself comment on incentive effects in Hooker 1993a.

[10] Brandt 1979: 287. For Brandt's stress on what he calls teaching costs, see (e.g.) his 1963: sect. 4, 1967 [1992: 126], 1983: 98, 1988: 346–7, 349–50 [1992: 140–3, 144–7], 1996: 126–8, 145, 148, 152, 223.

When this is the case, the code is not justified. And when a code is not justified, then of course complying with it is not required.

I am supposing that moral rules are inculcated pretty much as they are now—that is, by family, teachers, and the broader culture. I do *not* hold that the code is to be taught by some enlightened elite for blind acceptance by the uninformed masses. On the contrary, I assume the code is to be internalized *throughout* human society, without regard to socio-economic status or advanced educational qualifications. The importance of this will be more apparent later. For the moment, let me just emphasize that I accept Copp's (1995: 101) observation: '[G]iven human psychology, a code is unlikely to be socially enforced and widely subscribed to in a society unless it is or becomes part of the culture.'

Here is how the internalization costs can become crucial. Suppose we are evaluating two alternative possible codes, which we can call Code A and Code B.

First, consider the respective expected values of the consequences *after the codes have been completely internalized.* Suppose the expected value of the consequences after Code A has been internalized is n. Code A is simpler and less demanding than Code B. Suppose the expected value of the consequences after Code B has been internalized is $n + 5$.

Second, consider the respective expected *costs involved in getting the codes internalized.* Since Code A is simpler and less demanding, the internalization cost for Code A would be less than for Code B. Suppose the expected cost involved in getting Code A internalized would be -1, and the expected costs involved in getting Code B internalized would be -7.

Now consider the totals for each code. The total expected value of Code A is $-1 + n$. The total expected value of Code B is $-7 + n + 5$. This illustrates how counting the costs of internalization can change the ranking of codes.

Just as more complicated and demanding moral codes have higher internalization costs, so do they have higher 'maintenance' and 'reinforcement' costs. We must not jump to the conclusion that an expected-value comparison of different codes will favour the very simplest and least demanding ones. But we should recognize that internalization and maintenance costs militate against more complicated and demanding codes.

I formulated rule-consequentialism with reference to internalization costs *in each new generation*. The reason for this is that we should think about a code's inculcation in human beings who have no prior moral ideas. We should not take into account the costs of getting a code internalized by people who are already committed to some particular code. The costs of getting a non-racist and non-sexist code accepted by people who have already internalized racist and sexist rules, for example, should *not* be counted. To count them would be to give some influence, on the determination of which rules are best, to learned attitudes which rule-consequentialism itself takes to be avoidable and morally unjustifiable. For rule-consequentialism to do this would be misguided for the same reason that the theory's giving weight to 'external preferences' would be misguided.[11] (In a later chapter, I do give some weight to established moral practices, even where they are sub-optimal. This will not extend so far, however, as to let racist or sexist or homophobic attitudes influence the selection of a moral code.)

3.3 WHAT LEVEL OF SOCIAL ACCEPTANCE?

Another question about how to formulate rule-consequentialism is what level of social acceptance to hypothesize. My formulation refers to 'internalization by the overwhelming majority of everyone, everywhere, in each new generation'. Obviously, this phrase is awkwardly wordy. So I often use the shorter expression 'general internalization' as a stand-in.

I refer to internalization by the *overwhelming majority* rather than *universal* internalization because we should not imagine that the code's internalization extends to young children, to the mentally impaired, and even to every 'normal' adult. A moral code should be suited to the real world, where there is likely to be, at best, only partial social acceptance of, and compliance with, any moral code. An adequate ethic must provide for situations created by people who are malevolent, dishonest, unfair, or simply misguided. In short, for use in the real world, a moral code needs provisions for dealing with non-compliance.

But I do not mean to suggest that the reason for formulating the

---

[11] In Ch.2, n. 26, I gave some references to the literature on external preferences.

theory in terms of internalization by the overwhelming majority, rather than in terms of absolutely universal internalization, is simply a consequentialist one. Our reason for finding one formulation of consequentialism more plausible than another need not be itself consequentialist. We may favour one version of rule-consequentialism over any other because this version coheres best both with our general convictions about morality and with our convictions about what morality requires in particular cases. So what matters is not so much that the general internalization version would result in better consequences than the universal internalization version. Rather, what matters is that the general internalization version fits our convictions better.

A common thought is that, while independent moral convictions can legitimately help us choose *between* theories, moral convictions should have little or no role to play *within* Kantian, contractualist, and consequentialist moral theories. But, in saying that a moral belief can be our reason for favouring one version of a theory over another, I am not saying that independent moral conviction has a role *within* rule-consequentialism. Instead, as indicated in the first chapter, I start from the widely accepted idea that we must test competing theories against our convictions. I then add that we must likewise test competing versions of any given theory against our convictions. We might think of competing versions of a theory as highly similar competing theories. And just as we test highly dissimilar theories against our convictions, we test highly similar ones, too.

Let me then turn to the convictions that favour the general internalization version over the universal internalization version. We have (for example) the strong conviction that it is permissible to harm someone when necessary to defend oneself against physical attack. How can the universal internalization version accord with this conviction? Likewise, how can it accord with our convictions about what is allowed by way of deterring and punishing crime?

An ideal code for a world where everyone internalizes the code would certainly have rules against physically attacking others, taking or harming the possessions of others, and so on. And, even if every single person accepts these rules, there would presumably still be a need for rules for dealing with non-compliance. For, as I noted earlier, a code's *acceptance* by 100 per cent of the people does not guarantee perfect *compliance* with it. There will be people who fully accept the best rules and yet sometimes, seduced by temptation, act wrongly. So, a version of rule-consequentialism formulated in terms of 100 per cent acceptance does not imagine away the existence of murder, rape, robbery, fraud, and so on. Because of such actual and potential wrongdoing, the ideal rules will specify, for example, what penalties apply for what crimes. They might also specify what to do when those around you accept that they should be helping to save others but aren't.

I think we must formulate rule-consequentialism so as to make room for rules about situations where there is some non-acceptance as well as non-compliance with them. Think about what is needed to deter or rehabilitate someone who has a moral conscience and accepts the right rules but sometimes does not care enough about morality to ensure good behaviour. Contrast that with what is needed to deal with unmitigated amoralists (people who have no moral conscience at all). Likewise, contrast what is needed to deal with someone who has a moral conscience and accepts the right rules but sometimes does not care enough about morality to ensure good behaviour, with what is needed to deal with someone who has a moral conscience but accepts the wrong rules. If we imagine a world with acceptance of the best code by 100 per cent of the population, we have simply imagined out of existence unmitigated amoralists and those who are conscientious but misguided. Hence, we have imagined out of existence any rule-consequentialist rationale for having rules for deterring and dealing with such people.

Here is why imagining a world with acceptance of the best code by 100 per cent of the population precludes any rule-consequentialist rationale for rules for deterring and dealing with unmitigated amoralists and those who are conscientious but misguided. On the rule-consequentialist view, there is always at least some cost associated with every additional rule added to the code. Every additional rule takes at least a little time to learn and at least a little memory to store. Given this cost, we must ask whether there is some benefit from acceptance of the rule that could outweigh the cost. We can of course frame rules applying to non-existent situations: for example, 'Be kind to spiders with an IQ more than 150.' The situation described is of course purely imaginary. As far as I can see, there are no benefits from having such never-to-be-applied rules in a code. But there would be internalization and maintenance costs associated with such rules. Thus such rules fail a cost-benefit analysis.

As I suggested earlier, there are certain problems that are special

to cases where non-compliers lack the inhibitions that moral motivations spark, and other problems special to dealing with people
who have moral motivations but accept the wrong rules. It is one
thing to be dealing with people who do wrong but against what their
conscience tells them to do. It is another thing to be dealing with
people with no moral conscience to inhibit their behaviour. And it is
still another thing to be dealing with people with a strong moral conscience that is misdirected.

But how can the universal internalization formulation accord
with such distinctions? I am assuming that internalizing a moral
code involves developing moral motivations corresponding to the
code's rules. So, if we assume absolutely universal internalization, we
eliminate any room for rule-consequentialism to make prescriptions
about how to deal with people who completely lack moral motivation. Likewise, we eliminate any room for rule-consequentialism to
make prescriptions about how to deal with people who have moral
motivation but accept the wrong rules. But, intuitively, a moral
theory should make prescriptions about these (familiar) situations.
For rule-consequentialism to be able to do so, it needs to be formulated in terms of general, not universal, internalization.

I put off until a later chapter an explanation of why I have framed
the theory in terms of internalization by the majority of everyone
everywhere, rather than just everyone *in the agent's society*.

But we still have the question of whether 'overwhelming majority' is to mean 70 per cent of everyone, or 80 per cent, or 90 per cent.[12]
The first part of the answer is that the desirability of some rules does
not depend on precisely how widely they are internalized. Rules
against arbitrarily injuring others, theft, promise-breaking, and the
like, will obviously be desirable, whether they are internalized by 70
per cent of the people, or 99 per cent. The second part of the answer,
however, is that the desirability of other rules may well depend on
precisely how widely they are internalized.

So our question is, where the desirability of rules does depend on
precisely how widely they are internalized, should we run the cost-
benefit analysis on the basis of 99 per cent acceptance or 90 per cent
or 80 per cent, or even less? Admittedly, any precise number will of
course be somewhat arbitrary. Nevertheless, we do have some

---

[12] Earlier rule-consequentialists have addressed this question. See, for example,
Brandt 1967, section 8. For a more recent discussion by Brandt, see his 1992: 149–54.

relevant factors to consider. On one hand, we want a per centage close enough to 100 per cent to hold on to the idea that moral rules are for acceptance *by the whole society of human beings.*[13] On the other hand, we want a per centage far enough short of 100 per cent to make salient the problems about partial compliance—such problems should not be thought of as incidental. Acknowledging that any one per centage will nevertheless be somewhat arbitrary, I propose we take internalization by 90 per cent of each new generation as the figure to use in the cost-benefit analysis.

Let me clarify some aspects of this proposal. First, this distinction between the 90 per cent who do internalize the right rules and the 10 per cent who do not (either because they internalize no moral rules or because they internalize the wrong ones) is supposed to cut across all other distinctions, such as distinctions in nationality and socio-economic status. Second, my proposal is not at all that the 10 per cent who are imagined not to have internalized the rules are somehow allowed not to follow the rules that everyone else is required to follow. We should assume that everyone should follow the rules, but also that not everyone will.

I admit that the degree of arbitrariness in the 90 per cent figure is a weakness in rule-consequentialism. But this weakness does not seem fatal. First of all, there are the considerations I mentioned that should influence what the percentage should be. Second, while admittedly these considerations do not demand any one precise figure, the problem this creates is hardly unique to rule-consequentialism. On the contrary, most of the theory's leading rivals have the same difficulty.

For example, contractualism needs a rule about what to do in situations of partial compliance. In order to generate such a rule, contractualism must be framed so as to select rules for a world with some level of social acceptance less than 100 per cent. For, with 100 per cent social acceptance, the partial-compliance problems to which I pointed will be simply imagined out of existence; yet some guidance for dealing with these problems is certainly needed.

Virtue ethics will likewise have this difficulty of specifying how to behave towards those with the wrong attitudes. So will Kantianism

---

[13] Regan (1980) carefully develops a theory that focuses on the level of likely actual compliance, even if this is very low. In so doing, he abandons what I think we must retain—the idea that a moral code should be appropriate for internalization by the general population.

(Korsgaard 1986; Langton 1994). Act-consequentialism, on the other hand, does not face this difficulty of having to hypothesize some level of communal moral understanding and compliance other than the actual one. There are, however, other objections to act-consequentialism, as I shall discuss later.

3.4 PUBLICITY, YES; RELATIVIZING, NO

Sidgwick famously entertained the possibility that society should be divided. On the one hand, there would be an enlightened elite who understands the consequentialist test for the rules of popular morality, does the calculations, and then decides what these rules are to be. On the other hand, there would be the unenlightened masses, taught the popular morality but not its consequentialist underpinnings (Sidgwick 1907: 489–90).

Such paternalistic duplicity would be morally wrong, even if it would maximize the aggregate good. So consequentialism is frequently attacked for falsely maintaining that the wrongness of the duplicity and elitism depends on their consequences (Williams 1972: 111–12; 1973: 138–9; 1985: 108–9).

However, *rule*-consequentialism, at least as I have formulated it, rules out the objectionable elitism and duplicity from the start. The theory insists there are the same rules for internalization by the overwhelming majority of everyone. As indicated, this is to be thought of as 90 per cent of everyone, cutting across all social, economic, national, and geographical distinctions. There are the same rules for internalization by the social, economic, or educational elite as for the rest of us. Members of the educated (or any other) elite are not beyond the rules applying to everyone else. So members of the educated elite are not asked to mandate different rules for the less well educated. Much less is any deception of the masses endorsed. On the contrary, the rules are to be *public*.[14] For, as Kant plausibly assumed,

---

[14] The literature on the 'publicity condition' is voluminous. For a sampling, see Sidgwick 1907: 489–90; Baier 1958: 195–6; Donagan 1968: 194; Rawls 1971: 130 n. 5, 133, 181, 582, 1980, 517, 537–8, 555; Hospers 1972: 314–15; Scheffler 1982: 46–52; Railton 1984: 154–5; Parfit 1984: 40–3; Williams 1985: 101–2, 108–9; Brink 1989: 80 n., 259–62, 275; Gert 1998: 10–13, 225, 239–40. Brandt endorses publicity for rule-consequentialism in his 1967 [1992: 136], 1988: 348 [1992: 144]

if all (or even just most) subscribe to a given rule, sooner or later this fact will become public knowledge. Given this Kantian assumption, a theory which determines moral rightness by reference to a code to be accepted by everyone, or even just by the overwhelming majority of everyone, will be pointing to a code suitable for public consumption.

But now some people will object that there should not be the same rules for everyone.[15] Imagine a world with a million imbeciles and one genius. On my rule-consequentialism, an act is permissible in this world if it is allowed by the code whose internalization by the overwhelming majority in that world could reasonably be expected to produce at least as good consequences as any other identifiable code. Because almost all in that world are very unintelligent, they could not remember rules of even the least complexity. Their rules would have to be ultra-simple. But the one genius is capable of learning far more complex and finely grained rules, rules that would in fact enable her to produce far more good. Should the genius follow the code of ultra-simple rules?

Here I stick to the formulation I have put forward. The genius should follow the same rules as the rest. That is, the genius should follow the simple rules even if she could do somewhat more good by following more complicated rules. The 'even if she could do somewhat more good by following more complicated rules' clause does not address what she should do if following the ultra-simple rules would result in disaster. As I explain in section 4.2, one rule an ideal code would contain is a rule telling people to prevent disaster, even if they have to break other rules to do it. This rule is no counterexample to my claim about having the same rules for everyone. For anyone—imbecile or genius—should break any of the simple rules when necessary to prevent disaster.

Why do I think moral requirements should not be different for people with greater intellectual (or emotional) capacities? I shall say why in a moment. First, I want to acknowledge a certain line of objection to my insistence that moral requirements should not be different for people with greater intellectual (or emotional) capacities.

---

[15] This objection was succinctly and forcefully put to me by Margaret Little at the 1995 St. Andrews Conference on Practical Reason. A version of the objection that targets my views on famine relief appears in Mulgan 1996, which derives from his 1994 doctoral dissertation at Oxford.

This line of objection is that whether there are to be different rules for different groups should itself be a consequentialist question. The objection, in other words, is that any form of consequentialism must hold that we should ask what the consequences would be if society is divided one way with different codes being internalized by the different groups. Then we should ask if better consequences would result from dividing society in some other way with different codes being internalized by different groups. Consequentialists should favour whatever way of dividing society produces the best results, according to this line of objection.

Rule-consequentialism *could* be formulated so as to allow codes to be relativized to groups. My own formulation of rule-consequentialism, however, clearly does not allow for such relativization. Mulgan (1996: sect. 2) accuses me of the 'new vice' of assuming that an ideal society would be one where everyone has the same moral character and follows the same rules. He observes that this assumption 'renders it (comparatively) easy to discover what [rule-consequentialism] requires of us.' But he argues that the assumption he supposes I make is unwarranted.

A rule-consequentialist can accept the rule 'For all *x*, if *x* is rich, *x* ought to give to aid agencies'. Moral rules can certainly mention group membership.[16] The issue between Mulgan and me is not whether rule-consequentialism rejects any rule mentioning group membership, but rather whether people in different groups should accept different rules. Would rule-consequentialism hold that non-parents as well as parents should accept the rule 'For all *x*, if *x* has a child, *x* ought to support that child'?

There are some reasons for thinking the answer is yes. First of all, there are advantages in having just *one* code for internalization by everyone. These advantages include convenience. Secondly, the idea of relativizing codes to groups is on the road to relativizing them to sub-groups, and at the end of that road is relativizing them to individuals. To go down that road is to turn our backs on one of the traditional attractions of rule-consequentialism—namely, its basis in the idea that morality should be thought of as a *collective, shared* code. As Gert (1998: 216) writes, 'Morality should be taught to everyone, adherence to it should be endorsed by all members of

---

[16] Though of course membership of some groups (racial ones, for instance) is irrelevant to any moral question.

society whose endorsement counts, and everyone should be urged to follow it. The requirements of morality apply to all rational persons.'[17]

That thought is certainly not a peculiarly consequentialist one. But, as I argued earlier, we may favour one version of rule-consequentialism over any other because this version coheres best both with our *general* beliefs about morality and with our beliefs about what morality requires *in particular cases*. If rule-consequentialism is formulated so as *not* to relativize moral rightness to groups, the theory has more acceptable moral implications than it does if it is formulated so as to incorporate such relativization. I shall illustrate this when I later discuss in detail rule-consequentialism's strictures about how much the well-off are required to sacrifice for the needy.

3.5 THE OPERATION OF RULES

One common misconception about rule-consequentialism is that it is crude and mechanistic. The truth is that rule-consequentialists certainly believe that whether or not a rule applies *can* be unclear. About legal rules, Hart (1961: 12) famously stated, 'all rules have a penumbra of uncertainty'. The same seems true of moral rules. Rule-consequentialists are as aware as anyone that figuring out whether a rule applies can require not merely attention to detail, but also sensitivity, imagination, interpretation, and judgement.[18]

---

[17] Gert admits that the form of rule-consequentialism developed here 'is closely related to a correct account of moral reasoning' (p. 215). Rule-consequentialism is indeed very like Gert's account.

[18] Carritt (1930: 114) wrote, 'It will be agreed on all hands that no number of moral rules will save us from exercising intuition; it will always be necessary to satisfy ourselves that an act comes under the rule, and for this no rule can be given.' That we cannot escape entirely recourse to judgement in ethics is what Rawls (1971: 40) was acknowledging when he wrote, '[A]ny ethical view is bound to rely on intuition to some degree at many points.' See also Scheffler 1992: 43–51; Shafer-Landau 1997: 601; Scanlon 1998: 199, 225, 246, 299; and Crisp 2000b. I want to sidestep here deep philosophical questions about the nature of vagueness. One side holds that there simply are no true or false answers to some questions, such as whether the colour on my wall is blue or how many grains of sand it takes to make a heap. Others hold that there are answers to such questions, but these answers are unknowable (Sorensen 1988; Williamson 1994). Sidestepping this debate, I shall simply note that, whichever side is right, the implications for ethics are deeply troubling.

And, when rules do clearly apply, they can also clearly conflict. How should rule-consequentialism deal with conflicts between rules? There are two answers that at first seem tempting. On further reflection, however, both ideas prove to be mistaken.

One of these mistaken ideas is that, when rules conflict, agents should abandon the rules and do whatever act will produce the best consequences. This is mistaken because having the act-consequentialist principle 'Do whatever produces the best consequences' as the conflict-resolving rule would actually have bad consequences. One reason for this is the point about expectation effects: how much confidence would you have in others to keep their promises and to tell the truth, if you knew that they would abandon promises or the truth whenever a conflict with beneficence appeared?[19] Another reason is that the internalization costs of this conflict-resolving rule would be prohibitive. Since general duties regularly conflict (Ross 1930: 41), the act-consequentialist conflict-resolving rule would be regularly kicking in. People would therefore *regularly* be required to produce the best consequences. This requirement would be very demanding. To get such a requirement internalized by the overwhelming majority would involve enormous costs in terms of time, energy, psychological conflict, and so on. (Again, this is something I discuss much more fully later.)

A second misguided idea about how rule-consequentialism would resolve conflicts between rules is that it would build exceptions into the rules so as to keep them from conflicting. Admittedly, this idea may seem the obvious move, since the best rules certainly will have *some* exceptions built into them. Some exceptions can be built in without making the rules too complicated to be worth learning. For example, the rule about promise-keeping could have built into it an exception such that no one is required to keep a promise made to anyone who obtained the promise by lying. But rule-consequentialists should not try to prevent all conflict between rules by building exception clauses into the rules. The problem with building in

---

[19] As Scanlon (1998: 200) writes, '[T]he point of promising would be defeated if a minor inconvenience, or even a major cost that was clearly foreseeable at the time the promise was made, counted as adequate ground for failing to perform as promised.' And (1998: 223), 'To recognize ... [a] permission to break a promise or inflict a harm in every case in which this would benefit the person whose overall level of well-being was lower would prevent these principles [against promise-breaking and harming others] from offering the kind of assurance that they are supposed to supply.'

exception after exception is that the rules then become harder to learn. More demanding and more complex rules will have higher internalization costs.[20] At some point, the added costs involved in learning more complicated rules will outweigh the benefits.

A better approach to cases in which rules conflict points to the relative strengths of the motivations involved in accepting rules. As Brandt puts it, rule-consequentialists will

order the acceptable level of aversion to various act-types in accordance with the damage . . . that would likely be done if everyone *felt free* to indulge in the kind of behavior in question—not if everyone actually indulged. The worse the effect if everyone felt free, the higher the acceptable level of aversion. (1989: 95 [1992: 84–5]; cf. Schauer 1991: ch. 6; Frey 1976)

If an act would be prohibited by the moral aversions thus selected, it would be morally wrong, according to rule-consequentialism. When rules conflict, so do the aversions that are attached to them. The stronger aversion determines what action is permissible, according to rule-consequentialism. When moral requirements conflict, one should do, as Brandt writes, 'whatever course of action would leave morally well-trained people least dissatisfied'.[21]

There are four points we should note in this context. The first is that there is a striking similarity here with one of the claims prominent in recent discussions of virtue. This is claim that, at least sometimes, moral right and wrong cannot be determined except by reference to the dispositions of a virtuous person. The best version

---

[20] Epstein 1995 argues the case for simpler *legal* rules over more complex ones, given our motivational and informational limitations.

[21] Brandt 1963: sect. 6, p. 134. Brandt here mentions the similarity between his account and that of W. D. Ross, who pictured moral conflicts as balancing 'prima facie duties' against one another (Ross 1930: ch. 2). See also Aristotle *Nicomachean Ethics* 1107a1–2. I should add that Brandt has not always stuck to this line. Sometimes he seriously entertained the possibility that conflicts between rules should be adjudicated by a rule telling us to do whatever will produce the best consequences (Brandt 1979: 292; 1992: 146). This is in effect Hare's solution too (Hare 1981). But rule-consequentialists are unwise to embrace this solution. For, as I shall explain in Chapter 4, the line threatens (at least partial) collapse into act-consequentialism. Such a collapse would undermine rule-consequentialism's distinctiveness, as Brandt (1992: 130, 208) himself sometimes acknowledged. Such a collapse would also render rule-consequentialism prey to many of the intuitively compelling counterexamples to act-consequentialism. To the extent we think rule-consequentialism implicit in the moral reasoning of our society, we should not be surprised that relying on the built-in weights of the rules seems to be the conflict-resolving mechanism 'actually used in our society' (Brandt 1979: 292).

of rule-consequentialism accepts that this is true in some cases where different moral considerations pull against each other.

The second point to note here is that rule-consequentialism is *not* crippled by conflicts between rules. It has a method for determining what is right in such situations. And (as explained above) this method is not merely a retreat to the act-consequentialist view that the right act is the one that does the most good on that occasion. Although rule-consequentialism has a method for determining what is right when rules conflict, I do not mean that we can capture *all* the resolutions in some further set of rules. I take it that Brandt's point in referring to what would leave the well-trained moral agent least dissatisfied is to acknowledge the role of judgement in adjudicating conflicts between general duties in some situation. I shall return to this later.

The third point to note is that the rule-consequentialist approach is not simplistic or unsympathetic about moral conflicts. It leaves room for hard cases, where the conflicting moral motivations are of roughly equal strength. It even leaves room for tragic cases in which an agent's conflicting moral motivations are intense, and whichever loses the battle will take bitter revenge on the agent's psyche. Being a 'morally well-trained person' is not an inoculation against moral pain.

The fourth point to note here concerns the use of the word 'rule'. Rule-consequentialism takes the acceptance of rules to involve *more than* certain associated motivations. It also involves having sensitivities, emotions, and beliefs—indeed a particular cast of character and conscience. If you *accept* a rule against stealing, you will be motivated not to steal simply because it is stealing (not merely because you will get into trouble). You will also be disposed to feel guilty if you steal, disposed to resent stealing by other people, and disposed to blame them for it. You will want others to have these dispositions not to steal and to react negatively to those who do steal. And you will have associated beliefs, such as that stealing is morally prohibited and that this prohibition is justified. We might sum all this up by saying that to accept a code of rules is just to have *a moral conscience of a certain shape*. In other words, when rule-consequentialists consider alternative codes of rules, they are considering alternative possible contours for people's consciences.

Perhaps, in conceiving of the acceptance of a code of rules as having a moral conscience of a certain shape, rule-consequentialism uses the term 'rule' more broadly than normal. Some people might take 'rule' narrowly to mean something that must never be overridden or broken no matter how unusual and unfortunate the circumstances. On that narrow reading of 'rule', the version of rule-consequentialism I am discussing really contains vanishingly few rules. But there is a broader meaning of 'rule' which allows that something can count as a rule even if it can sometimes justifiably be broken.

I have now sketched the outlines of rule-consequentialism. I have already indicated something about how rule-consequentialism contrasts with one of its rivals, contractualism. My sketch of rule-consequentialism will develop into a fuller picture as I explore its ability to answer its critics and as I continue to contrast it with its rivals.

4
Is Rule-consequentialism Guilty of Collapse or Incoherence?

4.1 INTRODUCTION

For about thirty-five years now, rule-consequentialism has been widely thought to collapse into act-consequentialism. The charge is that rule-consequentialism will end up prescribing the very same acts that act-consequentialism does. The objection continues: if rule-consequentialism does escape collapse into extensional equivalence with act-consequentialism, it does so only by becoming incoherent. If rule-consequentialism either collapses or is incoherent, it is indeed untenable.

But I shall show in this chapter that the best form of rule-consequentialism neither collapses into act-consequentialism nor is incoherent. My explanation of how rule-consequentialism avoids incoherence, however, might provoke a further objection, namely that it is really just a version of its non-consequentialist rivals. I shall show that this further objection can also be answered.

4.2 COLLAPSE INTO EXTENSIONAL EQUIVALENCE WITH ACT-CONSEQUENTIALISM

The objection that rule-consequentialism collapses into extensional equivalence with act-consequentialism can take three different forms.

One form of the collapse objection claims that rule-consequentialism must favour just one simple rule—the rule 'always maximize expected value' (Smart 1973: 11–12). The objection assumes that, if each person successfully complies with a rule requiring the maximization of the good, then the good would be maximized.

This sort of objection may work against a version of rule-consequentialism that focuses solely on the consequences of people's
successful compliance with rules. That the best results would be
achieved under these conditions has been challenged (see Hodgson
1967: ch. 2; Regan 1980: ch. 5; Kagan 1998: 228–35; 2000). But
whether or not everyone's complying with the act-consequentialist
principle would produce the best consequences, the objection does
not work against a kind of rule-consequentialism that ranks systems
of rules in terms of the expected consequences of their *internalization*.[1] For, as I explained in the previous chapter, internalization of a
rule can have consequences over and above compliance with it.

To have internalized only the one act-consequentialist rule would
be to have just one moral disposition—the disposition to try to comply with act-consequentialism. To have just this one moral disposition would be to have act-consequentialism as the principle one
consults when making moral decisions. In contemporary philosophical jargon, the principle(s) one consults when making moral
decisions is one's 'moral decision procedure'.

In fact, act-consequentialism is *not* a good decision procedure. I
shall go into this in greater detail in later chapters. For the moment,
let me simply note that, if we had just the one rule 'Maximize the
good', sooner or later awareness of this would become widespread.
And becoming aware of this would undermine people's ability to
rely confidently on others to behave in agreed-upon ways. Trust
would break down. In short, terrible consequences would result
from the public expectation that this rule would prescribe killing,
stealing, and so on when such acts would maximize the good.[2]

---

[1] This line of response has been around since at least as Brandt 1963: sect. 4; see
also his 1967 [1992: 130]. Likewise, the objection will not work against versions of
rule-consequentialism that favour the rules whose *promulgation* would have the best
consequences, or against versions favouring the rules that, *if backed by social pressure*,
would have the best consequences. For discussion of the differences between promulgation and acceptance (internalization) versions of rule-consequentialism, see
Trianosky 1976; Witt 1984; and MacIntosh 1990. For a development of the social
pressure version, see Haslett 1994: sect. 1.6. In so far as the point of promulgation
and social pressure is to secure widespread internalization, these versions dovetail
with versions stated in terms of internalization. However, some differences may
remain. The best rules to promulgate might be harsher than the best rules for people
to internalize, just as the posted speed limit might be set a bit slower than the opti-
mum speed for people to drive (Brandt 1963: n. 7). Now, in so far as there is such a
difference between the best rules to promulgate and the best rules to internalize, right
and wrong should presumably be tied to the best rules to internalize.

[2] Hodgson 1967: ch. 2; Warnock 1971: 31–4; Brandt 1979: 271–7, 1992: 142–7,

Furthermore, apart from negative expectation effects, a morality comprised of just the one rule 'Maximize the good' would have extremely high internalization costs. The costs would not come from a difficult job of memorizing. Learning to recite such a simple rule could hardly be easier. The difficulty would come from getting the rule infused into people's motivations. For getting that one rule internalized amounts to getting people to be disposed always to do what would be impartially best. To get people to be always perfectly impartial is to push them a very long way from natural biases towards themselves and their loved ones. Of course, there are benefits to be gained from getting people to care about others, and to be willing to make sacrifices for those outside their circle of family and friends. But the time, energy, attention, and psychological conflict that would be needed to get people to internalize an overriding impartial altruism would be immense.

So rule-consequentialists have principled reasons for rejecting a code consisting of just the one rule 'Maximize the good'. Thus let us move on to the second version of the collapse objection.

The second version of the collapse objection asks us to suppose everyone were to internalize rules such as 'Don't kill *except when killing will maximize the good*', 'Don't steal *except when stealing will maximize the good*', 'Don't break your promises *except when breaking them will maximize the good*', etc. A code comprised of such rules is really nothing more than the simple rule 'Maximize the good'. Such a rule-consequentialist code does collapse into practical equivalence with act-consequentialism (Gert 1998: 214–15). But, for the reasons I outlined a few paragraphs ago, rule-consequentialists have principled reasons for rejecting such a code.

The third—and most common—version of the collapse objection starts by acknowledging that bad consequences would come from internalization of the one-rule code 'Maximize the good'. This third version of the collapse objection also acknowledges that bad consequences would come from internalization of a multi-rule code consisting of rules like 'Don't hurt others except when this will

1996: 126, 144; Harsanyi 1977, 1982: 58–61, 1993: 116–18; C. Johnson 1991, esp. chs. 3, 4, 9; Blackburn 1998: 42. For the view that useful practices such as promising and truth telling would not break down if there were perfect compliance with act-consequentialism, see P. Singer 1972b; Mackie 1973. But for conclusive arguments that in certain circumstances, act-consequentialists could not attain maximally beneficial co-operation, see Regan 1980: esp. chs. 2–4.

maximize the good', and 'Don't break promises except when this will maximize the good'. But the third version of the collapse objection maintains that the problem is not with having exception clauses, but with the overly general ones proposed. This third version of the collapse objection maintains that *more specific exception clauses would have good consequences*. For example, the rule could be 'Don't break promises *except when breaking a promise to meet one person will enable you to meet someone else who will benefit at least slightly more*'. If such specific exception clauses would have good consequences, then rule-consequentialists must embrace these exception clauses. And the same sort of reasoning will militate in favour of adding specific exception clauses aimed at each situation in which following some rule would not bring about the best consequences. Once all the exception clauses are added, rule-consequentialism will have the same implications for action that act-consequentialism has.

The rule-consequentialist reply to this way of developing the collapse objection is partly the same. How much confidence would you have in others if you knew they accepted such highly qualified rules? Mackie (1977: 156) observed, 'We are rightly sceptical about a man of principle who has a new principle for every case.'[3] The same is true about someone who has too many new exception clauses.

An additional problem comes into view when we remember that part of the comparison of different possible rules is the comparison of the costs of their inculcation. As Gert (1998: 214) notes, if we tried to list all the exceptions in the rules themselves, the rules 'must be so long and complex that they cannot possibly be formulated, let alone taught'. Even if such rules could be formulated and even taught, the costs of teaching and inculcating an overly long list of rules would be too high. The same would be true of overly complicated rules. Hence, the rules whose teaching and internalization would have the best results are limited in number and complexity.[4]

I do not mean to suggest that the list of rules has to be short and simple enough for most people to recite. We can learn things without being able to recite them. As Brandt writes,

---

[3] See also Blackburn (1998: 67).
[4] Sorensen (forthcoming) rightly remarks of the law, 'Law is a guidance system that must be sensitive to the costs as well as the benefits of constraining action. Guidance at the appropriate level of generality is an important skill. Part of learning law is learning techniques that pitch principles at the appropriate level of detail.' Likewise, a rule-consequentialist evaluation of proposed *moral* rules will be very keen to avoid both over-precision and under-precision.

[what matters is knowing the code of rules] well enough to recall the relevant rule when stimulated by being in a context to which it is relevant. Learning a moral code is thus like learning a complex route into a large city: we may not be able to draw it or explain to others what it is, but when we drive it and have the landmarks before us, we remember each turn we are to make. (1963: sect. 4, n. 6)

And as Copp (1995: 86) writes,

[I]t is possible to intend to conform to a rule, or to desire its currency, even if one does not know how to formulate it. One must be *aware* of the rule, but this does not require knowing its formulation. However, if a person subscribes to a moral standard, she must be able to recognize conformity with the standard in a wide range of circumstances and to see what would count as conformity. I do not mean that her recognition must be infallible without difficulty or doubt; I mean only that she can recognize what counts as conformity with rough accuracy.[5]

Although learning a code can fall short of being able to recite it, there remain limits on what we can learn. And even within the class of learnable codes, the costs of learning the ones with more rules and more complex rules will be higher. So the ideal code will contain rules of limited number and limited complexity. Such a code would not be extensionally equivalent with act-consequentialism. Thus, this kind of rule-consequentialism does not collapse into act-consequentialism.

But what if we could each carry around in our pockets a small computer containing lists of all the rules, with their exception clauses, and with an index? We wouldn't need to learn the rules, only how to operate the tiny computer. Here complexity of the rules would now not increase the internalization costs.

Yet, even if a highly complicated code of rules in the little computer is extensionally equivalent with act-consequentialism, there is the point about negative expectation effects. What we need is for people's responses in certain kinds of situations to be habitual, automatic, and therefore *easily* predictable. Everyone whipping out pocket computers to see how each other will behave does not fit this picture. Nor does the huge potential for misapplication of the

---

[5] Blackburn (1996: 99): '[A]ttitudes do not need to be reflected in a fully determinate propositional content, ascribing each act a determinate merit in any possible context. For most living it is enough to feel the everyday pressures: we are for benevolence and humanity, against ingratitude and lying.' See Ch. 3, n. 18, above.

computer's complicated rules militate in favour of the dependability that is so important for communal life.

Finally, we must again consider the cost of internalizing the motivation to comply with rules that end up requiring the same actions as act-consequentialism requires. Act-consequentialism is hugely demanding. If the computer's complicated rules are extensionally equivalent with act-consequentialism, then they too are hugely demanding. Hence, if people were motivated to comply with these rules, they would be motivated regularly to make enormous self-sacrifices. The cost of getting such motivation internalized would be too great. Rule-consequentialists would thus advocate a less demanding set of rules.

To be sure, one motivation that rule-consequentialism would endorse is a motivation to prevent disaster.[6] And this motivation should be stronger than other motivations.[7] For it is reasonable to expect that, in the long run, things will go better on the whole if people care more about preventing disasters than about breaking other rules. Thus the desire to prevent disaster should be stronger than the desire to keep promises and the desire to avoid lying. Rule-consequentialism therefore holds we should break the promise or tell a lie when necessary to prevent disaster.[8]

The fact that rule-consequentialism would incorporate a 'prevent disaster' rule capable of overriding other moral rules is relevant to one of the most common objections to rule-consequentialism. This is the objection that rule-consequentialism could result in disaster.[9] Rule-consequentialism of course endorses such rules as 'Tell the truth', 'Keep your promises', and so on. But blindly following such rules *can* result in disaster. For example, disaster will result if you tell the murderer the truth about where his target is. And disaster will

---

[6] Brandt 1988 [1992: 150–1, 156–7]; 1989 [1992: 87–8].

[7] Furthermore, along with motivations to keep promises, tell the truth, avoid harming others, prevent disasters, etc., rule-consequentialism will hold that we should be motivated to do good for others. But, unlike the motivation to prevent disasters, the motivation to do good for others should normally be *weaker* than the motivations to keep promises, tell the truth, avoid harming others, etc. So the motivation to do good for others is not relevant here.

[8] Compare this rule-consequentialist position with the contortions Korsgaard (1986) has to go through to make Kant's view about lying seem even vaguely plausible. I shall return later to the question of when promise-breaking is allowed.

[9] Note that this objection is incompatible with the objection that rule-consequentialism collapses into extensional equivalence with act-consequentialism.

result if you keep your promise about returning the chain-saw even when you can see that your crazed neighbour will kill someone with it. So if rule-consequentialism requires unswerving obedience to good rules like 'Tell the truth' and 'Keep your promises', rule-consequentialism is absurd. Yet what is even more absurd is the idea that rule-consequentialism would require blind obedience to such rules. But this is not to say that, by virtue of its rule about preventing disaster, rule-consequentialism collapses into extensional equivalence with act-consequentialism. Act-consequentialism holds that we should break the promise *whenever* doing so will produce more good. So, when breaking a promise would produce only *a little* more good, act-consequentialism tells us to break it. The 'prevent disaster' rule does not have this implication. On the contrary, the motivation to prevent disaster only comes into play when there is a sufficiently large difference in the amounts of expected value in the possible outcomes.[10] Thus, incorporating a 'prevent disaster' requirement into the ideal code is *not* a capitulation to act-consequentialism.

One objection I have just answered is that rule-consequentialism is highly *counterintuitive* in that it requires us to do certain things such as keeping a promise or telling the truth even when such acts would result in disaster. The answer is that better consequences will result if the code includes an overriding 'prevent disaster' rule. In the light of this move, rule-consequentialism gets attacked for collapsing into extensional equivalence with act-consequentialism. I have shown that this objection is also misguided. Rule-consequentialism does not collapse into act-consequentialism.

4.3 WHY RULE-CONSEQUENTIALISM NEED NOT BE INCOHERENT

Many philosophers who accept the arguments laid out above move now to yet another objection to rule-consequentialism. It is that rule-consequentialism is *incoherent* whenever it tells us to follow a rule though breaking it would do more good, if even only a little more good. If the ultimate goal is the maximization of good, is not it incoherent to follow rules when one knows this will not maximize

---

[10] I return to this matter later.

the good? If rules are really merely a means to an end, how can one coherently stick to rules when one knows they will not serve that end in the situation at hand?[11]

Many rule-consequentialists try to answer this objection by showing how general internalization of rule-consequentialism would actually produce *better* consequences than general internalization of act-consequentialism. The general internalization of rule-consequentialism would produce better consequences because of the points about the inefficiency, mistakes, and negative expectation effects that would result from an act-consequentialist decision procedure, and because of act-consequentialism's prohibitive internalization costs.

As against this line of thought, however, some act-consequentialists claim we must distinguish between two questions.[12] One is the question of whether a moral theory's criterion of rightness is correct. The other is the question of whether belief in that moral theory, and direct use of it in making decisions about how to act, would have good consequences. True, if the consequences of our believing in act-consequentialism are sub-optimal, then act-consequentialism would itself prescribe that we try to get ourselves *not* to believe in act-consequentialism. In other words, getting ourselves to disbelieve act-consequentialism would be morally right, according to act-consequentialism's criterion of moral rightness. But, many now argue, to show that belief in act-consequentialism is not optimal would not invalidate act-consequentialism's criterion of rightness. It might be said that likewise, if the results of general internalization of and belief in rule-consequentialism are optimal, this does not show that rule-consequentialism is actually correct, only that it is useful.

[11] For a sophisticated discussion, see Lyons 1965: chs. III, IV. See also Williams 1972: 99–102, 105–8; Mabbott 1956: 115–20; Smart 1956; Slote 1992: 59; Raphael 1994: 52; Scarre 1996: 125–26; Darwall 1998: 137–8. Relatedly, Regan (1980: 209) complains that rule-consequentialists 'are only half-hearted consequentialists'. For different answers to such objections than the one that I give, see Diamond 1997: sect. 7; and McClennen 1997: '[T]he logical structure of intrapersonal and interpersonal coordination problems is such that a viable version of consequentialism will be a version of *rule* consequentialism, in which the notion of a rational commitment to extant rules has a central place' (p. 258).

[12] Mill 1861: ch. II; Sidgwick 1907: 405–6, 413, 489–90; Moore 1903: 162–4; Smart 1956: 346, 1973: 43, 71; Bales 1971: 257–65; Parfit 1984: 24–9, 31–43; Railton 1984: 140–6, 152–3; Brink 1986: 421–7, 1989: 216–17, 256–62, 274–6, Pettit and Brennan 1986; Pettit 1991, 1994, 1997: 99–102, 156–61.

This debate ends in stalemate. One side says that what recommends a package composed of certain rules plus belief in rule-consequentialist theory is that this package promotes the good. The other side may agree that the components of this package promote the good, but go on to deny that this shows them to be correct (Kagan 1989: 37).

Most philosophers seem convinced that defending rule-consequentialism is a lost cause once one accepts an overarching commitment to maximize the good. Suppose rule-consequentialism is indeed a lost cause if one accepts an overarching commitment to maximize the good. This need not be the death knell of rule-consequentialism. For the best argument for rule-consequentialism is *not* that it derives from an overarching commitment to maximize the good. The best argument for rule-consequentialism is that it does a better job than its rivals of matching and tying together our moral convictions, as well as offering us help with our moral disagreements and uncertainties.

That rule-consequentialism might be defended by appeal to its match with our convictions is an old idea. Still, to dispel the objection about internal inconsistency, we need to show that rule-consequentialist agents need not have incoherent psychologies. And we need to show there is no internal inconsistency in the theory itself.

Rule-consequentialists need not have maximizing the good as their ultimate moral goal. They could have a moral psychology as follows.

> Their fundamental moral motivation is to do what is impartially defensible.
>
> They believe acting on impartially justified rules is impartially defensible.
>
> They also believe that rule-consequentialism is on balance the best account of impartially justified rules.[13]

This combination of moral motivation and beliefs would lead people to do as rule-consequentialism prescribes.

---

[13] Why is rule-consequentialism better than a list of the rules with no foundational principle? As I indicated in Chapter 1, an account that provides impartial justification of rules, and ties them together by exhibiting a common element, is better than one that does not.

I believe many people's fundamental moral motivation for complying with moral requirements is the desire to behave in ways that are impartially defensible. This desire seems more important even than benevolence, for two reasons: (i) it kicks in when benevolence gives out, and (ii) benevolence could sometimes motivate wrong action, as counterexamples to act-utilitarianism show.

Even if not already widespread, the desire to act in ways that are impartially defensible *could* become people's fundamental moral motivation. And having these moral beliefs is also obviously *possible*. (At this point in my argument, I am not saying the beliefs are correct; here, I am saying merely that some people could accept them.) Furthermore, having this combination of moral motivation and beliefs would make people rule-consequentialists, even though they would not have maximizing the good as their ultimate moral goal. For people with this combination of moral motivation and beliefs, there is nothing incoherent about following rules when this will not maximize the good.

Even if I am right that the rule-consequentialist *agent* need not have an overarching commitment to maximize the good, mustn't the *theory*—rule-consequentialism itself—contain such a commitment? The theory can be broken down into (i) a principle about which rules are optimal, and (ii) a principle about which acts are permissible. The theory selects *rules* by whether their internalization could reasonably be expected to maximize the good. The theory does not, however, evaluate *acts* this way. Rather, it evaluates acts by reference to the rules thus selected. This is all there is to say about how the theory stands with respect to maximizing the good. In other words, once we understand the theory's view about how rules are to be selected and its view about how acts are to be judged, there just is no further question whether the theory itself has an overarching commitment to maximizing the good.

4.4 IS RULE-CONSEQUENTIALISM REALLY CRYPTO-CONTRACTUALISM?

If rule-consequentialists deny an overarching commitment to maximizing the good and appeal instead to the desire to act in ways that are impartially defensible, are they thereby crypto-contractualists?

T. M. Scanlon's work on contractualism (1982; 1998) might lead some people to think the theory I have outlined *is* crypto-contractualism. His 1982 article contrasted utilitarianism with contractualism by pointing to the different concerns from which they grow. The article linked utilitarianism to concern for the well-being of (all) individuals. It linked contractualism to concern for reasonable agreement among all individuals who are concerned to reach reasonable agreement with one another.

I have suggested that the basic moral motivation of rule-consequentialists can be a concern with impartial defensibility. I have certainly not suggested that rule-consequentialism grows from a concern for reasonable agreement among all individuals who are concerned to reach reasonable agreement with one another. But if concern for impartial defensibility is construed as concern for reasonable agreement among those seeking agreement, then anyone appealing to impartial defensibility may be assumed to be some kind of contractualist.

Yet whereas Scanlon distinguished between concern for the well-being of (all) individuals and concern for reasonable agreement, I distinguished between the desire to maximize the overall good and the desire to act in ways that are impartially defensible. In two ways, my distinction is broader than his. One is that 'overall good' can be understood more broadly than just 'aggregate well-being'. The other is that 'impartial defensibility' can be understood more broadly than 'reasonable agreement among contractors': reasonable agreement among contractors is but one account of impartial defensibility.

Given my broader distinction, what reason could there be for thinking non-contractualist moral theories cannot appeal to the desire to act in impartially defensible ways? Is the answer that only contractualist theories can appeal to this desire because only they offer an account of impartial defensibility? Well, contractualism does offer an account of impartial defensibility. But it is hardly the only theory to do so (Scanlon 1982: 120–2). Various forms of impartial consequentialism clearly offer an account of impartial defensibility.[14]

Which theory offers the most plausible account of impartial defensibility is a further question, one not at issue in this section. Another further question, I admit, is whether any theory providing

---

[14] So might non-contractualist forms of Kantianism.

an account of impartial defensibility must hold that our overarching moral concern should be with impartial defensibility. A consequentialist theory could provide an account of impartial defensibility and yet go on to endorse concern for aggregate good as the overarching moral motivation. But, perhaps more naturally, a consequentialist theory can both provide an account of impartial defensibility and take concern for impartial defensibility as the overarching moral motivation. This is the kind of consequentialist theory I am exploring.

4.5 IS RULE-CONSEQUENTIALISM REALLY MERELY INTUITIONISM?

I claimed that the best argument for rule-consequentialism is that it does a better job than its rivals of matching and tying together our moral convictions, as well as offering us help with our moral disagreements and uncertainties. So, is my view really just intuitionism?

There are different senses of the term 'intuitionism' in ethics. 'Intuitionism' in one sense refers to the view that we should test moral theories by comparing what follows from them with our moral convictions. 'Intuitionism' in a second sense refers to a normative moral theory, a theory about which moral convictions are correct.

I accept that we should test moral theories by comparing what follows from them with our moral convictions. As I admitted right at the start of the book, I am looking for a theory that matches and makes sense of our considered convictions (or 'intuitions' in some metaphysically and epistemologically neutral sense of the term). I admit that we are more certain of some intuitions (moral verdicts) than we are of any theory. So I admit that, in moral theorizing our confident shared intuitions are central.[15] I am an intuitionist in the sense that I think that seeking a match between intuition and theory is the first (because most secure) step in moral theory building. Someone who ends up being convinced of rule-consequentialism can certainly think the *first* step in evaluating a moral theory is to see whether it can match our intuitions.

---

[15] Which, again, does not entail that they are infallible.

Turn now to the normative moral theory sometimes called intuitionism. This normative theory is a species of moral pluralism. The genus is:

MORAL PLURALISM

(1) There is a plurality of moral values or principles.

(2) There is no principle that underlies and provides justification for them.

The kind of moral pluralism that sometimes gets called intuitionism adds further theses to the above. Let me refer to this theory as

ROSS-STYLE PLURALISM

(1) There is a plurality of moral values or principles.

(2) There is no principle that underlies and provides justification for them.

(3) The different values or principles may conflict.

(4) The principles do not come in a strict order of priority that resolves all conflicts between them.

(5) There is an ineliminable need for the exercise of *judgement* in order to resolve some conflicts.[16]

Some other forms of moral pluralism accept (1) and (2) but then deny (3) because the values or (more likely) the principles or the world are such that conflicts are avoided. Since these forms of moral pluralism deny (3), they do not need to accept (4) or (5). There could be other forms of moral pluralism that deny (4), and thus do not need to accept (5).

As I have defined 'moral pluralism', all moral pluralists hold that there is nothing like rule-consequentialism or contractualism or act-consequentialism that ties together and justifies our various moral intuitions. Thus, obviously, moral pluralism is incompatible with rule-consequentialism, contractualism, and act-consequentialism. In fact, moral pluralism is a competitor of these theories.

As argued earlier, the most plausible form of rule-consequential-

---

[16] In this century, the *locus classicus* for this view is Ross 1930: ch. 2.

ism will select general duties with one eye on aggregate well-being and the other on the position of the worst off. In light of this, Ross-style pluralists might say that, however differently rule-consequentialism and Ross-style pluralism are dressed up, they are the same underneath. The accusation here is that rule-consequentialism has the same essential structure as Ross-style pluralism. The only difference is that rule-consequentialism has just two first principles where Ross-style pluralism has more.

This is not the only way in which rule-consequentialism is pluralistic. Ross-style pluralists ever since Ross have insisted that the most plausible forms of consequentialism are pluralistic about the good (Ross 1930: 23; Gaut 1993: 23–4). After careful reflection, most of us agree that an individual's well-being consists in an irreducible plurality of goods. If we are right about this, then rule-consequentialism should have not only a first principle that refers to both well-being and priority towards the worst off, but also a pluralistic theory of well-being.

Furthermore, rule-consequentialists are also pluralists about our general duties. We are required to do a plurality of different things— for example, avoid harming others, keep our promises, tell the truth, be grateful for what others have done for us, take special interest in the welfare of our own family and friends, do good for others generally up to some threshold of aggregate self-sacrifice. Many philosophers who think of themselves as *anti*-consequentialists assert that the right-making features of an act include such things as whether the act involves keeping a promise, telling the truth, returning a favour, helping a friend, protecting the innocent. Rule-consequentialists agree with this. Right and wrong are determined by the interplay of a plurality of general moral requirements.

Rule-consequentialists should also agree that the exercise of judgement is needed in at least the following four quite different broad areas:

(a) When evaluating alternative moral codes, rule-consequentialists will have to resort to judgement to determine when priority toward the worst off is more important than aggregate well-being.

(b) They will also need to use judgement to determine when one component of well-being is more important than another.

(c) Rule-consequentialist agents will have to rely on judgement to resolve some conflicts between general duties.

(d) Rule-consequentialists will have to rely on judgement even when trying to ascertain whether some one rule applies in a given case. For example, judgement is needed sometimes to ascertain whether an act would constitute breaking a promise, or whether an act would constitute destroying property, or stealing, or lying, or whether an event would make someone worse off, or whether someone's connection to you entitles her to special weight in your practical reasoning.[17]

Rule-consequentialism takes on board much of Ross-style pluralism. But this is not to say that rule-consequentialism fails to stand as an alternative to Ross-style pluralism. Again, rule-consequentialism disagrees with Ross-style and other forms of pluralism about whether there is a principle underlying the others. Ross-style pluralism holds that there is no one principle tying together the various general duties; rule-consequentialism holds that there is (see Table 4.1). Rule-consequentialism thus seems to have more systematic unity than Ross-style pluralism (cf. McNaughton 1996: 441).

TABLE 4.1

Ross-style pluralism	Rule-consequentialism
Implications for particular cases	Implications for particular cases
General duties/virtues (e.g.)	General duties/virtues (e.g.)
Non-maleficence	Non-maleficence
Trustworthiness	Trustworthiness
Beneficence	Beneficence
Loyalty	Loyalty
Gratitude and reparation	Gratitude and reparation
There is no deeper principle underlying the general duties listed above.	General duties to be selected on the basis of how much (weighted?) well-being would result from their internalization.

---

[17] See section 3.5 above.

4.6 IS RULE-CONSEQUENTIALISM NOT REALLY CONSEQUENTIALIST?

'Consequentialism' is often defined so narrowly that the term shrinks to synonymy with 'act-consequentialism'. Thinking rule-consequentialism inferior, many philosophers, when discussing consequentialism, have had act-consequentialism in mind. Having just one kind of consequentialism in mind has led them to use definitions of consequentialism that are really definitions of only act-consequentialism. Thus, for example, Derek Parfit used the term 'consequentialism' to refer to the view that 'What each of us ought to do is whatever would make the outcome best'.[18] And Philip Pettit writes that consequentialists say 'agents are required to produce whatever actions have the property of promoting a designated value' (1991: 231). And John Skorupski writes that 'consequentialism' is best used to refer to the view that 'an action is right just if it is optimal [results in the greatest possible value]' (1995: 52). By making the rightness of an act depend exclusively on whether that act max-imizes the good, these definitions of consequentialism point to act-consequentialism.

Furthermore, as John Broome observed (1991b: 5), '[A]gent-neutrality is often included within the *definition* of consequentialism.' A requirement is agent-relative (or, in other words, agent-centred) if it includes an essential reference to the agent in the description of the state of affairs the agent has to promote.[19] For example, you may be required to help *your* children. A requirement is agent-neutral if there is no essential reference to the agent in the description of the state of affairs the agent is required to promote. You may, for ex-ample, be required to help children *in general*, that is, whether or not they are yours. Given all this, Frances Howard-Snyder (1993: 271) is anything but idiosyncratic when she writes:

---

[18] Parfit 1984: 24. But Parfit is not trying to define 'consequentialism' as the term is used in contemporary ethics; rather, he is interested in a certain theory (which has traditionally been called act-consequentialism) and gives it the simpler name 'conse-quentialism'. That he is really just *stipulating* a definition is clear from the fact that he himself says a few pages later (p. 30) that there are other forms of consequentialism.

[19] The most careful discussion of the distinction between agent-neutrality and agent-relativity (or agent-centredness) is to be found in McNaughton and Rawling 1991. For influential earlier discussions, see Nagel 1972: 47–8, 90–6 and 1986: 152–3; and Parfit 1984: 143.

What makes consequentialism special is that the states of affairs it tells the agent to bring about can be described without essential reference to the agent. For example, the consequentialist tells the agent to produce the state of affairs which contains the most happiness, or the most peaceful state of affairs, or the state of affairs in which the fewest promises are broken. The deontologist, on the other hand, tells the agent to produce states of affairs such as '*Her* promises are kept' or '*Her* children flourish as far as possible' or '*She* does not kill'.[20]

As Howard-Snyder rightly noted, deontologists can include agent-neutral requirements within their theory.[21] Any attempt to explain the consequentialism/deontology distinction in terms of the distinction between agent-neutral and agent-relative requirements must respect this point. So she offers us the following definition of 'consequentialism':

A view is consequentialist if it does not include any agent-centred element. (1993: 274)

Her definition succeeds in making Ross, Nagel, and other familiar deontologists come out as nonconsequentialists because their theories include agent-centred (agent-relative) elements.

Her definition, however, also renders rule-consequentialism nonconsequentialist. For rule-consequentialism *does* give agents agent-relative goals (Howard-Snyder 1993: 272–3). Rule-consequentialism tells you to produce the state of affairs in which *you* follow the rules whose general acceptance would produce the most good. There might be some alternative state of affairs you could choose which would lead to greater compliance with the rules, even though you had to break the rules yourself. For example, cases could arise in which your keeping your promise would decrease the extent to which many other people keep theirs. In such cases, rule-consequentialism could tell you to keep your own promise, rather than maximize the extent to which everyone's promises are kept.[22] Thus, rule-

---

[20] Earlier, Donald Regan (1980: 208) complained that, under rule-consequentialism, 'the agent is encouraged to indulge in a sort of Pontius Pilatism, taking the view that as long as he keeps his own hands clean, the other agents as well as the consequences can take care of themselves'.

[21] See e.g. Ross 1930: ch. 2; Nagel 1979, 1986: chs. 8, 9, 1991; Gaut 1993: esp. p. 28; Raphael 1994: 54, 76, 78–80.

[22] I use 'could' instead of 'would' because, again, rule-consequentialists will endorse a rule require us to break any other rule when necessary to prevent a disaster (unless the self-sacrifice would be too great). So rule-consequentialism could tell us to break our promises in certain cases.

consequentialism contains an agent-relative element in its prescriptions about action. This agent-relativity makes rule-consequentialism nonconsequentialist, according to Howard-Snyder's definition of consequentialism.

I am not sure that Howard-Snyder and others are right to explain the consequentialism/nonconsequentialism distinction in terms of the agent-neutral/agent-relative distinction.[23] But even if they are, there is a perfectly good sense in which all forms of impartial consequentialism, including rule-consequentialism, share a commitment to *fundamental agent-neutrality*.[24] With this in mind, I offer:

> A theory is consequentialist if and only if it assesses acts and/*or* rules (or motives, social codes, virtues, or ways of life) in terms solely of the production of agent-neutral value.[25]

Act-consequentialism, for example, claims that an act's moral rightness is determined solely by whether that act would promote agent-neutral value. And rule-consequentialism claims that an act's rightness is determined solely by whether the general acceptance of a system of rules allowing that act would promote agent-neutral value. Clearly, the agent-relativity in rule-consequentialism is *derivative*.[26] Agent-relative rules are justified by their role in promoting agent-neutral value. So although Howard-Snyder is right that rule-consequentialism contains an agent-relative element at the level of requirements on action, rule-consequentialism contains no agent-

---

[23] For interesting arguments for the view that teleological moral theories can contain agent-relative demands, see Sen 1982; Broome 1991b: sect. 1.2; and Skorupski 1995: 49–51. For a powerful case for restricting the term 'consequentialism' in ways I find mostly persuasive, see Griffin 1992: 120–6.

[24] Egoism used to be called a form of consequentialism, because of egoism's identifying the right act as the one with the best consequences for the agent. Using the term 'consequentialism' so that it can incorporate egoism is now perhaps obsolete. In any event, by 'consequentialist theories' I shall mean forms of *impartial* consequentialism.

[25] Cf. Skorupski's definition of what he calls 'generic utilitarianism', which he uses to refer to a class of theories 'which hold that the good is some positive impartial function of the well-being of individuals and of nothing else' (1995: 54). Generic utilitarianism is a view about the good. There is a further question about the right. As far as I can see, generic utilitarianism leaves open whether the rightness of an act is determined solely by it own consequences, or at least partly by the consequences of something else such as rules or motives.

[26] As noted by Scheffler (1989: n.2 [1994: 155 n.]).

relative element at the deeper level where alternative systems of rules are assessed.

Is Howard-Snyder's definition of 'consequentialism' inferior to mine? Ideally, names should reveal important connections. So the question is whether rule-consequentialism has more important connections with other kinds of consequentialism, or more important connections with deontology. The answer is that it has important connections with both.

That rule-consequentialism is in some ways like familiar deontological views has always been a large part of the theory's attraction (Howard-Snyder 1993: 276–7). Rule-consequentialism's implications about which acts are morally right match quite closely our commonsense, deontological intuitions. Or, in other words, its rules seem to mirror familiar agent-relative requirements. And yet rule-consequentialism adds an impartial justification of these moral requirements. That it is wholly impartial at the fundamental level is something rule-consequentialism shares with other forms of consequentialism.

So how is it best, on balance, to define 'consequentialism'? This doesn't matter very much. What we should be interested in is the plausibility of a theory, not its name. Still, there is a rationale for preferring my definition over Howard-Snyder's. Hers makes rule-consequentialism's name mysterious. Mine makes rule-consequentialism's name unmysterious. Names—at least *last* names—should indicate family membership. And, as I have shown, there is a respectable way of defining the consequentialist family so that rule-consequentialism's name does just that.

5
Predictability and Convention

5.1 INTRODUCTION

In this chapter, I shall take up two questions about rule-consequentialism. One is a question about the upshot of the claim that we are only rarely able to predict confidently that changes to the conventionally accepted rules will be optimal. The second question is about cases where we can confidently predict that changes would be improvements. We might notice that conventionally accepted rules produce less *aggregate well-being* than would other rules with which they could be replaced. Or we might notice that conventionally accepted rules are less *fair* than possible alternatives. The question is whether in such cases rule-consequentialism implausibly says that the agent should always obey the better rules. The answer to both these objections requires a discussion of the status of conventionally accepted rules.

One possible view about the status of conventionally accepted rules is what I shall call *unrestricted conventionalism*. This is the view that complying with the rules conventionally accepted as morally binding is *always* morally required, because these rules are themselves what determine right and wrong. A second possible answer is that conventionally accepted rules determine right and wrong *as long as these rules reach some threshold of decency*. I shall refer to this view as *satisficing conventionalism*.

I shall argue against both these views. They are not idealistic enough. A moral theory should offer us hope of improvement, and not merely improvement in the level of conformity with established norms, but improvement in the norms themselves. Rule-consequentialism, properly conceived, does this, as I shall show.

Rule-consequentialism indeed has the opposite problem—of seeming *too* idealistic. In particular, rule-consequentialism might seem oblivious to the fact that complying with conventionally accepted rules is at least sometimes right even if these rules are less than ideal. I will reply to this objection by arguing that rule-consequentialism can itself contend that compromising with convention is sometimes right. Sometimes, complying with conventionally accepted rules is the only way to prevent a disaster with respect to aggregate well-being. But I shall show how rule-consequentialism can favour compromising with convention even when a great loss in aggregate well-being is not at stake.

5.2 PREDICTABILITY

Suppose we can't do the calculations, even to a reliable degree of probability, which would be necessary to decide which rules, feelings, dispositions are *best*. Would this truth kill rule-consequentialism?

As James Griffin notes, when we try to refine our crude, vague moral notions like benevolence and justice, we have to think like legislators who worry about the long-term consequences of changes in our practices and institutions. 'Moral legislators' will of course have to pay attention to basic facts about what individuals need, and pay attention to the affective and cognitive limitations of human agents. Moral legislators will also have to consider knock-on effects, such as the extent to which a change to one norm might undermine other norms.

But Griffin (1996: 106–7, 165–6) contends that we cannot calculate to a sufficient degree of reliability which set of rules and dispositions would, if they were to prevail in society, produce the most good in the long run. Or rather, he contends that we cannot do the calculation often enough to keep rule-consequentialism from being squeezed out of the centre of moral life:

We may know enough to identify fairly obviously inadequate rules and dispositions, but there will be many left that we cannot rank. And it is in the wide band that they would constitute that many of the hard choices in morality—choices, say, about the particular form that respect for life should take—would have to be made. (Griffin 1996: 107)

Is Griffin here attacking the best version of rule-consequentialism? One version claims that an act is wrong if and only if it is forbidden by the code of rules whose social prevalence would *actually* produce the best consequences. On this version of rule-consequentialism, in order to know what acts are wrong, we would have to know which rules actually would produce the best consequences. If Griffin is right that we often do not know which rules actually would produce the best consequences, then on this version of rule-consequentialism we often cannot know which acts are wrong. If we cannot know which acts are wrong on this version of rule-consequentialism, it falls under a dark shadow (but cf. Svavarsdóttir 1999: 168–9).

I already conceded that rule-consequentialism should be framed in terms of *reasonable expectations* about the consequences of the internalization of rules. So consider the version of rule-consequentialism holding that an act is wrong if and only if it is forbidden by a code of rules whose widespread internalization has an expected value no other code beats. This version of rule-consequentialism is also in trouble, if Griffin is right that we regularly cannot confidently predict which rules would be best.

At this point I think rule-consequentialism needs to be made even more modest. The most we can hope for is to find a code whose general internalization could reasonably be expected to result in at least as much good as could reasonably be expected to result from any other *identifiable* code. We would be silly ever to think we have found a completely unimprovable code—that is, a code whose internalization *would* in fact achieve as much good as possible.

So suppose we instead aspire to find a code whose general internalization could reasonably be expected to produce as much good as any other code we can identify. More than one code may pass this test. That is, more than one code may have unsurpassed expected value. Rule-consequentialism must have a way of selecting among the codes in this set. Suppose rule-consequentialism is formulated so as to claim that, of these codes with unsurpassed expected value, the one closest to conventional morality determines which kinds of act are wrong.[1] Call this view *wary rule-consequentialism*.

One thing that counts in favour of wary rule-consequentialism is its epistemological modesty. We start with what we know, with what has been already tried. Attempts at moral reform should begin with existing practices, and then prune, refine, and supplement these where changes seem very likely to increase the overall good.

---

[1] Cf. Sidgwick 1907: 467–71, 473–6, 480–4; Brandt 1979: 290, 1988 [1992: 147, 154], 1996: 143–4; Griffin 1986: 206, 302.

Another thing that counts in favour of this wary rule-consequentialism is that it solves a co-ordination problem: how do we make sure that everyone who will interact with one another picks the same code out of those that pass our test? Surely individuals cannot be allowed to pick for themselves. That would be like letting everyone decide which side of the road to drive on.

Let us now consider some possible objections to wary rule-consequentialism. Suppose that, when we are considering which set of rules to advocate, the best alternatives we can identify seem equally close to conventional morality. This case illustrates that the test I have advocated will not *necessarily* always determine exactly which set of rules to choose.

But how serious a problem is this? How often will we be presented with two or more possible codes which have not only just as much expected value as one another, but also the very same proximity to conventional morality? I think that this theoretical problem will rarely present itself in practice. Rather than blame our principle for not giving us an answer, we will think more about the expected values of the codes we might move to, and about their connections with conventional morality.

Another possible objection to wary rule-consequentialism is that it lets us down just where we need help. For if wary rule-consequentialism tells us that, as between codes with unsurpassed expected value, we should choose the one closest to conventional morality, then rule-consequentialism takes on board some of the problems with conventional morality. One of these problems is that there are situations where a conflict between moral requirements is stultifyingly difficult. Concerning some of these situations, conventional morality provides no determinate answer what to do. So, to the extent to which rule-consequentialism follows conventional morality, rule-consequentialism also lacks a determinate answer.

In reply, I concede that in some cases wary rule-consequentialism will be no more determinate than conventional morality. In other cases, however, wary rule-consequentialism is clearly better than conventional morality. (Remember that wary rule-consequentialism provides reasonable grounds for criticizing conventional morality if changes to conventional norms would produce greater expected (weighted?) well-being.) But is wary rule-consequentialism also sometimes worse than conventional morality? I shall argue later in this chapter that it is not. If I am correct, then wary rule-consequentialism is sometimes better and never worse than conventional morality. Thus, even if (as in the cases where wary rule-consequentialism mirrors the indeterminateness of conventional morality) wary rule-consequentialism *sometimes* is no better than conventional morality, wary rule-consequentialism may still be better overall.

Yet a further possible objection to wary rule-consequentialism is that it is too conservative. Why privilege the status quo? Admittedly, wary rule-consequentialism's inherent conservatism is troubling. But it is a modest conservatism. For example, wary rule-consequentialism does not count the costs of getting people who have already internalized one moral code to abandon that one and internalize a new one. That really would be too conservative (when we think how stupid and bigoted codes can be).

But I can see no alternative even half as good. For, in the first place, wary rule-consequentialism allows—indeed demands— reform whenever such reform seems likely to increase expected value. And, in the second place, more radical approaches will involve massive upset of people's innocent expectations. In other words, the suitably modest form of rule-consequentialism here under discussion holds that, if we *can* identify an alternative to the conventional code that we can confidently predict would have better consequences, then we should move to it. And if we *cannot* identify an alternative we can confidently predict would produce better consequences, then sticking with what we have and know seems reasonable.[2]

It is not that Griffin himself complains against wary rule-consequentialism that it is too conservative. For he himself gives conventional practice a large role in determining what is right. Where we cannot predict to a reliable degree of probability what the consequences of various codes would be, he holds that tradition and extant convention should be our guide (Griffin 1996: 96; see also 119–21).

Griffin's complaint is rather that for rule-consequentialism to rely to this extent on tradition and convention marginalizes rule-consequentialist thought (1996: 106–7, 165–6). He writes that

---

[2] Sidgwick was especially worried because 'here as elsewhere in human affairs, it is easier to pull down than to build up; easier to weaken or destroy the restraining force that a moral rule, habitually and generally obeyed, has over men's minds, than to substitute for it a new restraining habit, not similarly sustained by tradition and custom' (1907: 482).

rule-consequentialism, in relying to this extent on tradition and convention, can no longer plausibly claim to be the overall form of moral rationality.

I cannot see that this is the conclusion to reach. We are supposing that the only ground we have for making changes to conventional rules and norms is that we reasonably expect such changes to result in better overall consequences. We are also supposing that we should stick with conventional rules only when we cannot confidently identify which changes to them would result in better overall consequences. Given these two suppositions, wary rule-consequentialism provides the necessary and sufficient conditions for moral change. This is true even if we can only rarely predict with confidence that changes to moral rules will improve things overall.

5.3 UNRESTRICTED CONVENTIONALISM

Let us refer to the rules whose internalization really would result in the best overall consequences as the *ideal*, or *optimal*, rules. Allow me to refer to all other rules as *sub-optimal*. Obviously, there are different degrees of sub-optimality. At one end of the range are rules that are outrageously harmful or grossly unfair. Refer to these as *abominable* rules.

Now consider the view that right and wrong are determined by whatever rules are conventionally accepted as morally binding, even if these rules are abominable ones. According to this view, racist or sexist or even genocidal rules would, if conventionally established in a society, determine right and wrong in that society. Call this view *unrestricted conventionalism*.

Because unrestricted conventionalism can let abominable rules determine people's moral obligations, the view is highly counterintuitive. We do *not* think that, no matter how abominable the conventionally accepted rules are, complying with them is right as long as they are accepted by most people. On the contrary, most of us think that there are strong moral reasons for working to eliminate abominable rules, for example, by arguing against them and even publicly disobeying them as a way of expressing dissent.

Only the most hard-bitten relativists would defend the unrestricted conventionalist view that one is morally required to comply with

outrageously harmful or grossly unfair rules as long as these are conventionally accepted to be morally binding. So now consider
conventionally accepted rules that are not abominable (i.e. neither
outrageously harmful nor grossly unfair). These are, from the point
of view of theorizing about ethics, more interesting than abominable
conventions. Thus, the only conventionally accepted rules under
discussion for the rest of this chapter will be ones that are not
abominable in the senses specified.

Note here a complication. When conventionally accepted rules
that are not abominable nevertheless seem sub-optimal on the basis
of a preliminary review, sometimes these rules are actually better
than the alternatives, once all the complications and further effects
are taken into consideration. Indeed, public debate about morality is
often about whether this or that proposed change in social rules is
likely to increase well-being or fairness in the long run, all things
considered, given that large social changes typically have all sorts of
unforeseen effects. I accept that we need to be modest about our abilities to predict the effects of social change. But modesty can go too
far. It must not be used as an excuse for always opposing proposed
improvements.

5.4 SATISFICING CONVENTIONALISM

Of course many conventionally accepted rules do not fall into the
abominable category. One view holds that such rules, if they are
'good enough', determine right and wrong. Call this view *satisficing
conventionalism*.[3]

For those of us who think right and wrong must be tied to social
rules in some way, satisficing conventionalism may be initially
appealing. Its appeal is especially apparent when we think about
cases where complying with the conventionally established sub-

---

[3] I am assuming that, to be 'good enough', these conventional rules must themselves include a rule about preventing disaster. Some recent examples of apparent
endorsements of satisficing conventionalism are Mackie 1977: 148; Griffin 1992:
130–1. Arguably, Hume affirmed this view as well. In recent years, the philosopher
who has brought satisficing to the attention of others is Michael Slote (1984, 1985:
chs. 3, 5, 1989), though he focused on satisficing act-consequentialism, not satisficing
conventionalism.

optimal rule, rather than with an ideal rule, would produce greater overall benefit.

But further investigation reveals satisficing conventionalism is unsatisfactory. For there are cases about which it gives the wrong answer. Consider the possible moral code whose establishment in society would have highest expected value. Suppose this presumptively ideal code would permit lying to protect privacy—or, at least, to protect morally innocent privacy.[4] But suppose I live in a society whose conventionally accepted 'good enough' rules do *not* permit lying in order to protect privacy. My friend Linda has confided to me that she is having an affair with a famous person, an affair they both want to keep secret though it is morally innocent. Alas, rumours start to circulate, and reporters confront me with questions about her love life. For the sake of argument, suppose the only way I can protect her privacy is by lying. My refusing to answer the question would just confirm the reporters' suspicions. Is it not, then, *counterintuitive* to say that I must follow the conventional rule here?

Some philosophers will answer: 'Yes, it is counterintuitive. And this fact illustrates the attraction of direct appeals to simple utility. What makes obeying the conventional rule wrong in this case is simply that obeying it here will obviously produce lower aggregate well-being than not obeying it would.'

But when we explore the matter further, we find that what is operative here is not a simple appeal to utility. To make this more obvious, I need to fill out the example a little. My telling the truth or refusing to answer the question would have worse consequences for Linda and her lover. But it would benefit others. And suppose that the aggregate harm to Linda and her lover would be less than the aggregate benefit to everyone else concerned. (The reporters would

---

4 J. S. Mill wrote that the rule against lying, 'sacred as it is, admits of possible exceptions . . . the chief of which is when the withholding of some fact (as of information from a malefactor, or of bad news from a person dangerously ill) would preserve someone (especially a person other than oneself) from great and unmerited evil, and when the withholding can only be effected by denial' (1861: ch. II, para. 23). Mill claims this is 'acknowledged by all moralists'. For examples of philosophers who agree with Mill about lying to protect the innocent, especially the privacy of the innocent, see Sidgwick 1907: 315, 318, and Mackie 1977: 182–3. But, of course, not every moral philosopher agrees that lying is sometimes right (Kant, being the most notorious example). Be that as it may, what is crucial for my argument in the text above is not the assumption that the rules conventionally accepted here in our society actually forbid lying to protect the privacy of the innocent. All I need for a test case is an *imagined* society in which this is the situation.

advance their careers; very many people interested in celebrities would enjoy reading about the affair; I would get paid a lot by the reporters just for telling the truth.)[5] Because aggregate well-being would be maximized in this case by my failing to protect her privacy, a direct appeal to aggregate utility would tell me not to protect it. But, on reflection, it seems that—even in this case—lying to protect her privacy would be morally right. If we stick to this judgement, then this case illustrates that we believe that there are occasions when an agent should follow superior rules rather than conventionally accepted sub-optimal ones, even if (a) the conventionally accepted rule is not an abominable one and (b) in the situation at hand, compliance with the conventionally accepted sub-optimal rule would in fact maximize aggregate well-being.

Some people might object that my example about Linda does not show what I say it does. They might claim that what is really guiding our judgement about what to do in the example is merely another conventional rule—namely, a rule demanding that promises, even implicit ones, be kept. The suggestion would be that the reason I should protect Linda's privacy, even if I have to lie to do so, is that I explicitly or implicitly promised to protect it.

We should reject that analysis of the example. First of all, there may have been no implicit or explicit promise. Secondly, even if there were one, our conventional rules would consider the promise binding only if it was not a promise to do something *immoral*. According to conventional rules, lying in response to invasive questions *would* be immoral. Therefore, a promise to lie in response to such questions would not be binding, according to conventional morality.

Let me take stock. The example about Linda is obviously a counterexample to the thesis that act-utilitarian reasoning is what sways us against the conventionally established rule forbidding dishonest

---

[5] Might it be said that, on the best understanding of human good, the enjoyment for the gossips, the career advancement of the reporters, and the money for me would not outweigh the loss to Linda and her lover? Well, career advancement for the reporters and money for me almost certainly would not benefit us as much as the loss to Linda and her lover. But the enjoyment for the gossips? Enjoyment is an important good. And unless we discount the enjoyment for the gossips, then because there are many millions of these people, their enjoyment will aggregate to more benefit than the aggregate loss to Linda and her lover. And utilitarianism will be circular if we use it to make decisions about what to do, but then limit well-being to *morally* good enjoyment.

answers to invasive questions. In the example described, act-utilitarian reasoning would instead favour following the conventionally established rule. So, act-utilitarian reasoning cannot explain why breaking this rule is instead right. The Linda example also counts against satisficing conventionalism. Take whatever standard is proposed by satisficing conventionalists for determining what counts as a 'good enough' conventional rule. A conventional rule forbidding dishonesty surely meets the satisficers' standard. Nevertheless, a conventional rule forbidding dishonesty fails, we intuitively think, to determine right and wrong in the case I described.

5.5 COMPROMISING WITH CONVENTION OUT OF FAIRNESS

My conclusion was that we should *sometimes* follow ideal rules when they conflict with conventionally accepted ones that are recognizably sub-optimal. I did not claim we should never compromise with convention. Such a claim would itself be highly counterintuitive. The live question is not *whether* we should sometimes follow conventionally accepted sub-optimal rules. The live question is *why* we sometimes should. As I have already indicated, the reason is not that this would maximize overall utility (when it would). Nor is the reason derived from satisficing conventionalism. In fact, though this hardly seems immediately obvious, wary rule-consequentialism can explain why we should often follow conventionally established rules, though they are recognizably sub-optimal.

Earlier, I mentioned a rule requiring us to abandon other rules when complying with them would end in disaster. As I suggested, a strong requirement to prevent large losses in aggregate well-being would be a component of any code of rules with high expected value. There are limits to how much self-sacrifice can be demanded in the name of this rule. But that is a matter I want to put off until later. Here the important point is that, subject to qualifications about demandingness, we cannot follow a code with high expected value unless we comply with the requirement to prevent large losses in aggregate well-being. Thus, rule-consequentialists would claim that it is morally right to go against other rules when this is necessary to prevent disaster.

Similar things might be said about fairness. Just as in a world where things can go badly wrong we need a strong 'prevent disaster' rule, so we need a rule requiring us to comply with conventional suboptimal rules when our not doing so would cause serious unfairness. Consider a rule whose general internalization would produce no unfairness. This rule is thus ideal, at least with respect to fairness. But, in the real world, acting on this rule can actually cause serious unfairness if other people are not complying with it.

One kind of case involves people's 'innocent expectations'. For the sake of argument, suppose we thought an ideal rule about long-term contracts would insist on a period of reflection before consent. We might think that contracts about different kinds of things should be preceded by periods of different lengths. And we might think that, in certain kinds of cases where parties are trying to make binding bids for something before competitors do so first, the mandatory period for reflection can be quite short. But suppose we think that for a certain kind of contract to be binding, each party must have fourteen days to consider it in its final form before being able to give his or her binding consent to it, unless impending death or some other catastrophe threatens to cut short the fourteen-day period of reflection. Making the bindingness of a contract contingent on there having been a fourteen-day period for reflection would, let us suppose, promote aggregate well-being and fairness.

With this setting, I can now state my point about innocent expectations. Suppose Jack and Jill made a contract with one another while living in a society where conventionally established rules did *not* require a fourteen-day period of reflection. Their contract required each to give a quarter of the first million-dollar gift, payment, or winnings he or she receives to the other. Suppose Jack and Jill signed this deal after reflecting on it for only ten days. Suppose that ten years after signing this contract Jack is paid a million dollars to act in a movie.

Remember that we are supposing that an ideal rule about long-term contracts would require a fourteen-day period of reflection. Obviously, the application of such a rule to this case would free Jack from having to pay Jill. But, in the case at hand, can Jack appeal to the ideal rule? At the time Jack and Jill signed their deal, the socially established code of rules did not require a fourteen-day waiting period. Jill always thought she and Jack were bound by the deal they signed. Because of this, for the last ten years each has taken a particularly strong interest in the other's prospects and has repeatedly provided emotional support for the other.

For Jack to think himself let off the hook in this case by the ideal rule would be seriously unfair to Jill. She had perfectly reasonable expectations, and she reasonably relied on her deal with Jack. While an ideal rule about contracts may require a fourteen-day period for reflection, she had no idea of this. And she could not reasonably have been expected to know it at the time. The unfairness to Jill would be so bad if Jack did not honour their contract that he should honour it, even if ideal rules would not have sanctioned such a contract in the first place.

Of course, established rules can be so injurious that they should be abandoned immediately, even though this would upset people who formed expectations on the basis of those rules. But in other cases, the conventionally accepted rules are not bad enough to justify such measures, as the case of Jill in the preceding discussion illustrates. Where the line falls dividing the first set of cases from the second, I do not know.[6] However, the crucial point here is this: when people make agreements on the basis of conventionally accepted rules, albeit sub-optimal ones, to treat these people in a way that ignores the agreements can itself be seriously unfair.

Consider a rule that would be burdensome to follow but nevertheless would be ideal because an important public good would be secured if, though only if, most people were to comply with it. The results would be wonderful if everyone avoided polluting the river. But if I am the only one who makes the effort, then the river will remain dangerously polluted. In that case, I have imposed a cost on myself without any benefit to anyone. To take another example, it would be best if everyone supported the candidates from the Humanitarian Party. But if only a few do, they lose their time and money without reaching the threshold where some good is done.

Now, in such cases is an agent morally required to comply with the ideal rule if in fact nowhere near enough others are? By hypothesis, we are a long way away from the threshold of communal cooperation necessary to secure the public good. Suppose that there is no

---

[6] In this area, vagueness abounds. As we saw in sect. 2.5, fairness requires complying with agreements people actually made (not *would* have made) but only if the agreement was not elicited by fraud or by a threat to infringe someone's moral rights. Vagueness can appear in the context of an agreement, in the concept of fraud, and in the specification of what would count as a threat to infringe someone's moral rights.

serious chance of reaching that threshold. In such cases, the agent's complying with the ideal rule would be burdensome for her and put her at a disadvantage relative to others.[7]

But if morality would not require her to comply in these circumstances with the ideal rule, how can rule-consequentialism explain this? Suppose that the clear burden involved in complying with this rule would not be enough to count as a disaster in term's of the agent's own well-being. Nevertheless, it is unfair to require anyone to follow a burdensome rule for the sake of a public good when this rule is being ignored by most others.[8] Rule-consequentialism's attempt to tie morality to the best identifiable rules seems doomed unless it provides a way to avoid these kinds of unfairness.

5.6 PUBLIC GOODS AND GOOD DISPOSITIONS

When in a fairly ideal social world—that is, one where others are already following the ideal rules—rule-consequentialism seems unassailable. When the conventionally accepted rule is also the one that rule-consequentialism favours, clearly rule-consequentialism requires the agent to follow it (except when disaster looms).[9] Suppose that, before I come along, a sufficient number of people are already following some good rule to produce some public good beneficial to all. Suppose that following this rule is burdensome to me, as indeed their following the rule was to each of them. Since the benefits are already assured and my additional contribution is not needed, *act*-consequentialism might allow me not to conform with the good behaviour of the others. Whether act-consequentialism does allow me to shirk my duties as defined by the rules of the practice depends on whether I will set a bad precedent by shirking.

But *rule*-consequentialism would certainly not let me bypass a rule of a good practice to which others have already conformed. As Brandt (1967: n. 15) explained,

[7] Lyons 1965: 131.

[8] In David Lyons's terminology, rule-utilitarianism seems unfair if it requires one to comply with optimal rules when one is under 'minimizing conditions' (Lyons 1965: 128–32, 137–42). Cf. Murphy 1993.

[9] See Lyons's discussion of what he calls 'maximizing-conditions' (1965: 128, 141). See also Parfit 1984: 64–6; Griffin 1986: 206–15.

there could hardly be a public rule permitting people to shirk while a sufficient number of others work. . . . It would be all too easy for most people to believe that a sufficient number of others were working. . . . Would it even be a good idea to have a rule to the effect that if one absolutely knows that enough others are working, one may shirk? This seems highly doubtful. Critics of rule-utilitarianism seem to have passed from the fact that the best system would combine the largest product with the least effort, to the conclusion that the best moral code would contain a rule advising not to work when there are enough workers already. This is a non sequitur.

Lyons (1965: 141) rightly suggested that what he called 'minimizing-conditions' are harder for the rule-consequentialist. These are the cases where others do not accept and are not following the best rules. (See the literature on assurance problems, e.g. Rawls 1971: 270.) My examples about Linda and Jill illustrate this sort of case. Lyons was particularly concerned about cases where your following a rule that would be best if everyone followed it could be seriously unfair to you in a context in which others are not following it.

Rule-consequentialism must not require agents to make sacrifices for others who are able to follow the same rule but won't.[10] Rule-consequentialism aims to make people good, but not 'suckers'. As Mackie (1978, 1982a) and others (e.g. Axelrod 1984) have argued, the existence of suckers in a population enables 'cheats' to flourish. By 'cheats', I mean those disposed to free-ride on the kindness or self-denying restraint of others. To discourage people from becoming or remaining free-riders on the kindness or restraint of others, the ideal code does not require kindness or self-denying restraint towards people not disposed to reciprocate. (Exceptions will naturally be made for obligations towards those of diminished responsibility, such as young children.)

---

[10] Note that, in contrast with standard forms of Hobbesian contractarianism, rule-consequentialism holds that we can have burdensome duties toward those who cannot reciprocate (future generations, the very weak of current generations, animals). But like any plausible moral view, rule-consequentialism sees the enormous importance of reciprocity. This rule-consequentialist commitment is embodied in the proposition expressed in my text above. Note, incidentally, how well Sidgwick understood the gratification in treating well those who themselves have good dispositions. See especially Sidgwick 1907: 433.

6

Prohibitions and
Special Obligations

As I indicated earlier, most people confidently believe that harming others in certain ways is normally wrong. Morality imposes prohibitions on what we can do to one another. Most people also believe that individuals have special obligations to others with whom there are certain kinds of connections. This chapter explains how rule-consequentialism provides an impartial justification for familiar moral prohibitions and special obligations we have to particular others. A later chapter will discuss the general moral duty to help others.

6.1 BASIC RULE-CONSEQUENTIALIST PROHIBITIONS

We believe that, at least generally, physical attack, torture, theft, promise-breaking, lying, and the like are morally wrong. Rule-consequentialism agrees. On the whole, the consequences will be far better if there are generally accepted rules forbidding physical attack, torture, theft, promise-breaking, lying, and the like. Indeed, at least minimum forms of these rules are indispensable to society.[1] Just look at how things go in places where such rules are not generally accepted and followed. Life in such places descends into chaos and is nasty, brutish, and short, just as Hobbes predicted. H. L. A. Hart (1961: 192) observed, 'As things are, human altruism is limited in range and intermittent, and the tendencies to aggression are frequent enough to be fatal to social life if not controlled.' And, as he and so many others have pointed out, given the competition for resources and the 'inescapable division of labour and perennial need

[1] The best discussion of this I know of is in Hart 1961: 190–5.

for co-operation', rules protecting property and enabling people to bind their future actions by making promises are essential. Rule-consequentialism will thus prescribe rules 'protecting persons, property, and promises', to use Hart's phrase.

This has long and consistently been maintained by rule-consquentialists.[2] But even some non-consequentialists admit that rule-consequentialism does a good job of justifying such prohibitions and the correlative rights. For example, Thomas Nagel (1986: 177) writes, 'Rules against the direct infliction of harm and against the violation of widely accepted rights have considerable social utility, and if it ceased to be so, those rules would lose much of their moral attractiveness.'[3] Some philosophers would object, however, that the rules whose internalization could reasonably be expected to maximize aggregate *utility* might permit some kinds of intuitively prohibited behaviour toward some people. Indeed, I earlier tentatively renounced rule-utilitarianism in favour of a broader rule-consequentialism that evaluates rules in terms of not only aggregate well-being but also the position of the worst off. But is this enough? Are there any actions that (1) would be permitted by a code whose internalization would maximize expected value, and yet (2) on reflection clearly are immoral? At least initially, the answer seems to be No.

6.2 OUR INTUITIONS ABOUT PROHIBITIONS

Some people think that certain actions are wrong, *whatever the consequences* would be of not doing them. These people think that moral prohibitions must be obeyed even if disobeying them is the only way to prevent disaster. Suppose the only way to prevent a nuclear disaster is to lie, or break a promise, or take or harm the possessions of others, or even injure an innocent human being. Most of us believe it would be right to lie to a murderer if lying is the only, or even merely the best, means of sending him off in the wrong

[2] See Harrod 1936; Toulmin 1950; Urmson 1953; Harrison 1952/3; Rawls 1955; Brandt 1959: chs. 15–16, 1963, 1967, 1979: pt. II; 1988, 1989; Hospers 1972; Harsanyi 1982, 1993; Haslett 1987, 1994: ch. 1; C. Johnson 1991; Barrow 1991.

[3] See also Nagel 1991: 145, cf. 1995: 91–3, and Frankena 1993: 44. But this line of thought is opposed in McNaughton and Rawling 1998 and Montague 2000.

direction.[4] Or consider the case where I have promised my neighbour to return his chainsaw whenever he asks for it back, and he asks for it back while crazed with jealousy and threatening to murder someone (cf. Plato, *Republic* 331c). To keep the promise in this sort of case would be deeply misguided. So there certainly seem to be kinds of action that, though normally impermissible, are permissible— even obligatory—when they are necessary to prevent great harm. '[A]bsolute duties of allegiance, or respect for property, or truth-telling, promise-keeping, and the rest seldom appeal to the theoretically innocent when tyrants, axe-men, emergencies, and the other nightmares of ethics are introduced' (Blackburn 1996: 98).

How bad do the consequences have to be in order to justify doing something to someone that's normally impermissible? Judith Jarvis Thomson (1990: 153) writes:

There is no one size such that for any claim [right] you choose, the claim is permissibly infringeable if and only if infringing it would generate an increment of good of that size. . . . In short, the size of the required increment of good seems to vary with the stringency of the claim: the more stringent the claim, the greater the required increment of good.

This seems right. And, if it is, then at least the algorithm for moral judgement would have to be complex. But in fact many philosophers think such an algorithm either simply does not exist or at least is completely beyond our abilities. If this is right, there is an inelim-inable need for moral judgement to adjudicate conflicts when general moral considerations conflict in particular cases (cf. Aristotle, *Nicomachean Ethics* 1137a31–1138a3, 1142a11–15).[5] As Bernard Williams (1995: 189–90) writes,

Judgements of importance are ubiquitous. . . . It may be obvious that in general one kind of . . . ethical consideration is more important than another, but it is a matter of judgement whether in a particular set of circumstances that priority is preserved: other factors alter the balance, or it may be a very weak example of the consideration that generally wins.

---

[4] Kant held that lying would not be right even to save the victim. Most philosophers have taken this to show either that Kant's categorical imperative is implausible or that Kant himself misinterpreted what his categorical imperative requires. For an intriguing discussion, see Korsgaard 1986.
[5] The passage from Thomson just quoted leaves open the possibility that there are some claims so stringent that no amount of good could justify breaking them. I shall come back to her views about this.

The commonsense moral view goes further. It holds that, in some cases of conflict between the demands of different principles, there is a 'genuine indeterminacy' about what to do (Gaut 1993: 36). In section 6.3, I comment more extensively on the role of judgement in adjudicating conflicts of duties.

First, consider the view that some kinds of act can never be right, no matter how good the consequences. In *Othello*, Desdemona comments on adultery, 'Beshrew me if I would do such a wrong / For the whole world.'[6] In *The Brothers Karamazov*, Dostoevsky writes,

[I]magine that you yourself are erecting the edifice of human fortune with the goal of, at the finale, making people happy, of at last giving them peace and quiet, but that in order to do it it would be necessary and unavoidable to torture to death only one tiny little creature, that same little child that beat its breast with its tiny little fist, and on its unavenged tears to found that edifice, would you agree to be the architect under those conditions . . .?[7]

Take a case where as much as possible is at stake. Suppose that, because of some bizarre twist of fate, torturing to death a child who happens to be on a different planet is the only way to save the rest of *the entire human species* (and every other species) from excruciating suffering followed by painful death.[8] Suppose that this really is the *only* way: take as given that there is no benevolent God to save the day. Could we sincerely deny that torturing the child would be, all things considered, the thing to do, when the lives of every other present and future possible individual are at stake?

One view holds that this case is simple: sacrificing the child would clearly be right. Another view maintains that the case is simple in the opposite direction: refusing to sacrifice the child would clearly be right. A third view is there are certain moral dilemmas where anything the agent does is wrong. On this third view, the question

---

[6] Act IV, scene iii, emphasis added. Emilia replies to Desdemona: 'Why, the wrong is but a wrong i' th' world, and having the world for your labour, 'tis a wrong in your own world, and you might quickly make it right.'

[7] Pt. 2, bk. 5, ch. 4, p. 282 in the translation by David McDuff (Penguin, 1993). Dostoyevsky's direct focus here, I should mention, is not consequentialism, but the traditional problem of reconciling the existence of undeserved suffering with belief in an all-powerful, morally perfect God. For an elaboration of Dostoevsky's example with the focus on consequentialism, see James 1897 [1956: 188], and Le Guin 1980.

[8] Cf. Fried 1978: 31; Nagel 1986: 175–85; and on the idea that the hypothetical (advance) consent can justify harming some for the sake of saving others, see Rakowski 1993: 1105–7, 1129–50, and Reibetanz 1998.

is whether there is some one alternative in such situations that the agent really ought to choose, all things considered. If so, is this favoured alternative torturing the child to save the rest of humanity—or refusing to do that, with the foreseen but unwanted result that the rest of humanity is tortured and killed?

Maybe if God is there to protect us, we could refuse to torture the child in the hope that God would somehow come to the rescue (Pettit 1997: 150, 152). But that is not the case here considered. The case we are here considering contains no God to come to the rescue. Now in this case, refusing to save the world at the cost of one innocent child would, I believe, be morally worse than sacrificing the child. After all, this really is the only way to save *billions* of others, and indeed the very future of humanity.

But Elizabeth Anscombe (1958: 16) held that some kinds of act are wrong no matter what, and that even to entertain the question whether these things should be done 'shows a corrupt mind'.[9] Thomson, agreeing with Anscombe that there are certain things that are never permissible (1990: 168), expressed the suspicion that those who instead think horrible acts permissible if enough lives are at stake

are moved . . . by the feeling that where billions (or perhaps even just hundreds) could be saved from pain, a person ought to volunteer to suffer it, and that where the lives of billions (or perhaps even just hundreds) could be saved from death, a person ought to volunteer his or her life. (Thomson 1990: 167)

But Thomson herself went on to indicate, the point about volunteering is just irrelevant. It is one thing to consider a case where *you* could save lots of people only by sacrificing yourself. It is another thing to consider the kind of case where *someone else* could save lots of people only by imposing the sacrifice on you. People who confuse the two kinds of case may slide from the thought that you are obligated to make the sacrifice yourself to the thought that someone else is morally permitted to impose this sacrifice on you.

Suppose we now clearly see the difference between the two kinds of case. We may nevertheless believe that *all* normal prohibitions on harming others can be overridden in the most extreme (and unlikely) cases. Thomson has done nothing to cast doubt on this belief.

---

[9] Anscombe's quip, while perhaps amusing, is a paradigm case of arguing by begging the question at hand.

I do not pretend to have proven that even such horrible things as torture and killing the innocent can be morally right, all things considered, in certain extremely far-fetched possible cases. All I can do is to offer test cases. Think carefully about cases such as the one where torturing the child really is the only way to save the rest (and future) of humanity. Assume there is no God to prevent disaster. Don't you agree that, when so much is at stake, torturing or killing the innocent must be the 'lesser evil'? If so, you admit that normal prohibitions on harming others should be overridden in the most extreme (and unlikely) cases.

6.3 RULE-CONSEQUENTIALISM, PROHIBITIONS, AND JUDGEMENT

I suggest that (at least) lying and promise-breaking can be morally right, when not to do them would allow a disaster we could have prevented to occur. The implications of rule-consequentialism are consistent with this belief. Again, rule-consequentialism makes the moral permissibility of an act depend on whether it would be allowed by the set of motivations whose internalization could reasonably be expected to have as good consequences as any other set we can identify. As I argued in section 4.2, one motivation that rule-consequentialism would endorse is a motivation to prevent disaster. This motivation should be stronger than other motivations, since in the long run things would go better on the whole if people cared more about preventing disasters than about breaking other rules. Thus, rule-consequentialism holds we should break the promise or tell a lie when necessary to prevent disaster.

Rule-consequentialism's 'prevent disaster' rule does *not* prescribe that we should break a promise when breaking it would produce only *a little* more good. Rule-consequentialism holds, as I indicated in section 3.5, that rules should have attached to them different strengths (Brandt 1989: 95). To accept a rule against injuring others is in part to be averse to injuring others, with the degree of aversion correlating with the degree of injury. The worse the effect if everyone felt free to do a certain kind of act, the higher the level of aversion should be to this kind of act.

So, people with a good rule-consequentialist training would have an enormously strong aversion to killing others, a very strong aversion to doing serious bodily harm to others, but a much weaker aversion to doing very small harms to others. Likewise, they would have a very strong aversion to telling huge lies under oath and breaking solemn promises about important matters, but a much weaker aversion to telling small lies or breaking little promises. And as for the duty of beneficence, rule-consequentialist agents would have a very strong aversion to letting others suffer disasters (huge losses in well-being), but a much weaker aversion to letting others undergo small losses.

Again, rule-consequentialism holds that, when rules (and thus aversions) conflict, the stronger aversion determines what action is right. As I indicated in Chapter 3, the best form of rule-consequentialism holds that one should take, in Richard Brandt's words, 'whatever course of action would leave morally well-trained people least dissatisfied'. To illustrate, suppose people who have the pattern of aversions that rule-consequentialism prescribes face a situation in which their breaking a promise is the only way to prevent a loss in well-being. Would they break the promise? They would if the choice is between preventing a huge loss to someone and keeping a small promise. They would not if the choice is between preventing a small loss to someone and keeping a solemn promise about an important matter.

This approach does not entail that the duties and aversions can be lexically ranked in any sense denied by ordinary moral conviction. Rule-consequentialism agrees that the stringency of a general duty and the corresponding aversion varies with the circumstances—in particular, with what is at stake. Since the general duties are pro tanto, not absolute, the correct resolution of a conflict between two duties in one set of circumstances can differ from the correct resolution in other circumstances.

There are infinitely many possible circumstances in which general duties can conflict. So, in effect there are infinitely many possible particular conflicts between general duties. Nevertheless, there could be an infinitely long and complex ranking principle, one formed from the conjunction of all the resolutions of the infinitely many possible specific conflicts. But, as Berys Gaut (1993: 18) implies, no such ranking principle 'could be used and taught in coming to moral decisions in ordinary life'. Rule-consequentialists and everyday moral conviction agree that, in ordinary life, sometimes we have nothing to appeal to but judgement to determine what to do when rules conflict.

Both intuitively and by rule-consequentialist lights, there seem to be *some* general conflict-resolving principles. One example is that the duty not to injure others is *normally* stronger than the duty to benefit others (Ross 1930: 21). The qualification 'normally' allows that, if the difference between the size of the injury and the benefit is large enough, the priority is reversed.

Another example concerns promises. As T. M. Scanlon (1998: 199) writes,

the fact that keeping a promise would be inconvenient or disadvantageous is not normally a sufficient reason for breaking it, but 'normally' here covers many qualifications. There are, for example, questions of proportionality (the kind of disadvantage that may not be appealed to in order to justify backing out depends on what is at stake in the promise).

Certainly, solemn promises are more important than small losses of well-being, and huge losses of well-being are more important than small promises (Ross 1930: 19; Audi 1996: 106; McNaughton 1996: 445). Yet these conflict-resolving principles hardly eliminate the need for judgement. For, obviously, such general conflict-resolving rules refer to matters of degree. Judgement will be needed to determine whether for example a particular promise is a solemn one or only a small one or something in between, and whether a particular loss is small or huge or in between.

Judgement will also be needed to resolve conflicts where the degree of one consideration at stake is less dramatically different from the degree of the other consideration at stake. An example would be a choice between keeping a fairly strong (but not solemn) promise and preventing a significant (but not huge) loss in well-being. Some of these cases will have the 'genuine indeterminacy' to which Gaut points (see previous section).

Even the one rule-consequentialist rule that has the best claim to override any other rule—the rule requiring agents to prevent disaster—is not immune. For to determine what in a particular context counts as disaster will of course take judgement.[10] Here, too, there

---

[10] As Blackburn (1998: 44) writes, '[I]t will require judgement and training to know when a situation is a real emergency, one where for the sake of avoiding harm or doing good one should grasp the nettle and bend or abandon a prescribed role.'

may be cases where the vagueness in our concepts leaves us with no knowable right answer.

In all these kinds of conflict, precise formulae for mechanical application are not available. This insight makes deciding how to treat others very difficult sometimes, and it adds hugely to the difficulty of forming expectations about how others will treat us. So, repelled by these difficulties, we may start off trying to deny that vagueness and imprecision pervade morality.[11] But rule-consequentialism can certainly admit that there is no plausible way of wholly eliminating them.[12]

6.4 RULE-CONSEQUENTIALISM AND ABSOLUTE PROHIBITIONS

Yet whether rule-consequentialism would ever permit the intentional killing of unwilling innocent people, even for the sake of preventing disaster, may seem unclear. Consider three possibilities. (a) We could have *absolute* prohibitions on certain acts such as killing the innocent. (b) Or we could have very strong prohibitions with exception clauses added to them. (c) Alternatively, we could think of these very strong prohibitions without exceptions but with the potential to be overridden in some extreme cases by a 'prevent disaster' rule. In fact, I cannot see any real difference between (b) and (c) here.

A rule-consequentialist cost-benefit analysis of any code counts not only the benefits of its general internalization, but also the costs of inculcating and maintaining attachment to that code. Outside of wars, very few people are ever in a situation where they need to kill an innocent person in order to save many other lives. So, for any random individual, it is very unlikely that there will be benefits from that person's internalizing exception clauses allowing the killing of some for the sake of saving others.

---

[11] Hence the lines from Bob Dylan's 'My Back Pages':

'Good' and 'bad', I defined these terms,
'Quite clear', 'no doubt', 'somehow'.
But I was so much older then.
I'm younger than that now.

[12] So can contractualism. It can hold that judgement will be needed for resolving conflicts between the general rules that the contractualist first principle selects.

Now let us consider the costs. One is the sheer cost of teaching everyone these exception clauses. Another is that they will be misused. This is the danger of people's miscalculating that they are in a situation where the exception clauses become relevant, or where the prohibitions are overridden by a 'prevent disaster' rule.

If the miscalulations by common moral agents will probably be common and the benefits of teaching the exception clauses are unlikely, then the cost-benefit analysis seems to come out in favour of the absolute prohibitions. Rule-consequentialism could endorse absolute prohibitions.

Nevertheless, my own hunch is that the cost-benefit analysis comes down in favour of having very strong but not quite absolute prohibitions. Return to the issue of the benefits of not quite absolute prohibitions. The possibility is very remote of any random individual's ever facing a situation where the future of the human species could be saved only by his or her intentionally killing an innocent person. Yet the potential benefits of killing the innocent person in this sort of case are virtually infinite. So we have a very small probability of needing the provision, and this is to be multiplied by the virtually infinite possible benefits. On the assumption that any probability higher than zero, when multiplied by a virtually infinite value, comes out with a high expected value, I conclude that the cost-benefit analysis favours incorporating a provision about such extreme cases into the code. Such a provision would be supplied by a 'prevent disaster' rule that overrides other rules—including the rule about not taking innocent human life.[13]

Obviously, the ending of our species counts as a disaster, but what else counts as a disaster? The more important a moral rule, the larger the disaster at stake would have to be to justify breaking the rule. It takes the threat of a small disaster to justify breaking a small promise, a larger disaster to justify stealing, and a much larger disaster to justify inflicting serious physical harm on innocent people.

As foreshadowed in the previous section, this is not to say that rule-consequentialism will be *precise* about when an outcome is bad enough to justify breaking other moral rules. I acknowledge the theory will *not* be plausible if it insists on precision here. To be plausible, a theory of rules must allow the interplay between them to

---

[13] Mackie (1977: 167–8) likewise concludes that the 'object of morality', which he takes to be close to rule-consequentialist (see his pp. 199–200), is best served not by absolute prohibitions, but rather by ones that are 'nearly absolute'.

incorporate 'vague references to degree ("too much", "balances out", "does not pay enough attention to")'.[14] Obviously, this vagueness in rule-consequentialism's conflict-resolving rules limits the theory's ability to resolve our moral uncertainties. Here is a place where rule-consequentialism comes up short.

However, note that common moral consciousness seems similarly imprecise about how bad the consequences of keeping rules have to be in order to warrant breaking them.[15] Indeed, perhaps we would distrust any moral theory that was precise about just how bad consequences had to be in order to justify normally abhorrent acts necessary to prevent those consequences. As Stuart Hampshire (1992: 177) wrote, 'A philosopher in his study is in no position to lay down rules for justified murders and reasonable treachery.' Common moral consciousness does not specify any one cut-off point. And rule-consequentialism will, I take it, not be able to state any cut-off point either. Both common moral conviction and rule-consequentialism leave a large space for judgement to fill here.

6.5 SPECIAL OBLIGATIONS TO OTHERS

In addition to prohibitions on acts of certain kinds, morality contains some obligations to do good for others. There are obligations towards family, friends, and others with whom the agent has some special connection. There are also obligations towards individuals with whom the agent has no such special connection. Here my focus will be on the obligations towards those with whom the agent has some special connection.

As I noted back in Chapter 1, most of us think you should give your (at least close) friends and family some priority over others in the distribution of your own private resources. Of course, in many contexts, especially professional ones, strict impartiality is both legally and morally mandatory. But off duty, you are broadly allowed and indeed required to give special consideration to those with whom you have special connections. Suppose you have only enough money to buy a meal for your own hungry child, or a meal

---

[14] I borrow here from Williams 1985: 97.
[15] For an excellent discussion, see Ellis 1992; Shafer-Landau 1997: 602–3.

for some equally hungry stranger. There would be something perverse about devoting your private resources to securing benefits for a stranger when you could have used them to provide your own child with equally large benefits. The same could be said even if the benefits to your own child would be somewhat smaller than the benefits to the stranger.

Other factors can of course come into play. You may occupy a special role that requires complete impartiality. Or you may be in a situation where, while benefiting the stranger will in turn benefit many other people, the same is not true of benefiting your own child. In such cases, it can be right to benefit the stranger rather than your own child, because of the further benefits to others. Another kind of case in which you might be morally permitted to benefit the stranger rather than your own child is one in which your child has somehow forfeited any claim to be one of your priorities. Or you may have promised the stranger but not promised your child. But absent such special circumstances, friends and family should get special weight in your decisions about whom to benefit.

How can rule-consequentialism accommodate these common beliefs? At first blush, it might seem that rule-consequentialism would favour some such rule as, 'When trying to do good for others, always aim to maximize the aggregate good, impartially considered.' But we must be realistic. J. L. Mackie (1977: 132) writes, '[A] large element of selfishness—or, in an older terminology, self-love—is a quite ineradicable part of human nature.'[16] Whether selfishness is ineradicable or not, realism demands we acknowledge that it is pervasive and recalcitrant.

True, it is hardly the whole of human motivation. Human beings naturally develop attachments to particular others, starting typically with members of their own families. These attachments involve concern for the particular others, i.e. altruism towards those within the circle, or, to use David Hume's phrase, 'confined generosity' (1740: bk. III, pt. ii, sect. 2, p. 495). Even these most natural kinds of altruism militate against complete impartiality. As James Griffin (1996: 87) writes,

[T]here is genetic bonding to a few others. Many species, humans among them, are capable of great self-sacrifice, especially to protect offspring. But

---

[16] See also Brandt 1979: 287.

how can we expect beings like that, profoundly self-interested and of very limited altruism, to be capable of complete impartiality, counting everybody for one and none for more than one?

Mackie admits that he doesn't know whether human nature can be changed. He writes,

Of course, given the techniques of mass persuasion adolescents can be turned into Red Guards or Hitler Youth or pop fans, but in each of these we have only fairly superficial redirection of what are basically the same motives. It is far more doubtful whether any agency could effect the far more fundamental changes that would be needed to make practicable a morality of universal concern. Certainly no ordinary processes of education can bring them about. (1997: 133)

Nagel (1991: 26) writes, '[P]eople are motivationally complex, and a moral argument cannot transform them into beings of a completely different kind. Neither can a revolutionary new political arrangement.' He adds, 'Altruism appears to be just as scarce in socialist as in capitalist societies, and the employment of strong-arm methods to make up the deficit has not been a success' (Nagel 1991: 28; see also 72–3, 110.) Neither moral education and argument nor political change are likely to transform human nature so as to make impartial altruism prevalent.

Nor should we be too influenced by the fact that people *in the pitch of excitement* are capable of making huge sacrifices. That people in the pitch of excitement are capable of making huge sacrifices does not show that they can be trained to make large sacrifices for the impartial good on a day in, day out basis (Griffin 1996: 88–90).

And natural human partiality is not the only thing pulling us constantly to focus on our own good. Careful reflection on the nature of our own good does so as well. For among the central components of the good life are accomplishment and deep friendships.[17]

Accomplishment and deep friendships are relevant to our discussion here because they involve 'long-term, life-structuring' aims and focus:

To have deep attachments to particular persons is to acquire motives that shape much of one's life and carry on through most of it. To accomplish

---

[17] Moore 1903: ch. 6; Griffin 1986: chs. 2, 4, 1996: ch. 2; Brink 1989: 233; Hurka 1993: ch. 8, and sect. 10.3. My 1999b discusses the role of reciprocity in non-instrumental friendship.

something with one's life requires dedication to particular activities that typically narrow and absorb one's attention. Many prudential values involve commitments—to particular persons, institutions, causes, and careers. One cannot live a prudentially good life, one cannot fully flourish, without becoming in large measure partial. That partiality becomes part of one; it is not something one can psychologically enter into and exit from at will. (Griffin 1996: 85. See also his 1986: 196, 198, 199).

So two components of personal good are accomplishment and deep friendship, and these components require partiality. This partiality precludes one's *always* aiming to do what maximizes the impartial good (Griffin 1996: 104).

Why does seeking accomplishment require a kind of partiality? Griffin is of course right that building one's life around certain goals requires dedication and focus. To focus on your career or on helping the local school or on developing your artistic talents takes your attention away from other things, including the impartial good. But what if you made maximizing the impartial good your overriding personal goal? If you did make this your overriding personal goal, then personal accomplishment would require, rather than compete with, maximizing impartial good. As Griffin (1996: 86) rightly notes, however, this accomplishment is but one personal good, and it would probably come at the expense of others, such as deep friendships and varied enjoyments (cf. Hurka (1993: ch. 7) on the well-rounded life).

Why is deep friendship incompatible with constant impartiality? Jonathan Dancy (1993: 191) writes, 'To want to treat all impartially is to love nobody.' Why? Because of the conjunction of two facts. The first is one I noted earlier: deep friendships necessarily contain strong affection and concern. The second is the empirical fact that human beings cannot have strong concern for any and equal concern for all. This truth is widely noted. Sidgwick (1907: 434) wrote, '[I]t seems that most persons are only capable of strong affections towards a few human beings in certain close relations, especially the domestic: and that if these were suppressed, what they would feel towards their fellow-creatures generally would be, as Aristotle says, "but a watery kindness".' Ronald Dworkin (1986: 215) put it thus: 'If we felt nothing more for lovers or friends or colleagues than the most intense concern we could possibly feel for all fellow citizens, this would mean the extinction not the universality of love.'

In short, the combination of *strong* concern for any and *equal* concern for all is empirically impossible. Human beings can of course care *strongly* about *some* others. Or they can perhaps care *equally* about *all* others. But they are not able to care *equally and strongly* about *all* others. Therefore, as Griffin (1996: 77) writes, 'One can raise one's capacity for complete impartiality and generalized love of humanity only by reducing one's commitments to particular persons and projects.'[18]

Consequentialists who hold that deep attachments among family members and friends are themselves partly constitutive of a person's good have a very strong reason for thinking any good moral code must protect and promote such attachments. This will require leaving some space for the attendant partiality to operate.

Furthermore, consequentialists will note that attachments among family members and friends are some of the chief sources of pleasure (Parfit 1984: 27, 30).[19] This provides another consequentialist reason to avoid eliminating them. True, one can also get pleasure out of the successful pursuit of impartial good. But a life focused exclusively on increasing the impartial good will very probably contain less enjoyment than one involving a wider variety of projects, including some close friendships.

Virtually everyone needs the special concern of some others. Indeed, people need assurance that their welfare will *consistently* get special weight in someone else's practical deliberation. And we cannot depend on affection to secure this attention and deliberative priority every time they are appropriate. Affection isn't reliable enough, being so easy to forget or ignore when anger, jealousy, or

---

[18] See also Parfit 1984: 27–8, 30, 32–5; Crisp 1992: 149. Susan Wolf (1982: 424 [1997: 83]) makes a more general observation: '[W]hen one reflects . . . on the Loving Saint easily and gladly giving up his fishing trip or his stereo or his hot fudge sundae at the drop of the moral hat, one is apt to wonder not at how much he loves morality, but at how little he loves these other things.'

[19] More generally, as Williams (1973: 131) writes, '[M]any of the qualities that human beings prize in society and in one another are notably non-utilitarian, both in the cast of mind that they involve and in the actions that they are disposed to produce. There is every reason to suppose that people's *happiness* is linked in various ways to these qualities.' Similarly, Susan Wolf (1982: 420 [1997: 80]) identifies moral sainthood with having a life 'dominated by a commitment to improving the welfare of others or of society as a whole', and then (1982: 427 [1997: 87]) writes, 'A world in which everyone, or even a large number of people, achieved moral sainthood—even a world in which they *strove* to achieve it—would probably contain less happiness than a world in which people realized a diversity of ideals involving a variety of personal and perfectionist values.'

disappointment intrude. Moral requirements of loyalty are thus needed for the common enough occasions when affection isn't up to the job.[20] In other words, special moral obligations towards family and friends can then be justified on the ground that internalization of these obligations gives people some assurance that some others will consistently take a special interest in them. Such assurance answers a powerful psychological need.

Let me summarize. The cost of having equal concern for all is that there would be no more than weak concern for any. To have but weak concern for others would preclude the obtaining of deep personal attachments. To lack deep personal attachments would in itself be a loss. In addition, it would deprive us of much pleasure and of much of our sense of security.

Even if these *ongoing* costs of successfully raising people to be equally concerned about all others did not in fact exist, the *transition* costs would be astronomical. Imagine what psychological and financial resources would have to be devoted to getting the overwhelming majority of children in each new generation to internalize an overriding equal concern for all others! The costs would outweigh the benefits. I will defend this view in the chapter on rule-consequentialism's requirements about doing good for the world (Chapter 8). If my argument there is correct, rule-consequentialism provides an intuitively appealing answer to the notoriously difficult question of how much morality requires the comfortably off to do for needy strangers.

---

[20] Brandt writes, 'Michael Stocker seems to think that interiorizing the aversions (etc.) of an optimal morality is incompatible with the existence of motives like love, friendship, affection, and community. I fail to see why. The moral motives here will operate as a "back-up" system when direct affections fail' (Brandt 1989: n. 22 [1992: 85 n.]). See also Sidgwick 1907: 434–5. Railton 1984; Pettit 1994, 1997: 97–102; Mason 1998; Powers 2000.

7
Act-consequentialism

To repeat, act-consequentialism is the view that an act is morally right if and only if the act maximizes (actual or expected) value, impartially construed. But act-consequentialism tells us to make the vast majority of our moral decisions by recourse to rules—indeed, much the same rules that rule-consequentialism endorses. This blurs the contrast between act-consequentialism and rule-consequentialism. Indeed, rule-consequentialism is often presented as merely a special part of act-consequentialism, or even as merely a confused bastardization of act-consequentialism. In this chapter, however, I shall lay bare the conflict between act-consequentialism and rule-consequentialism.

7.1 ACT-CONSEQUENTIALISM AS A CRITERION OF RIGHTNESS, NOT A DECISION PROCEDURE

One might at first think that act-consequentialism is the view that

> On every occasion, an agent should decide which act to do by ascertaining which act has the greatest expected value.

Actually, no consequentialist I know of holds that view. Consequentialists instead agree that our *decision procedure* for day-to-day moral thinking should be as follows:

> At least normally, an agent should decide how to act by referring to tried and true rules, such as 'Don't harm others', 'Don't take or harm the possessions of others', 'Keep your promises', 'Tell the truth', etc.

Why? For a number of reasons. First, we frequently lack information about the probable effects of various acts we might do.

Second, we often do not have the time to collect this information. In either case, if we could not decide what to do until we knew which act had the greatest expected value, our ability to make decisions, especially fairly quick ones, would be severely restricted.

Third, human limitations and biases are such that we are not accurate calculators of the expected consequences—for everyone—of our alternatives. For example, most of us are biased in such a way that we tend to underestimate the harm to others of acts that would benefit us. So if we use 'maximize expected value' as our decision procedure, our natural biases will frequently lead us to make mistakes.

Fourth, expectation effects are again relevant. If others know we standardly use an act-consequentialist decision procedure, and especially if they bear in mind we are biased in ways that distort our attempts at impartial calculation, they may then be unwilling to trust us. They would fear that we would willingly break our promises or take their property or lie to them or even physically harm them whenever (we convinced ourselves that) this would maximize expected value impartially considered. Certainly, trust in society would be destroyed by the common knowledge that agents, on the one hand, standardly use an act-consequentialist decision procedure and, on the other, are systematically biased in ways that distort impartial calculation.

For all the four reasons I have just outlined, act-consequentialists prescribe that we inculcate and maintain in ourselves and others firm dispositions to follow certain rules, including firm dispositions not to harm others, not to take or harm the possessions of others, not break promises, etc. Thus, D. W. Haslett (1994: 21) writes,

because of mistaken calculations and rationalizations, because of the unpredictability in people's behaviour and thus insecurity throughout society that would inevitably result, in short because of human fallibility, for people to take it upon themselves to contravene these norms whenever they believed that doing so maximized utility would cause far more harm than good.[1]

And Donald Regan (1997: 132) writes,

Any sane consequentialist (*pace* readers who will regard that as an

---

[1] See also Brandt 1979: 271–7; Harsanyi 1982: 56–61; and C. Johnson 1991: esp. chs. 3, 4, 9.

oxymoron) must believe in a 'two-level' theory in some fashion and must admit that deliberation does not proceed always and only in terms of what is *ultimately* valuable. Many decisions may quite properly be made without any conscious attention to the ultimate good at all. But when it comes to justifying habits of mind, or modes of deliberating, that do not attend consciously to the ultimate good, it is to the ultimate good that any justification must finally appeal.

The assumption is that our day-to-day moral thinking will be dominated by our pattern of dispositions and concerns. And, as Henry Sidgwick (1907: 413) indicated, if there will be greater overall good where people have patterns of concern in which nonconsequentialist motivations predominate, then consequentialism itself prefers these other patterns of concern.[2] Indeed, given our psychological limitations, act-consequentialism may favour our moral dispositions' running so deep that we could not bring ourselves to do the kinds of act in question even in some cases in which they *would* bring about the best consequences, impartially calculated. Of the sets of dispositions that are psychologically possible, these might be the ones that would produce the most good.

So act-consequentialists and rule-consequentialists by and large agree about how people should do their day-to-day moral thinking. What they disagree about is what makes an act morally permissible, that is, about the criterion for moral rightness.

> ACT-CONSEQUENTIALISM claims that an act is morally permissible if and only if the actual (or expected) overall value of *that particular act* would be at least as great as that of any other act open to the agent.[3]

Having distinguished between act-consequentialism's criterion of rightness and the patterns of concern it favours, I shall mostly focus on its criterion of rightness. Where I am concerned with act-consequentialism's strictures about patterns of concern rather than its criterion of rightness, I shall say so.

---

[2] See references in Ch. 4, n. 12 above. For criticism of the mileage some have tried to get from this, see C. Johnson 1989; Griffin 1992: 123–4, 1996: 105.

[3] Contrast the version of rule-consequentialism developed in this book. This version of rule-consequentialism claims that an act is permissible unless it is forbidden by the code of rules whose internalization by the overwhelming majority of everyone everywhere in each new generation has maximum expected value in terms of weighted well-being.

7.2 ACT- VERSUS RULE-CONSEQUENTIALISM ON PROHIBITIONS

Whatever act-consequentialism says about day-to-day moral thinking, act-consequentialism's criterion of moral rightness implies that *whenever* killing an innocent person, or taking or harming the possessions of others, or breaking a promise, and so on, would maximize the good, such acts would be morally right. Rule-consequentialism denies this. It claims instead that individual acts of murder, torture, breaking promises, and so on, can be wrong even when they result in somewhat more good than not doing them would. Morality, according to rule-consequentialism, is not a matter of the (expected) consequences of individual acts, but rather a matter of the expected value resulting from the general internalization of codes of rules. And general internalization of a code prohibiting physical injury (except when necessary for defence of the innocent or as part of competitive games played voluntarily), prohibiting stealing and vandalizing property, and prohibiting promise-breaking and lying would clearly result in more good than general internalization of a code with no prohibitions on such acts.

In the 1930s, W. D. Ross put forward the following example suggesting that keeping your promises can be right even when this would produce *slightly* less good (Ross 1930: 34–5).[4] Here is his example (numbers represent units of good (or of expected good)):

	Effects on person A	Effects on person B	Total good
Keep your promise to A	1,000	0	1,000
Break your promise to A	0	1,001	1,001

But is Ross's example realistic? Wouldn't the person to whom the promise was made lose in some way if the promise were broken? Normally, someone to whom a promise is made is at least inconvenienced if the promise is broken.

To take account of this, let us then modify Ross's example. (Ross himself indicated this sort of modification is possible.) So suppose:

---

[4] In claiming that we ought to repay a debt (i.e. keep a certain kind of promise) even when not repaying it would have resulted in somewhat more utility, Ross is echoing Joseph Butler and Richard Price.

	Effects on person A	Effects on person B	Total good
Keep your promise to A	1,000	0	1,000
Break your promise to A	−100	1,101	1,001

We might have more worries about the artificiality of Ross's example. Only two people are considered. Aren't other people almost always involved, at least potentially? For example, what about the effects on you of your breaking your promise? Breaking it might make you feel guilty, or start the destruction of your own character and reputation.

As Ross rightly stressed, however, all such effects on others, including the agent himself, can be neutralized in the example. We simply build in assumptions that all effects on others cancel one another out. So let us turn at last to the real lesson of the example.

Most of us would agree with Ross that keeping the promise would be morally right when the total good produced by breaking the promise is only slightly greater than the total good produced by keeping the promise. Act-consequentialism, of course, disagrees. It holds that breaking the promise is morally right here, since that is the alternative with the most good. So, if we agree with Ross about this, we must reject act-consequentialism, that is, reject the view that what maximizes good is always morally right.

Most of us also believe (as Ross went on to say) that, if breaking the promise would produce *much greater* good than keeping it, breaking the promise could be right. We believe parallel things about other kinds of acts—for example, inflicting harm on innocent people, taking or harming the possessions of others, lying, and so on. As I said earlier, act-consequentialism of course accepts that it is right to break promises, take or harm the possessions of others, lie, or harm innocent people *when doing so is necessary to prevent a disaster*. But act-consequentialism also holds that it is right to do these things *when doing them would produce only slightly greater good* than not doing them would. This idea most of us do not accept. Rule-consequentialism, on the other hand, would agree with our beliefs both about when we can, and when we cannot, do normally forbidden acts for the sake of the overall good. (That is what I argued in the previous chapter.)

7.3 THE ECONOMICS OF WORLD POVERTY

In the next section, I will address the question of how much act-consequentialism requires you to do for the needy, including the needy in the poorest countries. Before I take up that question, I want to address the question of whether there is anything you or anyone else can do for the needy in the poorest countries.

The differences between the world's rich and poor are striking. Gross Domestic Product per year in the twenty wealthiest countries is over $20,000 per head. In the poorest fifteen countries, it is under $250 per head. These differences in GDP correlate strongly with more important things. Life expectancy is over 76 in Japan, virtually all of Europe, Australia, New Zealand, the United States, and the United Kingdom. It is under 40 in Sierra Leone, Malawi, and Uganda, and under 50 in Zambia, Zimbabwe, Afghanistan, Rwanda, Mozambique, Angola, Somalia, Ethiopia, Chad, Botswana, and a few other countries.[5]

The vast majority of people in economically developed countries are affluent relative to the world's poorest billion. In this book, the vast majority of people in economically developed countries I am calling the 'relatively affluent' or 'relatively well off'. And, by 'poor', I mean the very poor, those living in severe poverty, which comes to between 1 billion and 1.5 billion people, at the moment.

An influential argument against transferring resources from the relatively affluent to the very poor has been around for about two hundred years. Thomas Robert Malthus argued at the end of the eighteenth century that if the starving are given the resources they need, they will simply multiply to the point where population growth outruns growth in the supply of food. Food shortages will thus only get worse, he predicted.

He was completely wrong. While world population explodes, not only the percentage but even the absolute number living in poverty are falling. In other words, the average material standard of living and life expectancy have continued to rise even while population was rapidly expanding. Furthermore, food has become much cheaper,

---

[5] These numbers all come from *The Economist Pocket World in Figures 2000 Edition*, 40, 86–7.

relative to manufactured goods—about 38 per cent between 1982 and 1992.[6]

This is not to deny that expanding population can contribute to (though it also is caused by) other social and economic problems.[7] But note that the 'low-income' countries have had an average growth rate of GNP per head (3.9 per cent per year for 1980–92) that is much faster than that of 'high-income' countries (2.4 per cent).[8] In other words, poor countries have been getting 'richer' faster than rich countries.

The problem is that a country's economy can grow while leaving some people worse off. Or, obviously, disaster can strike some even while most others are getting by, or even getting richer.

Donations can help the poor and protect the vulnerable. To be sure, the effectiveness of attempts to help is largely hostage to the policies pursued by the governments of the countries whose people need help. Donations that end up funding feuds or enriching the already affluent in poor countries can worsen the position of the worse off. Donors thus need to be careful to pick good charities.

True, countries with low per capita GNP can make enormous strides themselves in raising their citizens' life expectancy and literacy rates (e.g. China). How can poor countries afford to do so much for their citizens? Jean Drèze and Amartya Sen (1989: 270; see also chs. 11–12) point out that

[b]oth elementary education and health care are extremely labour-intensive in their provisioning, and one of the characteristics of a poor economy is the cheapness of labour—and of training labour for elementary education and basic medical services. Thus, the poorer economies not only have less money to spend on providing these services, they also *need* less money for making these provisions.

---

    [6] See Sen 1994: sect. 2, esp. n. 21.

    [7] And environmental problems. Many people nowadays seem traumatized by the thought that the expanding world population will soon bring about environmental degradation to the point where the planet is uninhabitable. But note that the average person from North America or Western Europe is responsible for something like fifteen times more pollution than the average person from India, China, or other low-income countries. From the point of view of conservation of the environment, changing the rich's patterns of consumption may be more important than the fertility rate of the world's very poor. But this does not gainsay the point that an expanded world population isn't good from the point of view of conservation of the environment.

    [8] Here I am merely paraphrasing Sen 1994: sect. 2.

A relatively small amount of contributed money can go a long way in those economies. And the most effective way to prevent people's losing the ability to obtain an adequate supply of food is usually not the direct provision of food. The direct provision of food tends to induce a collapse of local food prices, which then leaves local food producers with inadequate economic incentives to devote their capital and labour to further food production. What usually works is instead the public provision of employment with cash wages for those who can work, supplemented by unconditional relief for those who cannot either work or rely on someone else to provide support (Drèze and Sen 1989: ch. 7. Cf. Lucas 1990: 640). And if the main provision of resources comes from public provision of employment, not from unconditional handouts, then we have two kinds of benefits to consider. First, of course, there are the benefits to the needy of getting the wages they need to buy food. Second, there are the benefits produced by the work they do.

A person in one of the poorest countries can keep from starving on less than $250 per year, as long as the country's poverty inhibits demand *and inflation*. What would be the effects of lots of money flowing into a very poor country's economy? Channeled properly, the money can have excellent effects. Donations to the best charities really do save lives.

7.4 ACT-CONSEQUENTIALISM AND THE NEEDY

Act-consequentialism is normally taken to be unreasonably demanding, construing as duties what one would have thought were supererogatory self-sacrifices.[9] To fully appreciate this objection, we must keep in mind the following four points. First, as I have just contended, donations can save lives. Second, money and other material goods *usually* have diminishing marginal utility. Third, each dollar can buy vastly more food in, for example, Ethiopia than it can in one of the industrially developed countries. Fourth, other relatively

---

[9] This objection is addressed in most contemporary discussions of act-consequentialism. Important early discussions are Godwin 1793: 325; Mill 1861: ch. 2, para. 19; Sidgwick 1907: 87, 434, 492, 499; Baier 1958: 203–4.

well-off people will not give much. Given these facts, we must accept that good would be maximized if I gave away most of my material goods to the appropriate charities. Therefore, giving away most of my material goods is what act-consequentialism requires of me. To be sure, I should not give in ways that create or sustain a 'culture of dependency'. But this is no excuse for not giving to the best charities, since their projects avoid this problem and instead aim to promote self-sufficiency. And I must, of course, take into account the effects of my present actions on my future capacity to give—for example, I need to be both presentable and healthy enough to avoid losing my job (P. Singer 1993: 223, n. 1). Still, if I am well off by world standards, then what I am allowed to keep for myself is probably very little.

Perhaps I should even change to some more lucrative employment so that I would then have more money to give to charity.[10] I probably could make much more money as a corporate lawyer, banker, stockbroker, accountant, gossip columnist, or bounty hunter. If one should be willing to make any sacrifices that are smaller than the benefits thereby secured for others, then I should move to the better-paying job so that I will have a bigger salary to contribute to the needy. I would then have to give an even larger percentage of my earnings to aid agencies. The result would be a life of devoted money-making—combined with denying myself virtually all the rewards I could buy for myself with the money. After all, the enjoyment and comfort and convenience and other benefits I could buy for myself are all insignificant compared to the very lives of those who would be saved if I instead contributed the money to aid agencies.

Given all this, Shelly Kagan must be right that, 'Given the parameters of the actual world, there is no question that [maximally] promoting the good would require a life of hardship, self-denial, and austerity' (1989: 360).

But many of us may on reflection think that it would be *morally unreasonable* to demand this level of self-sacrifice for the sake of others.[11] This is not to deny that morality can from time to time

---

[10] Unger (1996: 151–2) likewise stresses this point.

[11] See Crisp 1992, and Quinn 1993: 171: 'We think there is something morally amiss when people are forced to be farmers or flute players just because the balance of social needs tips in that direction. Barring great emergencies, we think people's lives must be theirs to lead.'

require significant self-sacrifice for the sake of others. Nor is it to deny that giving most of what one has to the needy is both permissible and extremely praiseworthy. But, however praiseworthy such self-sacrifice may be, most of us are quite confident that perpetual self-impoverishment for the sake of those outside one's circle of family and friends is supererogatory—something 'above and beyond the call of duty', not something morality *requires* of us.[12]

I admit there is something unsavoury about objecting to a moral theory because of the severity of its requirements. The demandingness objection might seem aimed at people who have a lot to lose from a strong requirement to aid others and who are letting their self-interest cloud their moral judgement (Carson 1982: 243). But to dismiss the objection on such grounds would be inappropriate. An objection cannot legitimately be dismissed as 'guilty by association'. It has to be evaluated on its own merits. And, even after we acknowledge that the demandingness objection may appeal to some disreputable characters, the objection seems eminently forceful (Murphy 1993: 274).

I have been discussing the objection that act-consequentialism requires us to make huge sacrifices in order to maximize our contribution to famine relief. This feature of act-consequentialism is a consequence of a more general feature. The more general feature is that act-consequentialism requires self-sacrifice *whenever* this maximizes aggregate good. And this more general feature has another consequence—that act-consequentialism requires self-sacrifice even when the benefit to the other person is only *slightly* larger than the cost to the agent. But that is additionally implausible.

Consider, for example, the corner office in our building. Offices are allotted on the basis of seniority. Suppose you are the most senior person who might want this corner office. But if you do not take it, it will go to an acquaintance who spends ten per cent more time in her office than you do in yours. Suppose we therefore reasonably guess that she would benefit a bit more from moving into this office than you would. This is not a life-and-death matter. Nor will she be so depressed by not getting the corner office that her

---

[12] If something is above and beyond the call of duty, not doing it is blameless. It is not something for which someone should be punished by law, by public opinion, or by 'the reproaches of his own conscience'. If something is required, however, then failure to do it is blameworthy, unless there is some good excuse.

work or domestic life will be seriously compromised. Nevertheless, she would get a bit more enjoyment out of the better office than you would. But, having the required seniority, you still take it for yourself. No one would think you unreasonable or immoral for doing so. Morality does not, we think, really require you to sacrifice your own good for the sake of only slightly larger gains to others (except in special circumstances).

So now I have offered two objections about the demandingness of act-consequentialism. (1) Act-consequentialism requires *huge* sacrifices from you. (2) Act-consequentialism requires you to sacrifice your own good even when the aggregate good will be only *slightly* increased by the your sacrifice. We can amalgamate these more specific objections into one and call it the objection that act-consequentialism is *unreasonably demanding*.

One act-consequentialist reply here might be to point out that we often act selfishly, or alternatively in the interests of those with whom we have special connections, when we should instead be working for the good of all. This is of course true. But it hardly eliminates the objection. To object that act-consequentialism is unreasonably demanding, we need not deny that people are often selfish.

Likewise, in order to object that act-consequentialism is unreasonably demanding, we need not specify just when an agent has done as much for others as morality demands. In other words, we need not specify just where the dividing line is between duty and supererogation. We do not need to know just where a dividing line is in order to know where it is not. And we know the dividing line is *not* right at the altruistic end of the spectrum that runs from completely impartial altruism to complete egoism.

Actually, act-consequentialism itself entails that there really is no line between duty and supererogatory altruism. For the act-consequentialist, where duty stops, so stops permissibility.[13] In other words, act-consequentialism entails that there is no such thing as morally permissible self-sacrifice that goes above and beyond the call of duty. On the act-consequentialist view, a certain very high degree of altruism is required, but any beyond that degree is wrong. This is extremely counterintuitive.

---

[13] This needs a slight qualification. In cases where the agent has two or more options with unsurpassed expected value, none of these options is the agent's duty but each of them is permissible.

Some defenders of act-consequentialism may claim that the counterexamples above are wrong about the theory's practical implications. We know far more about how to help ourselves and our near and dear than we do about how to help those who are far and unfamiliar, and we have more opportunity to satisfy our own needs and those of family and friends.[14] Because we know more about those right around us, so this defence goes, we will maximize the overall good by focusing on ourselves and them. J. S. Mill (1861: ch. 2, para. 19) claimed that only on rare occasions can anyone ('except one in a thousand') multiply happiness on an extended scale—that is, be a 'public benefactor'. Only on these rare occasions is the agent, according to Mill, 'called on to consider public utility; in every other case, private utility, the interest or happiness of some few persons, is all he has to attend to'. Hence, this defence concludes, we will not have to sacrifice so much for needy strangers.

This defence of act-consequentialism should be far less persuasive now than it was when Mill and Sidgwick wrote.[15] People in their day rarely had detailed information either about the current needs of disaster victims, or about the relative effectiveness of different charities. In contrast, current news about natural disasters appears all around us. And we can do something to help victims just by phoning in a credit card number to someone at a highly effective charity such as Oxfam or UNICEF or Care.

Can act-consequentialists adequately answer the objection about demandingness by invoking the distinction between their criterion of rightness and their recommendations about decisions, patterns of concern, and dispositions? Act-consequentialists typically claim that some degree of everyday partiality towards ourselves and those close to us is consistent with act-consequentialism, because act-consequentialism is a criterion of right action, not a procedure for day-to-day moral thinking and not a prescription about how one should be motivated. While act-consequentialism holds that an act is morally right only if it maximizes overall good, act-consequentialism need not claim that one should always be *motivated* by the concern for maximum overall good or that one should always be *consciously aiming* at it.

But this line of defence is open to a number of objections. It is

---

[14] Sidgwick 1907: 431, 434; Brink 1989: 266, 275; Jackson 1991.
[15] A similar point is made by Mackie (1977: 123).

one thing to claim that there will be more good overall if *everyone* retains their special concerns for themselves, their family, and their friends than there would be if everyone's patterns of concern were absolutely impartial. It is quite another thing to claim that, given that everyone else will have more or less the same special concerns they do now, there will be more overall good if you or I retain our special concern for ourselves, our families, and our friends than there would be if our patterns of concern were absolutely impartial. As will become clear, the difference between these two claims matters.

I have already argued that, if the cost of everyone's being motivated by an equal concern for all is the elimination of strong affections and deep attachments, greater good will result if everyone keeps their greater concern for themselves and their family and friends. But this claim is about the consequences of *everyone's* retaining their special concerns versus the consequences of *everyone's* being impartial. Act-consequentialists sometimes try to use these claims in order to defend their theory against the charge that it is excessively demanding. However, they should not be allowed to get away with it.[16] For even if my life would be miserable without strong affections and deep attachments, this state of affairs might benefit others enough to outweigh my loss.

How could that be the case? No matter what happens to me, the vast majority of the people in the world will continue to have something roughly like their present patterns of concern. The elimination of my special concern for my family, my friends, and myself would not jeopardise that. Admittedly, I have suggested that the world might well be a poorer place if *all people* lost their strong affections. But only I and the comparatively tiny circle of people with whom I am connected would lose if *only my* strong affections were eliminated. Meanwhile, the benefits to others of my becoming impartial would be as follows. With my present special concerns for my family, my friends, and myself, all of whom are already relatively well off, I do relatively little to help relieve the enormous suffering in the world. But if I came to care no more about myself or those close to me than I do about each and every other person, I would devote my money and energy to helping the most needy. I would thereby relieve

---

[16] Here I borrow from Parfit's matchless discussion (1984: 30–1). See also Wolf 1982: 428 [1997: 87].

the suffering of quite a lot of people. Thus, although the elimination of (or even just a severe reduction in) my special concern for my family, my friends, and myself would threaten my relationships with these people and lead me to make other great personal sacrifices, the benefits would be greater than the losses, impartially considered.

In the face of this fact, act-consequentialism does not allow one to have much greater concern for friends, for family, and for oneself than for each other person. On the contrary, act-consequentialism requires that one should *not* have much greater concern for friends, family, and self than for others. Thus, its requirements about what pattern of concern one ought to have are severely demanding.

Roger Crisp (1997: 106–7) questions whether the sort of impartiality in question here is something people are able to achieve. He observes,

Children are brought up within traditions and cultures, and all the traditions and cultures that have yet developed among human beings have embodied partiality. Parents, teachers and others in society establish special relationships with children which make it possible to bring them up to be rational. It is hard to imagine a system of education which did not rest on such partialities, or to imagine partialities and attachments which could be shed once the capability to think rationally were achieved.[17]

If this is correct, and if people cannot be morally required to do what they cannot do, then people cannot be required to be wholly impartial.[18]

But even if there is a level of impartiality which is beyond human capacity, and therefore beyond what act-consequentialism (or any other moral theory) can require, the degree of impartiality that act-consequentialism demands might nevertheless be more than morality seems really to require. (I am not suggesting that this is something Crisp denies.)

I earlier argued that act-consequentialism's requirements concerning *acts* are extremely demanding. I have now argued that act-consequentialism makes severe demands concerning *patterns of concern*. It is important to see, however, that act-consequentialism's requirements on action are too demanding even if its requirements on patterns of concern are far less severe than I believe they are.

---

[17] See also LaFollette 1996: 208.
[18] Cf. Scheffler 1992: 59 and Horton 1999.

So, for the sake of argument, assume there is some fatal flaw in my attack on act-consequentialists' attempts to rationalize your having something like your present pattern of concern, that is, one dominated by special concerns for your friends and family, and your own projects. Assume that act-consequentialism would allow you to have this pattern of concern. If that is right, then act-consequentialism may be off the hook with respect to patterns of concern. Still, it may be on the hook with respect to its criterion of right action.

Act-consequentialism maintains that an act is right only if it maximises good overall. As Samuel Scheffler (1982: 9) writes about act-utilitarianism, it

requires the agent to allocate energy and attention to the projects and people he cares most about *in strict proportion* to the value from an impersonal standpoint of his doing so, even though people typically acquire and care about their commitments quite independently of, and out of proportion to, the value that their having and caring about them is assigned in an impersonal ranking of overall states of affairs.

I argued above that, in order to do what is right on this criterion of right action, you must regularly perform acts of *extreme* self-sacrifice for the sake of strangers. I also argued that act-consequentialism requires you to make sacrifices for others even when the benefit to them is only *slightly* greater than the cost to you. Act-consequentialism's requirements on action are thus unreasonably demanding. And this objection about act-consequentialist requirements on action holds no matter what act-consequentialism says about patterns of concern. So the objection cannot be avoided by appeal to a distinction between the theory's criterion of rightness and its prescriptions about motivation.

There is one more way of trying to defend act-consequentialism against the objection that it is unreasonably demanding. David Brink writes:

We have social capacities for sympathy, benevolence, love, and friendship whose realization makes our lives better than they would otherwise be. . . . Family relations, friendships, and social relations involving mutual concern and respect exercise these capacities. (1989: 233)

I have already mentioned that some theories of well-being would count friendship as partly constitutive of one's own well-being. This is what gives some credibility to Brink's idea that realizing one's social capacities is a constitutive part of one's own well-being. But does this idea support Brink's claim that act-consequentialism 'will not enjoin great self-sacrifice'? (1989: 242) Brink argued:

For pursuit and realization of one's projects to be valuable, these projects must be, among other things, morally acceptable. The pursuit of projects that would impose avoidable hardship on others is not intrinsically valuable. Moreover, personal and social relationships that involve mutual concern and commitment are *part of* an agent's welfare. An agent's welfare, therefore, is directly related to the welfare of others in certain ways. One is better off when another's welfare is enhanced, and especially when one enhances another's welfare, and, similarly, one suffers when others suffer, and especially when one causes the suffering of others. (1989: 243)

There seem to be two lines of argument here. I shall take them in turn.

One line claims that the successful completion of one of my projects cannot constitute a benefit to me unless it avoids imposing avoidable hardships on others. This seems implausible. Suppose Sarah develops some brilliant theory in an extremely esoteric corner of pure mathematics. Add that, in the course of her single-minded pursuit of this achievement, she wins positions, grants, promotions, and recognition that, had they gone to other people, would have prevented hardships for those other people. Hardship for others could have been avoided if she had not succeeded in her projects.

Someone might reply that, in this example, hardship was bound to be visited upon some people, whether that group includes Sarah or not. So there is a sense in which, even if the hardship *for others* was avoidable, hardship for *some* was not.

Then, let us suppose that those hardships that Sarah's rivals had to endure were worse than what Sarah would have had to endure if she had not won the positions, grants, promotions, and so on. So there is a recognizable sense in which her success imposes worse hardships than would have occurred had she not been successful. We might say her success imposes avoidable *levels* of hardship for others.

Still, on any plausible view of well-being, Sarah's achievement makes her life go better in self-interested terms. Indeed, the successful completion of projects often enhance the agent's life even if they involve the imposition of avoidable hardship on others.

The other line of argument in the passage from Brink is that one reason act-consequentialism will not require much self-sacrifice is that personal and social relationships involving mutual concern and commitment are part of an agent's own welfare. Thus, when for the sake of my relationships with family or friends I sacrifice money or comfort or career opportunities, I may be sustaining relationships which constitute a large benefit for me. Indeed, I may be doing what adds to my own welfare more than would anything else I could have done.

But act-consequentialism constantly requires me to donate my money and energy to campaigns to help people *other than* my friends and family—that is, people with whom I have no relationship of mutual concern and commitment, such as victims of famine on the other side of the world. Nothing Brink says about the benefits to me of relationships of mutual concern and commitment can undermine the thought that my donating a huge amount of my time or money to help those people would be a huge sacrifice. For all Brink has argued, act-consequentialism remains outrageously and implausibly demanding.

8

Rule-consequentialism and Doing Good for the World

8.1 INTRODUCTION

In both the first and second chapters of this book, I claimed that rule-consequentialism provides intuitively attractive answers to questions about how much the relatively well off are obligated to do for the needy. Other writers have disputed this claim.[1] The question how much the relatively well off are obligated to do for the needy is one of the most interesting areas in the discussion of rule-consequentialism—indeed, in moral theory as a whole. Rarely do most civilized people seriously consider physically injuring others.[2] But we frequently wonder whether we are doing what morality requires of us in terms of helping others. And it is far from obvious that any familiar moral theory has an intuitively acceptable line on this matter.

I have already attacked the act-consequentialist requirement to keep making sacrifices for others until further sacrifices would result in less overall good in the long run. This chapter starts by briefly exposing the inadequacy of a few other approaches to the problem. The rest of the chapter shows that rule-consequentialism's approach is in fact intuitively acceptable.

8.2 THE LARGE GAP PRINCIPLE

Consider the following principle of aid: we are required to come to the aid of others as long as the benefit to them is very great in

---

[1] Kagan 1989: 35, cf. 395–7; Carson 1991, 1993; Mulgan 1994b, 1996.
[2] Near the beginning of the book, I noted that certain competitive sports allow or even require players to physically attack one another (within limits). This is justifiable

comparison to the sacrifice to us. Henry Sidgwick remarked that this principle is part of 'common-sense morality' and even, 'broadly speaking, unquestionable'.[3] On the contrary, the principle seems unreasonably demanding. Most of us would have to sacrifice most of our welfare in the course of helping others before we reached the point at which the sacrifice to us would no longer be very much smaller than the benefits produced for them.[4] Yet a requirement that we sacrifice *most* of our welfare for the sake of strangers whose suffering is not our fault seems unreasonably demanding, particularly when most others in a position to help are not doing so.

8.3 BENEFICENCE AS AN IMPERFECT DUTY

For many centuries, a distinction has been drawn between two kinds of moral duties, perfect and imperfect.

Perfect duties are ones with which everyone should *always* comply, that is, take every opportunity to comply. Everyone should always refrain from making false promises, being violent towards innocent others, taking the legitimately acquired possessions of others without their consent (unless one is enforcing court orders). And everyone has moral rights that these things not be done to them. In other words, perfect duties everyone has not to do certain kinds of things to others are mirrored by rights everyone has not to have these things done to them.

In contrast, *imperfect* duties are ones that everyone has to comply with in general, but gets to choose the occasions. You cannot help everyone in need. But you have an imperfect duty to help some others—and which ones you help is up to you. I have no right that you help me instead of others.

---

only because the players want to play a game with those rules. I also acknowledged that doctors are allowed to cut into patients. This is justified only when it is for the benefit of the patient and with the patent's consent, if the patient is able to consent. In addition, members of the army and police have to consider physically injuring others but they should injure others only when necessary to defend the innocent.

[3] Sidgwick 1907: 348–9; see also 253, 261.

[4] This claim is similar to one of the central points in Fishkin 1982. See also Nagel's observation that, given existing world circumstances, not just act-utilitarianism but any morality with a substantial impersonal component will make voracious demands (1986: 190).

The distinction between perfect and imperfect duties—as a distinction between duties mirrored by rights and duties not mirrored by rights—goes back to the founder of so-called modern natural law theory, Hugo Grotius (1625). Samuel Pufendorf (1672) then pointed out that the distinction between perfect and imperfect duties correlates with another distinction.[5] General compliance with perfect duties is necessary for the very existence of society. In contrast, general compliance with imperfect duties is beneficial but not absolutely necessary for the existence of society. Roughly these same distinctions have been widely endorsed since Grotius and Pufendorf (most famously by Immanuel Kant (1785) and J. S. Mill (1861: ch. 5)).

The distinction between perfect and imperfect duties has obvious appeal. You can avoid killing innocent people without their consent. You can avoid taking or harming other people's possessions. If careful, you can avoid breaking your promises and telling lies. So these can be things you must always avoid. But there are too many needy people for you to be able to help them all. What you cannot do, you cannot be obligated to do. So you cannot be obligated to help every needy person. Yet you are obligated to help some. Which ones are you obligated to help? Is not the reasonable answer that morality should leave this to your discretion?

Underneath the surface plausibility of the imperfect duties view, however, lurk serious problems. Suppose I am faced with two strangers who each need help, but one of whom has greater needs and can be helped a lot more than the other. According to the imperfect duties view, I can simply choose which to help. But that answer seems wrong. Other things being equal, I should help the needier one. The imperfect duties view leaves too much room here for arbitrary choice.

Or suppose I saved someone's life this morning, and now I can save someone's else's life at no cost to myself. Is it really morally optional whether I go on to save the second person? Surely not!

Now consider cases where helping others does involve some self-sacrifice. Imagine there are overwhelmingly many people to save, and for each one I save I have to make some additional self-sacrifice.

---

[5] I learned these facts about Grotius and Pufendorf from Schneewind (1990: 49).

How much am I morally required to sacrifice here? The imperfect duties view gives us no help.[6]

I do not deny that the duty to do good for others may be quite complicated and its application require careful judgement. The root problem with the imperfect duties view is that it ignores questions of how much help to provide, how much sacrifice to make, and how to choose between potential beneficiaries.

The imperfect duties view can fail to require people to do enough for others. To see this, focus on two (of the many possible) alternative policies you might have. One policy would be to do good for others at least sometimes, but only *in minor ways* and only when the *sacrifice to you is trivial* (not only on that occasion but also even when totaled with all your other such sacrifices). The other policy would be to do good for others at least sometimes in ways that would *transform their life prospects*, and to do this even if the *costs to you would be more than trivial*. The imperfect duties view implies that the first policy would be enough. That implication is counterintuitive. A plausible view must allow that you can be required to make significant sacrifices to help the needy, and that, at least when other things are roughly equal, you should do what helps the needy more rather than less.

8.4 DOING WHAT, IF EVERYONE DID IT, WOULD MAXIMIZE THE GOOD

Consider the rule requiring you to do what, if everyone did it, would produce the most good.[7] Suppose that, if each relatively well-off person followed a rule requiring the contribution of at least some relatively small percentage of his or her income to the best charities, there would be enough not only to feed the world but also to deal with most other basic needs. Making any contribution at all seems difficult for many people, but the demand that one should contribute

[6] For the view that, on the contrary, it gives considerable help, see Schaller 1990: 198–200. Other important discussions include Hill 1971; Baron 1987; Nagel 1991: ch. 5; O'Neill 1986: ch. 8; Murphy 1993: 272 n. 13; Cummiskey 1996: ch. 6.
[7] For a particularly important discussion, see Parfit 1984: 31. Compare P. Singer 1972a: 233, 1993: ch. 8, esp. pp. 244–6; Fishkin 1982: 162–3; Kagan 1991; and Murphy 1993, 1997.

at least some small percentage of one's income does not seem unreasonable. So if small contributions from all the well off would effectively end world hunger and satisfy most other very basic needs, then rule-consequentialism might seem to offer a plausible line on the question of duties to aid.

But is it true that the combined effect of fairly small contributions from each of the well off would really be so good? I am not a development economist. Nevertheless, I submit that the combined effect of fairly small contributions from each of the well off would have excellent effects, as long as these contributions were made to the best charities.[8]

I acknowledge that rule-consequentialism is implausible if it requires us to be experts in political economy in order to determine what morality requires of us. Rule-consequentialism should be formulated in terms of the *expected* value of general internalization of rules, not in terms of the value of their *actual* consequences. If morality requires us to comply with the rules whose general internalization has as much expected value as any other rules we can identify, what rule about aid to the needy will this involve? The answer might be a rule requiring contributions of at least 1 per cent to 10 per cent of annual income from those who are relatively well off by world standards.

The amount of required contributions should be 'progressive'. Thus those who are themselves very poor by world standards are rarely (but sometimes) obligated to make contributions. The reason they would rarely have to make contributions is that, because they are so close to the edge, most contributions they could make would involve, for them, large sacrifices. Those who barely qualify as relatively well off by world standards are required to contribute at least 1 per cent. Those who are even better off are obligated to give more, not only in absolute terms but also as a percentage of their income.

Let me stress the following about the rule requiring contributions of at least 1 per cent to 10 per cent of annual income from those who are relatively well off by world standards. I am not claiming this rule would result in the best consequences. I am claiming merely that, of

---

[8] Note that the teams of economists at the World Bank and the United Nations call for contributions from the rich countries of 0.7 per cent of their GDP. With all due humility, I tried my hand at doing the economics in my 1991a. Brandt (1996: ch. 8) discusses the economics from an explicitly rule-consequentialist perspective, but takes issue with my calculations.

the alternative possible rules, this one has at least as much *expected* value as any other, given the economic disruptions and mismanagement that would probably result if *all* the relatively rich gave a greater percentage.

8.5 BEHAVING DECENTLY IN A SELFISH WORLD

But is complying with such a rule really defensible, given that in fact others aren't following it? If rule-consequentialism requires no more than that, the obvious complaint against rule-consequentialism is that it evaluates an act by reference to the *hypothetical* consequences of everyone's accepting ideal rules, and ignores the *actual* consequences of the act. (Virtually never do the consequences of an act include everyone's accepting ideal rules.)

Rule-consequentialism is implausible if it holds that how much I should contribute is completely insensitive to how much others are actually contributing. Suppose I and nine other people see ten people fall from the ship's deck into the sea. Each of us still on deck could easily throw one or more lifejackets to the people overboard. Suppose I throw one lifejacket to the people in the water but then notice that the other people on the deck are doing nothing to help. Intuition is clear about this case: I should continue throwing lifejackets overboard until everyone in the water has one. Here, because others aren't helping, I should do more.

Or take a more famous case, one that has indeed been central to the contemporary debate about beneficence.[9] A and B are on their way to the airport for long flights when they see two small children drowning in a shallow pond. A and B could each easily wade in and save the children, at no risk to themselves. The two children are positioned in the pond in such a way that A and B could each save one and still make their flights. But if either A or B takes the time to save both children single-handedly, then that person will miss the flight.

---

[9] This debate was initiated in Singer 1972a. See also Kagan 1989, esp. 3–4, 231–2; Cullity 1994, esp. 104–5; Unger 1996: chs. 1, 2, 6. For the variant of the example in the text above, see Singer 1972a: 231–3, 1993: 229; Kagan 1991: 224–5; and Murphy 1993: 291.

Suppose A saves one child but B does nothing. Surely, A should now save the other child.

Rule-consequentialism certainly agrees. Remember my argument, in section 4.2, that rule-consequentialism would prescribe a requirement to prevent disaster. Since I can prevent a disaster by throwing more lifejackets to the people in the sea, or by saving the second child, I should do so. Since A can prevent disaster by rescuing the second child if B won't, A should rescue that child. Thus, by incorporating a rule about preventing disaster, rule-consequentialism makes how much the agent should do sensitive to how much others are doing.

Should we therefore conclude that, whenever others in a position to help are not doing so, the rule-consequentialist view is that the rule about preventing disasters applies and so you must give more than you would have to give were everyone else complying with rule-consequentialism? That conclusion threatens to make rule-consequentialism itself too demanding (according to commonsense moral conviction).[10] For the starvation of innocent people counts as a disaster. And often you can save some of these lives by contributing to the best charities. But there is an overwhelming number of lives to be saved. Thus, an *unlimited* requirement to prevent disaster seems to entail that you should keep making contributions—at least to the point where you yourself are impoverished. Going that far might well be admirable, even saintly. But it does not really seem to be morally *required*.

Rule-consequentialism may not be compelled to defend the view that so much self-sacrifice is morally required. For, as I argued in sections 4.2 and 6.5, the theory can point to the psychological and other costs of inculcating and sustaining in everyone the disposition to make severe self-sacrifices for the sake of needy strangers. More demanding rules about preventing disasters and aiding others would be far more difficult and costly to inculcate and sustain in everyone

---

[10] The idea that there are limits on the demandingness of morality has implications not only for the duty to prevent disaster but also for other duties. This was implicit in my earlier discussion of reciprocity. One is not required to follow certain rules when dealing with those who refuse to do likewise. But even beyond this, my duty to tell the truth, for example, may stop short of requiring me to reply honestly to the Inquisition's question about whether I am an atheist. This sort of limit may be implicit in the law of some countries where self-incrimination and testifying against a spouse are not required.

than would less demanding ones. The time, energy, attention, and psychological conflict that would be needed to get people to internalize a very demanding rule would be immense.

And these internalization costs would be incurred with each new generation. It is not as if infants begin with as much altruism as their parents eventually internalized. Rather, each new generation starts with roughly the same genetic makeup as the previous generation. Each new generation would need to be transformed from beings concerned mainly with immediate gratification, personal comfort, and self-assertion to impartial beings willing to make virtually endless sacrifices for others. So the internalization costs would not be a one-off event; instead, they would be repeated indefinitely.

I have contended that the costs of getting internalized an extremely demanding rule about preventing disasters would be huge. If I am right about these costs, they would be so large that trying to get each new generation to internalize a completely impartial altruism could not plausibly be thought to maximize expected value. There is some point short of this where the costs of going further outweigh the benefits.

With these points clearly in view, let me indicate what rule about aid I think rule-consequentialism would prescribe:

> Over time agents should help those in greater need, especially the worst off, even if the personal sacrifices involved in helping them add up to a significant cost to the agents. The cost to the agents is to be assessed aggregately, not iteratively.

Agents would of course *be allowed* to make sacrifices beyond the 'significant aggregative personal cost' threshold. But agents would not be required to go beyond this threshold, even to save lives.[11]

What is a significant aggregative personal cost? This is obviously vague. The person who regularly gives a little wealth or time to good

[11] The distinction between aggregative and iterative cost comes from Cullity 1995: 293–5. I first endorsed Cullity's distinction in my 1998a and 1999a. And Scanlon (1998: 224) writes, '[I]f you are presented with a situation in which you can prevent something very bad from happening, or alleviate someone's dire plight, by making only a slight (or even moderate) sacrifice, then it would be wrong not to do so. It is very plausible to suppose that this principle . . . could not reasonably be rejected, at least not if the threshold of sacrifice is understood to take account of previous contributions (so that the principle does not demand unlimited sacrifice if it is divided into small enough increments).'

charities, or sometimes gives a great deal of time or wealth to them, seems to reach the required threshold. But this threshold is not so high that it would require agents to forgo any other personal projects or deep personal relationships.

The point about assessing personal sacrifice aggregately rather than iteratively is meant to suggest that the rule does not require one to help another in great need whenever the sacrifice involved in helping *on that particular occasion* is relatively little.[12] For such a requirement, carried to its logical extreme, is immensely demanding. Small sacrifices, repeated indefinitely, can add up to a huge sacrifice. If on every occasion on which you can help the needy you have to ignore whatever sacrifices you made in the past and to sacrifice a little more of what you have left, then, if there are enough such occasions, you will end up with only a very little yourself.

So, if the rule about aiding others assessed the amount of sacrifice made by the agent iteratively rather than aggregately, the rule would be extremely demanding. Thus, the costs of getting the rule internalized by the overwhelming majority would be extremely high. A rule-consequentialist theory that takes these internalization costs into account will thus favour the less demanding, aggregative assessment of personal sacrifice, rather than the iterative one.

The rule proposed would apply in very wide variety of cases. It is not merely about famine-relief cases. And this rule is not about merely what the rich should do. So, although it would apply when a rich person can help a poor one, it would also apply when a poor person can help another poor one, and when a poor person can help a rich one. It would even apply when a rich person can help another rich one. (Joe might be rich—but if he is drowning in the river, he has a very great need for the life preserver that Joanna could easily toss to him.)

The rule that I have argued rule-consequentialism will favour may seem close to the idea that the duty of beneficence is an imperfect duty. After all, both the rule-consequentialists' rule and the idea that beneficence is an imperfect duty focus on patterns of action over time, rather than on individual decisions abstracted from those patterns. But I think the rule-consequentialists' rule is more specific

---

[12] Actually, an exception needs to be added here for cases where sacrifice of one's life is necessary to save the world, or even just some significant proportion of humanity. I shall come back to this sort of case below.

than the idea that beneficence is an imperfect duty. The rule-consequentialists' rule points to the superiority of helping the more needy over the less needy, and it tries to indicate the rough level of lifetime self-sacrifice one should be willing to make.

Let me immediately address an objection not about the rule's rule-consequentialist backing, but about its intuitive plausibility. This is an objection to *any* limit on the amount of self-sacrifice that can be required in the cause of helping strangers, or at least to any limit short of a severely demanding one. Suppose that, having already done what the principle I have proposed required of you, you notice yet another person whom you could save.[13] Here, any principle which allows you to say that you have done your part to help others and now want to work on other interests of yours can sound counterintuitively mean. How could it ever be morally permissible to 'shut the gates of mercy on mankind'?

On the other hand, any principle which tells you that you must take *every* opportunity to come to the rescue will look counterintuitively demanding, once we realize the virtual infinity of opportunities you have to come to the rescue. I cannot see how to keep morality from being outrageously demanding without drawing some kind of line limiting your duty to help strangers. But any such line will be opposed by the objection about meanness.[14] A compromise must be struck. Given the pressure to compromise, the rule about aiding others I think rule-consequentialism would endorse seems intuitively plausible. Why? Consider the following.

Most of us believe that morality certainly requires one to come to the aid of the needy, even at non-trivial cost to oneself. Most of us also believe there are limits on how much self-sacrifice morality can reasonably demand, except in very exceptional cases. In other words, our shared moral opinion seems to accept a lower and an upper threshold for how much morality requires in everyday cases. Between these thresholds, there are many different levels of self-sacrifice that morality might require. Most of us are very uncertain which of these levels is the right one. But I think we can be fairly confident that, in light of the internalization costs I mentioned, a rule-consequentialist cost-benefit analysis of the alternative possible rules about aiding others and preventing disasters would arrive at

---

[13] For an example of this kind of objection, see Unger 1996: 59–61.
[14] This is noted by Murphy 1993: 290 n. 41; 1997: 84.

something between these thresholds. Thus intuition and rule-consequentialism would not be in conflict here.[15]

I have argued that rule-consequentialism's rule about preventing
disasters contains a qualification about the cost to the agents.
Another qualification needs to be added, in order to deal with the
most extreme cases. Presumably, rule-consequentialism will favour
some such rule as 'When necessary to save the world, or even just
some significant proportion of humanity, one may be required to
make an extreme—even the ultimate—self-sacrifice.' Most people
will probably never find themselves in a situation in which they
could save huge numbers of people by sacrificing their own lives.
True, the probability of anyone finding herself or himself in such circumstances is very low. But consider how much *might* turn out to be
at stake. Someone might find herself able to save millions of innocent people by sacrificing her life. She might even be able to save the
human species from extinction by sacrificing herself. Given how
much could be at stake, I think expected value would be maximized
by the inculcation of a rule requiring extreme self-sacrifice in those
exceptional cases where such self-sacrifice is the only way to secure
some good on the order of the saving of a significant proportion of
humanity. (Note the parallel here with my earlier discussion of prohibitions.)

Cullity (1995) suggests that the aggregate sacrifice required by
morality over a series of cases would be at least as much as the sacrifice morality would demand in an exceptional, that is, non-iterated,
case. I think this more than rule-consequentialism would demand,
because of the points about differential internalization costs. I also
think that, on careful reflection, it seems more than intuition suggests.

8.6 OTHER POSSIBLE WORLDS

Let us now consider the implications of rule-consequentialism for
hypothetical (i.e. other possible) worlds. Even if rule-consequential-

---

[15] For other discussions of how much rule-consequentialism requires the comfortably off to do for the world's needy, see Ihara 1981; Carson 1991, 1993; Mulgan
1994b, 1996; Haslett 1994, 2000; Brandt 1996: 199–236.

ism is not terribly demanding in present world conditions, might conditions be such that it would be terribly demanding? Imagine a world containing only ten thousand very affluent people and a billion starving ones. Imagine that the billion could all be saved if each of the affluent donated everything he or she had to the starving. In this possible world, might not the optimal rule about aid be one requiring the affluent to make such a sacrifice?

Rule-consequentialists might appeal to the inculcation costs of an extremely demanding rule about aid. But can such an appeal succeed? Thomas Carson (1991: 119) has pointed out that the needs of the many people in extreme poverty would certainly outweigh the costs of inculcating in the few rich a very demanding rule about aid.

His point is correct—but far from decisive. Carson focuses on the costs of inculcating the very demanding rule in the few rich. But the version of rule-consequentialism I have been discussing holds that an act is right if and only if it is allowed by the code whose internalization by the overwhelming majority of everyone has as high an expected value as any alternative code we can identify. We thus must consider the costs of its being inculcated in the overwhelming majority of *everyone*—that is, not only in the relatively affluent but also in the poor themselves. The costs of inculcating in the overwhelming majority of the poor as well as the relatively affluent the disposition to follow a very demanding rule about aid would be astronomical. A large share of resources, especially if they are scarce, would have to be devoted to inculcating and sustaining commitment to this rule. Therefore, the consequences of getting internalized in everyone a less demanding rule might well be better.

The point about the costs of getting the poor to internalize a demanding rule about aid is crucial to my defence of rule-consequentialism against the charge that it can be implausibly demanding in possible worlds with a different ratio of affluent to poor. So let me elaborate on how this defence is supposed to work.

When comparing alternative possible rules about aid, all versions of rule-consequentialism count the benefits to the poor of getting the food, medicine, and so on that they would not otherwise get. All versions also count the costs to the relatively affluent of their donations. As I mentioned in section 2.8, material goods have diminishing marginal utility. Thus, donations by the relatively affluent to efficient charities typically benefit the poor much more than they cost the relatively affluent.

But I have also maintained that we should consider the costs of getting the rule about aid internalized *by the relatively affluent*. Because of natural human selfishness, these costs are higher with more demanding rules than with less demanding ones. Yet, if the only costs in play are the costs to the relatively affluent of giving and the costs of inculcating rules in the relatively affluent, then rule-consequentialism's rule about aid will vary widely depending on the ratio of relatively affluent to poor. And, on these assumptions, rule-consequentialism might be extremely demanding in a world with fifty billion poor.

The point I am stressing in this section, however, is that the costs of inculcating rules *in the poor* also should get counted. If these costs are counted, then as the number of poor increases, not only does the number of people who would benefit from a rule about aid increase, so does the aggregate cost of inculcating a rule about aid.

Is that true? Or is the truth instead that getting the poor to accept a stronger rule about aid would be *easier* than getting them to accept a less demanding rule? After all, the poor stand to gain more from everyone's accepting a stronger rule than from everyone's accepting a weaker rule. Since they would benefit more from the stronger rule, why would not it be easier to teach them the stronger rule?

Presumably, inculcating a rule in someone who is mainly going to benefit from that rule is generally easier than inculcating that rule in someone who is mainly going to be disadvantaged by it. Hence, inculcating the stronger rule about aid may be easier in the poor than it is in the relatively affluent. But that is not the relevant comparison. The relevant comparison is between the cost of inculcating a stronger rule in the poor and the cost of inculcating a weaker rule in them.

The poor would benefit more from internalization by the overwhelming majority of a stronger rule about aid. Yet the costs of getting the poor themselves to internalize the stronger rule could still be higher. Inculcating a moral code in real human beings is not really like negotiating a binding social contract. Many familiar moral rules are such that a perfectly rational agent would happily internalize them, were this *really* a necessary and sufficient condition for getting everyone else to internalize them. But getting real human beings to internalize those very same rules is difficult. For one thing, all human beings have powerful, non-rational instincts, feelings, and impulses to subdue. For another thing, their rationality can itself get in the way. After all, even small children are wise enough to suspect that their taking any particular set of rules to heart is neither a necessary nor a sufficient condition of everyone else's doing so. I have been attacking a broadly contractualist view about what would determine the relative difficulty of inculcating a stronger or a weaker rule about aid in the poor. My own view is that what deter- mines the relative difficulty of inculcating a rule is how much self- denial it would require of that agent, not how much the agent would benefit from *others'* following the rule. A stronger rule about aid will require more self-sacrifice. This makes stronger rules more difficult to get internalized. Hence, getting a more demanding rule internal- ized by the poor would involve greater psychological and other costs. And once we include these costs in the calculations, it is unclear that the rule about aid that rule-consequentialism would mandate for a world with fifty billion poor will be exponentially more demanding than the rule it would mandate for a world with a small fraction of that number of poor.

To be sure, there may well be some difference between the demandingness of the two rules. But the fact that how much rule- consequentialism demands of us can increase as the number of people starving increases does not necessarily count against rule- consequentialism. Suppose that, important as inculcation costs are, world conditions were such that the rule about aid whose internal- ization has the highest expected value would be an extremely demanding one. In this case, rule-consequentialism would indeed prescribe an extremely demanding rule about aid. But that possibil- ity on its own seems to me no objection to rule-consequentialism. Indeed, the possibility is a consequence of the idea that moral rules are to be selected from an impartial point of view. And this impar- tiality is a deeply attractive feature of rule-consequentialism.

Another deeply attractive feature of rule-consequentialism is the considerable extent to which rule-consequentialism coheres with our convictions about what is right in specific circumstances. Opponents of rule-consequentialism can try to set these two attractive features against each other. They can try to do this by introducing a possible world in which rule-consequentialism would favour a rule about aid whose demands go significantly beyond what we intuitively think would be morally required of people *in that world*.[16]

---

[16] Mulgan in particular tries to set these two features against each other. See his 1996.

To do this, rule-consequentialism's opponents must not merely describe a world in which rule-consequentialism is extremely demanding. Indeed, I have already acknowledged that rule-consequentialism can require extreme self-sacrifice in the actual world. What rule-consequentialism's opponents must do is describe a possible case in which the theory's rule about aid is *counterintuitively* severe. Possible worlds in which rule-consequentialism prescribes extremely demanding rules about aid are no embarrassment to rule-consequentialism—as long as those rules match our convictions about what morality would require of people in those worlds.

8.7 WHY COUNT THECOSTS OF GETTING RULES ABOUT AID INTERNALIZED BY THE POOR?

I have pointed to the costs of getting the poor to internalize rules about aiding the needy. But why should the costs of inculcating such rules in the poor be counted at all? We could instead count only the costs of inculcating and maintaining such rules in everyone *who could reasonably be expected to have opportunities to follow them.*

Some rule-consequentialists accept the idea that moral codes should be relativized to societies and even groups within societies. I resist this idea, for reasons I gave in section 3.4. Instead, I favour one code applying to everyone. But even if we think that a moral code should apply to everyone, why worry about the cost of getting it *internalized* by the overwhelming majority of everyone, which might include people who will not have an opportunity to act on it?

A general consequentialist answer would be that better consequences would result from inculcating fairly general moral rules in everyone than from teaching different rules to different groups. In the case of rules about aiding the needy, there is the consequentialist point that a rule requiring one to come to the aid of others in desperate need is a rule the very poor might sometimes have occasion to follow. Even the terribly poor have opportunities to rescue others sometimes. Furthermore, there is the possibility that a poor person could become relatively affluent.

I do not rest my case, however, on such consequentialist considerations. As I said before, our reason for finding one version of con-

sequentialism more plausible than another need not itself be consequentialist. We may favour one version of rule-consequentialism
over any other version of consequentialism because this version has
implications about right and wrong that are more intuitively plausible.

I have argued that a version of rule-consequentialism that
includes the costs of inculcating rules about aid into the poor yields
the following rule. Agents are required to help those in greater need,
especially the worst off, even if the personal sacrifices involved in
helping others add up to a significant cost to the agents over the
course of their lives. Agents who accept this rule will be disposed to
help those in greater need, and to do so up to at least the threshold
of 'significant aggregative personal cost', though agents are of
course allowed to make sacrifices beyond this threshold.

This rule is intuitively plausible. Coming up with an intuitively
plausible rule about aiding the needy is something that (as far as I
am aware) no other consequentialist theory does. So we (at least I)
have a nonconsequentialist reason to favour this version of rule-
consequentialism.

9
Help with Practical Problems

My last criterion for the assessing of moral theories (section 1.2) was that they should help us deal with moral questions about which we are not confident, or do not agree. Rule-consequentialism does indeed give us a way of addressing our moral disagreements and uncertainties, a way that is intuitively appealing, relatively accessible, publicly defensible, and indeed often actually used (especially by those people who do not expect to find in religion clear answers to all moral questions). One difficult question is the one of how much you are required to do to prevent disasters for strangers. The previous chapter attempted to show how rule-consequentialism answers the question of how much self-sacrifice is morally required for the sake of the world's needy. The present chapter will illustrate how rule-consequentialism can help with some other moral problems.

9.1 RULE-CONSEQUENTIALISM AND SEX

One example of how rule-consequentialist arguments have a place in the moral thought of western culture concerns pre-marital sex. A century ago, one of the strongest moral prohibitions concerned pre-marital sex. This prohibition was, of course, firmly endorsed by most western religions. But the prohibition may well have had a rule-consequentialist rationale, prior to the advent of reliable methods of birth control.

Of course, risking a pregnancy outside marriage was highly imprudent, because of the attendant social penalties if one were found out. Given those social penalties, we might say the prohibition on sex between the unmarried was justified on rule-consequentialist grounds. But why take the social practices and moral beliefs of that era as givens? If the moral code could be redesigned from the ground up, and thus *could* eliminate the social penalties for sex outside marriage, shouldn't those social penalties be eliminated?

The ideal moral code needs some mechanism for making both parents responsible for their children. Presumably, a prohibition on intercourse between unmarried men and fertile women could be justified only when life expectancy was short, little social safety net existed, no reliable methods of birth control were available, and there was no reliable mechanism for making both parents responsible for their children except marriage. Imagine the prospects for babies in an era in which parents' life expectancies were so short as to make it improbable that both parents would survive until the baby had grown into a self-sufficient adult. The best moral code, under those conditions, would need to find some way of making *both* parents responsible for their children. Making marriage the precondition for sex was one way of trying to do this.

I am certainly not saying that this line of thought prevailed at the time. Most people at the time would have appealed to religion for the justification of their moral prohibitions. Still, as reliable methods of birth control became available, most people's commitment to the prohibition waned. Or in other words, when they could no longer see harms associated with pre-marital sex, the prohibition seemed uselessly obstructive. When the prohibition seemed to have outlived its secular function, it was abandoned.

And if we insist that moral prohibitions should have defensible secular purposes, some other sexual prohibitions will also fall away. For one example, a moral prohibition on homosexuality works against rather than promotes weighted well-being. Certain kinds of homosexual acts are harmful (e.g. homosexual rape, recklessly spreading disease)—but this is equally true of the same kinds of heterosexual acts. Rape, recklessly spreading diseases, and certain other kinds of act are thus rightly prohibited, independently of whether they are heterosexual or homosexual.

One terrible argument that is often used against permitting homosexual activity is that, if everyone had sex only with others of the same gender, the human species would die out. This argument wrongly reads a proposed permission as a requirement not to make babies with the opposite sex. Of course rule-consequentialism's permitting homosexuality neither requires people to have homosexual relations, nor prohibits all heterosexual intercourse. As I indicated at the very beginning of the book, for the rule-consequentialist, the question is not, 'What if everyone *did* X?' Even more, the question is not, 'What if everyone never did anything but X?' The question is, rather, 'What if everyone *felt free* to do X?' Morality's allowing homosexual intercourse will hardly lead to the extinction of hetero-sexual intercourse.

Consider an analogy. Suppose my nephew tells me he refuses to have children. If everyone refuses to have children, the human species will die out. This would be a disastrous consequence. But it is irrelevant to the morality of my nephew's decision. What is rele-vant is that everyone's feeling free not to have children will not lead to the extinction of the species. Plenty of people who do not feel obligated to have children nevertheless *want* to—and, if free to do so, will. Thus, there is no need for a moral obligation to have children. Neither is there any need for a general moral obligation to have heterosexual intercourse.

9.2 KINDS OF EUTHANASIA

I hope the preceding discussion shows how rule-consequentialism offers an intuitively plausible approach to moral issues concerning sex. I think rule-consequentialism likewise offers a promising per-spective on moral questions about embryo experimentation, genetic engineering, capital punishment, surrogacy, gun control, mandatory drug testing, euthanasia, physician-assisted suicide, and so on into business ethics, legal ethics, and other areas.

To discuss all those issues would require another book (and vastly more knowledge than I have). Let me focus on just one of them in order to illustrate at greater length how rule-consequentialism provides a helpful approach to practical problems. I shall focus on the debate about euthanasia.

The term 'euthanasia' derives from the Greek term for an easy, painless death. However, we often now hear the term 'passive euthanasia', which refers to passing up opportunities to save an indi-vidual from death, out of concern for that individual. If passive euthanasia is indeed one kind of euthanasia, then 'euthanasia' can-not mean 'killing painlessly'. For to pass up an opportunity to save someone, that is, passive euthanasia, is arguably not *killing*. Furthermore, the death involved in passive euthanasia is often *painful.* So let us take the term 'euthanasia' to mean 'either killing or passing up opportunities to save someone, out of concern for that person'. (Note that, on this definition, what the Nazis called 'euthanasia' was not euthanasia, because it was not done out of concern for the patients.)

We need to distinguish three different kinds of euthanasia, or rather three different ways euthanasia can be related to the will of the person killed. Suppose I ask you to either kill me or let me die should my medical condition get so bad that I am delirious and won't recover. If you then comply with my request, we have what is commonly called *voluntary euthanasia*. It is voluntary because the person killed or allowed to die literally asked for this.

Now suppose that I slip into an irreversible coma without ever telling anyone what I wanted to happen in such circumstances. If I am then killed or let die, we have what is commonly called *non-voluntary euthanasia*. The distinguishing characteristic of non-voluntary euthanasia is that it is euthanasia on someone who did not express a desire on the matter.

But what if I do express a desire neither to be killed nor to be let die no matter how bad my condition gets? Then killing me would constitute what is called *involuntary euthanasia*. Quite apart from its moral status, involuntary euthanasia can seem puzzling. To be euthanasia, it must be done for the good of the person killed. Yet if the person desired that it not be done, how can it be done for this person's own good? Well, involuntary euthanasia may be morally wrong (we will discuss why in a moment), but we must start by acknowledging that people are not always in the best position to know what is best for themselves. Someone could be mistaken even about whether he or she would be better off dead than alive in a certain state. And other people could think that the person in front of them had made just this kind of mistake. If they not only thought this but also were motivated to do what was best for this person, they might contemplate euthanasia. What they would then be contemplating would be involuntary euthanasia.

As I have already remarked, passive euthanasia involves *passing up opportunities to prevent the death* of someone out of concern for that person's own good. Active euthanasia involves *actively killing* someone out of a concern for that person's own good. The distinction between active and passive euthanasia cuts across the distinction between voluntary, non-voluntary, and involuntary euthanasia.

In other words, either with my consent, or without knowing what my wishes are or were, or against my wishes, you might kill me. Likewise, either with my consent, or without knowing what my wishes are or were, or against my wishes, you might pass up an opportunity to keep me from dying. Thus we have:

Active voluntary euthanasia
Active non-voluntary euthanasia
Active involuntary euthanasia

Passive voluntary euthanasia
Passive non-voluntary euthanasia
Passive involuntary euthanasia

9.3 EUTHANASIA AS A PRIMARILY MORAL MATTER

We also need to distinguish between questions about law and questions about moral rightness, permissibility, and wrongness. Consequentialists, as well as moral philosophers of many other stripes, can think that there may be some moral requirements that the law should not try to enforce. A relatively uncontroversial example concerns the moral requirement forbidding people to break contracts with their spouses. There may be good consequentialist reasons for not lumbering the law with the duty or ability to enforce contracts between spouses that were made verbally but not in writing. To police the give and take of such relationships might be too difficult and too invasive. This isn't to deny that breaking verbal contracts with spouses is usually morally wrong, only that the law shouldn't poke its nose into this matter.

So, initially at least, there is the potential for divergence in what the rule-consequentialist says about the law and about morality. There is less scope for this on rule-consequentialism, however, than there is on some other theories. For both in the case of law and in the case of morality, the first thing rule-consequentialism considers is the consequences of our *collective* compliance with rules. (See Mill 1861: ch. 5.) Normally, where rule-consequentialism holds that some kind of act is morally permissible, the theory will hold that this kind of act should be legally permissible as well.

With respect to euthanasia, rule-consequentialism is especially likely to take the same line on law as it does on morality. That is, if rule-consequentialists think that active or passive euthanasia in certain kinds of case would have generally good consequences, then they will think such acts are *morally* allowed in these kinds of case. They will also think the *law* should allow them in the specified conditions. And if they think the consequences would be generally bad, then they will think morality does, and the law should, prohibit the acts in question.

But, in the following discussion of the rule-consequentialist approach to euthanasia, I will focus on just one realm, morality. I think many people presume that, in most cases, if something is morally permissible, it ought to be legally permissible. Most opponents of euthanasia certainly believe that the reason it should be illegal is that it is immoral. So let us ask: are there kinds of euthanasia that an ideal moral code would allow?

9.4 POTENTIAL BENEFITS OF EUTHANASIA

Perhaps the most obvious potential benefit of permitting euthanasia is that it could be used to prevent the unnecessary elongation of the suffering experienced by many terminally ill people and their families. What about painkilling drugs? I believe that, until medical technology develops further, there are some kinds of pain that cannot be controlled with drugs, or at least not with drugs that leave the patient conscious and mentally coherent. And in addition to physical agony, there is often overwhelming emotional suffering for the patient, and derivatively for friends and family in attendance. All this could be shortened if euthanasia were allowed.

However, the moral norms in this area should be shaped in light of the truism that people suffering from terminal illness and intense pain are often not in a good state to make rational decisions. Often, tragedies would ensue if there were a general willingness on the part of doctors to authorize *immediate* implementation of what might be only a temporary wish of the patient's to die. For often the patient would have changed her mind if not prevented by the immediate granting of the patient's ill-considered request to die. Rule-consequentialists will therefore want doctors to be committed to a waiting period between the patient's request to die and active euthanasia.

Should there also be a waiting period between the patient's request to die and passive euthanasia? One view is that there need not be such a waiting period, since merely withholding of food and fluids will give the patient a chance to change her mind anyway. And yet I cannot see why the argument for a waiting period does not work—albeit to a lesser extent—even with respect to passive euthanasia. Suppose my terminal illness is so painful and degrading that I request death. If the hospital I have just been admitted to starts immediately withholding food and fluids from me, this is hardly likely to make me more clear-headed and reasonable. I may soon be too dehydrated and hungry to think straight—or to rescind my earlier request to die.

So, if there is to be a waiting period with active or passive euthanasia, then it remains true that one advantage of active over passive euthanasia is that active euthanasia brings about a quicker and perhaps less painful termination of the patient's suffering. There may, however, be especially large costs associated with allowing active euthanasia. I shall consider these later.

For consequentialists who count personal autonomy as a value over and above whatever feelings of satisfaction it brings and frustration it prevents, there is an additional consideration. It is that *voluntary* euthanasia must increase personal autonomy, in that it gives people some control over *when* their lives end. And if *active* voluntary euthanasia were allowed, this would give people some control over *how* their lives end. Concern for people's autonomy obviously counts only in favour of voluntary euthanasia. It is irrelevant to the discussion of non-voluntary euthanasia of any kind, and opposes involuntary euthanasia of any kind.

9.5 THE POTENTIAL HARMS OF ALLOWING INVOLUNTARY EUTHANASIA

The importance of autonomy is not the only rule-consequentialist reason to oppose active *involuntary* euthanasia. Another is that many people would be scared away from hospitals and doctors if they thought that they might be killed against their wishes. Allowing involuntary euthanasia could not begin to generate benefits large enough to offset this loss. The last thing moral permissions should do is scare people away from trained medical experts. A related point is that allowing involuntary euthanasia would terrify many people taken to a hospital while unconscious. Imagine waking up to find that you had been taken to a hospital where people can, against your wishes, kill you, as long as they claim to think this would be best for you.

Furthermore, to allow the killing of innocent people against their wishes would be difficult to square with other moral prohibitions of supreme importance. In particular, the general feeling of abhorrence for the killing of innocent people against their wishes is the bedrock of social existence. Without communal acceptance of that prohibition, life would be precarious and insecure. It cannot be wise to include in a moral code a rule that undermines people's commitment to the general prohibition on killing the innocent against their wishes.

At this point someone might say, 'Ah, but we can distinguish between killing innocent people *against their wishes* but *for their own good*, and killing them against their wishes for some other reason.' True, we can make that distinction. But is it a distinction we would be wise to incorporate into a rule for use by human beings? No, again because people would not feel secure in a society where they might be, against their wishes, killed for their own good.

These points about insecurity add up to a very persuasive rule-consequentialist argument against permitting *active* involuntary euthanasia. But do they count against *passive* involuntary euthanasia? Consequentialists have long argued that their doctrine is generally anti-paternalistic (Mill 1859). Grown-up human beings are generally the ones who know which of the ways their lives might unfold would be best for themselves, because they are generally the ones who know best their own aspirations, tastes, talents, sensitivities, vulnerabilities, and so on. Of course there are general exceptions—for example, children, and people with permanent or temporary mental impairments. But, by and large, people are the best guardians of their own well-being.

As noted at the very end of the previous section, rule-consequentialists can have another reason for opposing involuntary euthanasia, passive just as much as active. This reason comes from the idea that autonomy is an important component of well-being. As

Eric Rakowski (1993: 1113) notes, there is 'the delight we take in our own agency'. Indeed, having control over our own lives is itself a part of our own good.[1] This seems to be the strongest rule-consequentialist reason for disallowing passive involuntary euthanasia.

9.6 POTENTIAL HARMS OF ALLOWING VOLUNTARY AND NON-VOLUNTARY EUTHANASIA

Turn now to the harms that voluntary and non-voluntary euthanasia might involve. Suppose the doctors tell Jones he has disease X. This disease almost immediately produces excruciating pain, dementia, and then death. Jones asks to be killed, or at least allowed to die, before the pain gets too severe. The doctors comply with Jones's wishes. Later, however, a post-mortem reveals that he didn't have disease X at all, but instead some curable condition. As this story illustrates, euthanasia can inappropriately take a life after a mistaken diagnosis.

And yet how often do medical experts misdiagnose a condition as a terminal illness when it isn't? And how wise is it now to go against expert medical opinion? And are there ways of minimizing the risk of the doctors' acting on misdiagnoses? Euthanasia could be restricted to cases where three independent medical experts—and I mean *real* experts—make the same diagnosis. (Many hospitals today do this with established committees.) With such a restriction, the worry about misdiagnoses fades.

But closely associated with the point that doctors sometimes misdiagnose someone's condition is the point that doctors are sometimes wrong about what will happen to someone whose condition is correctly diagnosed. Suppose the doctors rightly believe that there is now no treatment known to prevent a disease from bringing acute pain followed by a painful death. But a cure or more effective pain

---

[1] Rakowski (1993: 1114) is excellent on this as well: '[R]anking ends and selecting means is ultimately what defines us as persons. The construction and reworking of our higher-order desires is what integrates us over time, shaping our more immediate urges and longings and lending contour to our lives. The evident importance of autonomy to our identity and well-being is the main reason paternalism is only tolerable in exceptional situations. We resent others' choosing for us and fear tyranny that dons the mantle of benevolence.'

block might soon be discovered. If people were killed or allowed to die today and the medical breakthrough comes tomorrow, euthanasia amounted to giving up on those people too soon—with tragic results.

Again restrictions could be put in place to prevent the losses envisaged. One restriction could specify that euthanasia is completely out of the question until someone is fairly near the final stages of a disease, since in such cases new cures or treatments are very unlikely to be able to change the fatal path of the disease. (One way of approximating this restriction would be to allow *passive* but not *active* euthanasia. But this seems an unnecessarily crude way of ensuring that people aren't killed before they could be cured.) Another restriction could specify that euthanasia should be out of the question until after a thorough and disinterested investigation into the state of research on cures and treatments. When this investigation shows that the development of a cure or new treatment is a *realistic* possibility during the life of the patient, euthanasia would again be prohibited.

From a rule-consequentialist perspective, the points about mistaken diagnoses and future cures mandate restrictions on when euthanasia would be considered, but they do not preclude euthanasia altogether—even active euthanasia. Something else, however, does threaten to add up to a conclusive case against allowing any kind of euthanasia, especially active euthanasia. This is the danger of intentional abuse.

Think of the people who might be in a hurry for some ill person's death. Some of these might be people who have to care for the ill person, or pay for the care and medicine the person receives. Another group, often overlapping with the first, is made up of the person's heirs. The heirs might even include the hospital in which the person lies. With so much to gain from an early death of the ill person, these people might easily convince themselves that the ill person would be better off dead. Left up to these people, many ill people might unnecessarily be killed or allowed to die. Any system allowing this would both result in unnecessary deaths and terrify the ill.

Even without these points about intentional abuse, rule-consequentialists have enough reason to disallow *in*voluntary euthanasia. But do the points about intentional abuse add up to a compelling rule-consequentialist argument against *voluntary* euthanasia? Certainly they necessitate severe restrictions, at the very least.

One sensible restriction would be that, with a single exception, the people given authority in the decision about euthanasia must be people with nothing to gain directly or indirectly from their decision. The single exception is of course the patient himself or herself. But heirs and those who stand to benefit from heirs could be denied any authoritative say in the matter. Thus, if a hospital is itself an heir, its doctors could be precluded from having any role, including that of making or confirming the diagnosis. The rule could be designed to ensure that the decision to perform euthanasia on a patient is made by people focusing on the wishes and best interests of the patient. Of course the patient may ask loved and trusted others, including heirs, what they think. But the rule could insist that doctors with nothing to gain certify that the patient really would be, by the time of the euthanasia, thereafter better off dead. And the rule could insist that the patient be asked on a number of occasions whether he or she really does want euthanasia. Patients will need the rule to protect them against coercive pressures by family and other heirs (not that morality can ever protect people completely from their families).

Focus now on *non-voluntary* euthanasia—euthanasia performed on people who have not indicated whether or not they want their lives to be prolonged. Some patients have never been in a position to give or withhold consent. This is true of individuals who never developed sufficient rationality to be capable of consenting. Any euthanasia performed on such people will be non-voluntary euthanasia. Rule-consequentialists might well think that a cost-benefit analysis of this sort of euthanasia would end up supporting it—given that the rule is designed so as to ensure that the people making the final decision are experts with nothing but the best interests of the patient in mind.

But what about patients who were once rational enough to consent or withhold consent but never made their wishes known and now are incapable of prolonged rationality? Rule-consequentialists can think that allowing euthanasia would be best here too (but only if all the safeguards are in place).

A more important question, however, might be whether the rule should require adults now in possession of their faculties to indicate formally whether they want euthanasia under certain conditions. It might actually increase autonomy to get people to decide whether they would want euthanasia for themselves before they are unable to make such decisions. Obviously, the system for doing this would have to involve informing people what they were being asked to decide about. It would also need to be designed so as to make sure people's decisions are their own, that is, not the result of some sort of coercion. Furthermore, ideally the system would annually ask for confirmation that people have not changed their minds (there could be a box to check on annual tax returns).

Some people will think that, no matter how clever rule-conse-quentialists are in adding safeguards to a rule allowing euthanasia, there will be at least a few people who manage to subvert it, and so abuses will occur. Rule-consequentialists may grant this, but then ask how many such abuses there would be. Would there be so many abuses as to terrify the general population? These questions are ones of sociology and social psychology. If the answers to them are that the abuses would be extremely rare and the general population wouldn't become paranoid over them, then a rule-consequentialist might be willing to accept that, if some abuse is inevitable, this cost of a few abuses would be worth the benefits of allowing euthanasia.

There is one more potential harm associated with allowing vol-untary and non-voluntary *active* euthanasia. To allow them might seem to be a step onto a slippery slope to a very undesirable posi-tion. As I have already noted, the prohibition on killing the innocent against their will is an immensely valuable, indeed essential, prohib-ition. Would people slide away from a firm commitment to that pro-hibition if they came to accept the permissibility of voluntary and non-voluntary active euthanasia?

9.7 RULE-CONSEQUENTIALIST CONCLUSIONS ABOUT EUTHANASIA

It is hardly an a priori question whether allowing euthanasia would erode communal inhibitions on killing the innocent against their will. This question, like the question of whether the level of inten-tional abuse would be unacceptably high, is really one for social scientists. Furthermore, any answers to such questions have to be partly speculative. We ought to know by now that large social, economic, or legal changes often have unexpected results. We cannot be *certain* what the results would be of a moral permission to perform voluntary and non-voluntary active euthanasia. Rule-consequentialists have to make a judgement based on what they think the probabilities are.

The recent history of medical practice in Holland should throw light on the likelihood of abuse and the slide down slippery slopes. However, there is dispute about what exactly has happened there.[2] Perhaps, the policy design and policing in Holland have been too vague and too trusting.

But discovering the flaws in the design and implementation of new rules does not compel us to return to one or another code of rules from the past. We must not forget the benefits to be had from moving forward to a code permitting some kinds of euthanasia: prevention of suffering and respect for autonomy. And the moral codes from the past were hardly flawless. To be sure, experience teaches that any new moral code people try long enough will also prove imperfect in some ways. The question for us now is whether a new code allowing euthanasia under some conditions must have lower expected value than a moral code forbidding euthanasia.

Human beings are susceptible to cognitive error and impure motivation. These facts provide rule-consequentialist reasons for tight restrictions on the use of euthanasia, and for rigorous enforcement of those restrictions. With rigorously enforced restrictions, a rule allowing euthanasia, even active euthanasia, has (I believe) greater expected value than a complete ban (Frey 1988; G. Dworkin 1998).

---

[2] Van der Maas *et al* 1991 and the references in Frey 1998: n. 13.

AFTERWORD

In this book, I have tried to show that rule-consequentialism is distinct, plausible, and helpful.

As I have stressed, rule-consequentialism is not new. But my case for this theory comes from a new combination of arguments, and this combination itself contains some new elements. In particular, my formulation of the theory did not come from earlier rule-consequentialists. Likewise, as far as I am aware, no previous rule-consequentialist has explicitly argued that we should choose among different formulations of the theory, not on the basis of purely consequentialist considerations, but on the basis of intuitive plausibility.

And my account of the rule-consequentialist agent's psychology does not come from earlier rule-consequentialists. Furthermore, this account provides a compelling answer to the one objection that has done most to push philosophers away from rule-consequentialism. This objection was that rule-consequentialism can avoid collapse into act-consequentialism only by becoming incoherent. My account of the rule-consequentialist agent's psychology answers the objection. Someone with this psychology would neither behave like an act-consequentialist nor have an overarching moral aim to maximize the good. Without that overarching aim, the rule-consequentialist agent can *coherently* refuse to harm others, to take others' possessions, to break a promise, or to make further sacrifices, even when in the circumstances such a refusal will not maximize the good.

Again, the rule-consequentialist agent can have, as an overarching moral aim, the desire to act in ways that are impartially defensible. And of course a rule-consequentialist agent will believe that following impartially justified rules is impartially defensible, and that rule-consequentialism is the best account of impartially justified rules. How can anyone believe that following rule-consequentialism is impartially defensible? My book amounts to an extended answer to this question.

I am unsure what to think of the answer. My formulation of rule-consequentialism selects rules by reference to the expected value of their being internalized by the 'overwhelming majority' in each future generation. I am worried by the question of what exactly constitutes the overwhelming majority. I am also worried by questions about whether rule-consequentialism should be formulated so as to make room for some kinds of relativity. Alas, there are probably other, even bigger problems I have overlooked.

REFERENCES

Adams, R. M. 1976. 'Motive Utilitarianism', *Journal of Philosophy* 73: 467–81.

Anscombe, Elizabeth. 1958. 'Modern Moral Philosophy', *Philosophy* 33: 1–19.

Aristotle. *Nicomachean Ethics*, trans. W. D. Ross, revised J. O. Urmson (Oxford: Clarendon Press, 1975).

Arneson, Richard. 1999a. 'Human Flourishing versus Desire Satisfaction', *Social Philosophy and Policy* 16: 113–42.

—— 1999b. 'Egalitarianism and Responsibility', *Journal of Ethics* 3: 225–47.

Attfield, Robin. 1987. *A Theory of Value and Obligation* (London: Croom Helm).

Audi, R. 1996. 'Intuitionism, Pluralism, and the Foundations of Ethics', in W. Sinnott-Armstrong and M. Timmons, eds., *Moral Knowledge?* (New York: Oxford University Press), 101–36.

Austin, John. 1832. *The Province of Jurisprudence Determined*, ed. H. L. A. Hart (London: Weidenfeld, 1954).

Axelrod, Robert. 1984. *The Evolution of Cooperation* (New York: Basic Books).

Ayer, A. J. 1936. *Language, Truth and Logic* (London: Gollancz).

Baier, Kurt. 1958. *The Moral Point of View* (Ithaca, N.Y.: Cornell University Press).

Bailey, James Wood. 1997. *Utilitarianism, Institutions, and Justice* (New York: Oxford University Press).

Bales, R. E. 1971. 'Act-Utilitarianism: Account of Right-Making Characteristics or Decision-Making Procedure?', *American Philosophical Quarterly* 8: 257–65.

Baron, Marcia. 1987. 'Kantian Ethics and Supererogation', *Journal of Philosophy* 84: 237–62.

—— 1991. 'Impartiality and Friendship', *Ethics* 101: 836–57.

—— 1997. 'Kantian Ethics', in Marcia W. Baron, Philip Pettit, and Michael Slote, *Three Methods of Ethics* (Oxford: Blackwell).

Barry, Brian. 1995. *Justice as Impartiality* (Oxford: Oxford University Press).

Barrow, Robin. 1991. *Utilitarianism: A Contemporary Statement* (Aldershot: Edward Elgar).

Bentham, J. 1789. *Introduction to the Principles of Morals and Legislation*.

Berkeley, G. 1712. *Passive Obedience, or the Christian Doctrine of Not Resisting the Supreme Power, Proved and Vindicated upon the Principles of the Law of Nature.* Repr. in D. H. Monro, ed., *A Guide to the British Moralists* (London: Fontana, 1972), 217–27.

Berlin, Isaiah. 1969. *Four Essays on Liberty* (Oxford: Oxford University Press).

Blackburn, Simon. 1984. *Spreading the Word* (Oxford: Clarendon Press).

—— 1985. 'Errors and the Phenomenology of Value', in T. Honderich, ed., *Morality and Objectivity: A Tribute to J. L. Mackie* (London, Routledge & Kegan Paul). Repr. in Blackburn 1993: 149–65.

—— 1993. *Essays on Quasi-Realism* (New York: Oxford University Press).

—— 1996. 'Securing the Nots', in W. Sinnott-Armstrong and M. Timmons, eds., *Moral Knowledge?* (New York: Oxford University Press), 82–100.

—— 1998. *Ruling Passions* (Oxford: Clarendon Press).

Blanshard, Brand. 1939. *The Nature of Thought* (London: Allen & Unwin).

Bradley, F. H. 1914. *Essays on Truth and Reality* (Oxford: Oxford University Press).

Brandt, Richard B. 1959. *Ethical Theory* (Englewood Cliffs, N.J.: Prentice-Hall).

—— 1963. 'Toward a Credible Form of Utilitarianism', in H.-N. Castañeda and G. Nakhnikian, eds., *Morality and the Language of Conduct* (Detroit: Wayne State University Press), 107–43.

—— 1967. 'Some Merits of One Form of Rule-Utilitarianism', *University of Colorado Studies in Philosophy*, 39–65. Repr. in Brandt 1992: 111–36.

—— 1979. *A Theory of the Good and the Right* (Oxford: Clarendon Press).

—— 1983. 'Problems of Contemporary Utilitarianism: Real and Alleged', in N. Bowie, ed., *Ethical Theory in the Last Quarter of the Twentieth Century* (Indianapolis: Hackett), 81–105

—— 1988. 'Fairness to Indirect Optimific Theories in Ethics', *Ethics* 98: 341–60. Repr. in Brandt 1992: 137–57.

—— 1989. 'Morality and its Critics', *American Philosophical Quarterly* 26: 89–100. Repr. in Brandt 1992: 73–92.

—— 1992. *Morality, Utilitarianism, and Rights* (New York: Cambridge University Press).

—— 1996. *Facts, Values, and Morality* (New York: Cambridge University Press).

Brink, David O. 1986. 'Utilitarian Morality and the Personal Point of View', *Journal of Philosophy* 83: 417–38.

—— 1989. *Moral Realism and the Foundations of Ethics* (New York: Cambridge University Press).

—— 1993. 'The Separateness of Persons, Distributive Norms, and Moral Theory', in R. Frey and C. Morris, eds., *Value, Welfare, and Morality* (Cambridge: Cambridge University Press), 252–89.

Broad, C. D. 1916. 'On the Function of False Hypotheses in Ethics', *International Journal of Ethics* 26: 377–97.

—— 1930. *Five Types of Ethical Theory* (London: Routledge & Kegan Paul).

Broome, John. 1991a. 'Fairness', *Proceedings of the Aristotelian Society* 91: 87–102.

—— 1991b. *Weighing Goods* (Oxford: Blackwell).

—— 1994. 'Fairness versus Doing the Most Good', *Hastings Center Report* 24: 36–9.

Buchanan, James. 1975. *The Limits of Liberty* (Chicago: University of Chicago Press).

Butler, J. 1726. *Fifteen Sermons Preached at the Rolls Chapel*. Repr. in Raphael, ed., 1969: vol. i, paras. 374–435, pp. 325–77.

Carritt, E. F. 1930. *A Theory of Morals* (London: Oxford University Press).

—— 1947. *Ethical and Political Thinking* (Oxford: Clarendon Press).

Carruthers, Peter. 1992. *The Animals Issue: Moral Theory in Practice* (Cambridge: Cambridge University Press).

Carson, Thomas. 1982. 'Utilitarianism and World Poverty', in H. Miller and W. Williams, eds., *The Limits of Utilitarianism* (Minneapolis: University of Minnesota Press), 242–52.

—— 1991. 'A Note on Hooker's "Rule Consequentialism"', *Mind* 100: 117–21.

—— 1993. 'Hare on Utilitarianism and Intuitive Morality', *Erkenntnis* 39: 305–31.

Clarke, Samuel. 1728. *A Discourse of Natural Religion*. Repr. in Raphael, ed., 1969: vol. i, paras. 224–61, pp. 191–225.

Copp, David. 1995. *Morality, Normativity, and Society* (New York: Oxford University Press).

Cottingham, John. 1998. 'The Ethical Credentials of Partiality', *Proceedings of the Aristotelian Society* 98: 1–21.

Crisp, Roger. 1990. 'Medical Negligence, Assault, Informed Consent, and Autonomy', *Journal of Law and Society* 17: 77–89.

—— 1992. 'Utilitarianism and the Life of Virtue', *Philosophical Quarterly* 42: 139–60.

—— 1996. *How Should One Live? Essays on the Virtues* (Oxford: Clarendon Press).

—— 1997. *Mill on Utilitarianism* (London: Routledge).

—— 2000a. 'Griffin's Pessimism', in Crisp and Hooker, eds., 2000: 115–28.

—— 2000b. 'Particularizing Particularism', in Hooker and Little, eds., 2000.

—— and Hooker, Brad, eds. 2000. *Well-Being and Morality: Essays in Honour of James Griffin* (Oxford: Clarendon Press).

Cullity, Garrett. 1994. 'International Aid and the Scope of Kindness', *Ethics* 105: 99–127.

Cullity, Garrett. 1995. 'Moral Character and the Iteration Problem', *Utilitas* 7: 289–99.

—— 1996. 'The Life-Saving Analogy', in W. Aiken and H. LaFollette, eds., *World Hunger and Morality* (Upper Saddle River, N.J.: Prentice-Hall), 51–69.

—— 2001. *The Demands of Morality* (forthcoming).

Cummiskey, David. 1996. *Kantian Consequentialism* (New York: Oxford University Press).

Dancy, Jonathan. 1981. 'On Moral Properties', *Mind* 90: 367–85.

—— 1983. 'Ethical Particularism and Morally Relevant Properties', *Mind* 92: 530–47.

—— 1985. *Contemporary Epistemology* (Oxford: Blackwell).

—— 1993. *Moral Reasons* (Oxford: Blackwell).

Daniels, Norman. 1979. 'Wide Reflective Equilibrium and Theory Acceptance in Ethics', *Journal of Philosophy* 76: 256–82.

—— 1980. 'Reflective Equilibrium and Archimedean Points', *Canadian Journal of Philosophy* 10: 83–110.

—— 1985. 'Two Approaches to Theory Acceptance in Ethics', in D. Copp and D. Zimmerman, eds., *Morality, Reason and Truth* (Totowa, N.J.: Rowman & Littlefield), 120–40.

Darwall, Stephen, 1998. *Philosophical Ethics* (Boulder, Colo.: Westview Press).

Davidson, Donald. 1969. 'How Is Weakness of the Will Possible?' in Joel Feinberg, ed., *Moral Concepts* (Oxford: Oxford University Press), 93–113. Repr. in D. Davidson, *Essays on Actions and Events* (Oxford: Clarendon Press, 1980).

DePaul, Michael. 1987. 'Two Conceptions of Coherence Methods in Ethics', *Mind* 96: 463–81.

—— 1993. *Balance and Refinement: Beyond Coherence Methods of Moral Inquiry* (New York: Routledge).

Diamond, Cora. 1997. 'Consequentialism in Modern Moral Philosophy and in "Modern Moral Philosophy"', in D. Oderberg and J. Laing, eds., *Human Lives: Critical Essays on Consequentialist Bioethics* (London: Macmillan), 13–38.

Donagan, Alan. 1968. 'Is There a Credible Form of Utilitarianism?', in M. Bayles, ed., *Contemporary Utilitarianism* (Garden City, N.Y.: Doubleday), 187–202.

Drèze, Jean, and Sen, Amartya. 1989. *Hunger and Public Action* (Oxford: Clarendon Press).

Dworkin, Gerald. 1998. 'Public Policy and Physicial-Assisted Suicide', in G. Dworkin, R. G. Frey, and Sissela Bok, *Ethanasia and Physician-Assisted Suicide: For and Against* (Cambridge: Cambridge University Press), 64–80.

Dworkin, Ronald. 1985. *A Matter of Principle* (Cambridge, Mass.: Harvard University Press).

—— 1986. *Law's Empire* (Cambridge, Mass.: Harvard University Press).

—— 1996. 'Objectivity and Truth: You'd Better Believe It', *Philosophy and Public Affairs* 25: 87–139.

Ebertz, Roger. 1993. 'Is Reflective Equilibrium a Coherentist Model?', *Canadian Journal of Philosophy* 23: 193–214.

Economist. 1999. *Pocket World in Figures 2000 Edition* (London: Economist Publications).

Elliot, Robert. 1984. 'Rawlsian Justice and Non-Human Animals', *Journal of Applied Ethics* 1: 95–106.

Ellis, A. J. 1992. 'Deontology, Incommensurability and the Arbitrary', *Philosophy and Phenomenological Research* 52: 855–75.

Epstein, Richard. 1995: *Simple Rules for a Complex World* (Cambridge, Mass.: Harvard University Press).

Ewing, A. C. 1947. *The Definition of Good* (New York: Macmillan).

—— 1951. *The Fundamential Questions of Philosophy* (London: Routledge & Kegan Paul).

Feinberg, Joel. 1970. *Doing and Deserving* (Princeton: Princeton University Press).

—— 1974. 'Non-Comparative Justice', *Philosophical Review* 83: 297–338.

—— 1978. 'Rawls and Intuitionism', in Norman Daniels, ed., *Reading Rawls* (Oxford: Blackwell), 108–24.

Feldman, Fred. 1997. *Utilitarianism, Hedonism, and Desert* (Cambridge: Cambridge University Press)

Finnis, John. 1980. *Natural Law and Natural Rights* (Oxford: Clarendon Press).

—— 1983. *Fundamentals of Ethics* (New York: Oxford University Press).

Fishkin, James. 1982. *The Limits of Obligation* (New Haven, Conn.: Yale University Press).

Fletcher, George P. 1993. *Loyalty: An Essay on the Morality of Relationships* (New York: Oxford University Press).

—— 1996. *Basic Concepts of Legal Thought* (New York: Oxford University Press).

Foot, Philippa. 1978. *Virtues and Vices* (Oxford: Blackwell Publishers).

—— 1985. 'Utilitarianism and the Virtues', *Mind* 94, pp. 196–209.

Frankena, William. 1973. *Ethics*, 2nd edn. (Englewood Cliffs, N.J.: Prentice-Hall) [1st edn. 1963].

—— 1993. 'Brandt's Moral Philosophy in Perspective', in Hooker, ed., 1993b: 189–205.

Frazier, Robert. 1995. 'Moral Relevance and *Ceteris Paribus* Principles', *Ratio* 8: 113–27.

Frey, R. G. 1976. 'Moral Rules', *Philosophical Quarterly* 26: 149–56.

—— 1998. 'The Fear of a Slippery Slope', in G. Dworkin, R. G. Frey, and Sissela Bok, *Euthanasia and Physicial Assisted Suicide: For and Against* (Cambridge: Cambridge University Press), 43–63.

Fried, Charles. 1978. *Right and Wrong* (Cambridge, Mass.: Harvard University Press).

—— 1981. *Contract as Promise: A Theory of Contractual Obligation* (Cambridge, Mass.: Harvard University Press).

Gaut, Berys. 1993. 'Moral Pluralism', *Philosophical Papers* 22: 17–40.

—— 1999. 'Ragbags, Hard Cases, and Moral Pluralism', *Utilitas* 11: 37–48.

—— 2001. 'Justifying Moral Pluralism', in P. Stratton-Lake, ed., *Moral Intuitionism* (Oxford: Clarendon Press).

Gauthier, David. 1986. *Morals By Agreement* (Oxford: Clarendon Press).

Gert, B. 1998. *Morality* (New York: Oxford University Press).

Gewirth, A. 1988. 'Ethical Universalism and Particularity', *Journal of Philosophy* 85: 283–302.

Gibbard, Allan. 1990. *Wise Choices, Apt Feelings: A Theory of Normative Judgement* (Oxford: Clarendon Press).

Glover, Jonathan. 1984. *What Sort of People Should There Be?* (Harmondsworth: Penguin).

Godwin, William. 1793. *An Enquiry Concerning Political Justice*, ed. I. Kramnick (Harmondsworth: Penguin, 1985).

Griffin, James. 1986. *Well-Being: Its Meaning, Measurement and Moral Importance* (Oxford: Clarendon Press).

—— 1992. 'The Human Good and the Ambitions of Consequentialism', *Social Philosophy and Policy* 9: 118–32.

—— 1996. *Value Judgement* (Oxford: Clarendon Press).

Grotius, Hugo. 1625. *On the Law of War and Peace*, transl. by Francis Kelsey (Oxford: Clarendon Press, 1925).

Hampshire, Stuart. 1992. *Innocence and Experience* (Harmondsworth: Penguin).

Hampton, Jean. 1986. *Hobbes and the Social Contract Tradition* (Cambridge: Cambridge University Press).

Hardin, Russell. 1988. *Morality Within the Limits of Reason* (Chicago: University of Chicago Press).

Hare, R. M. 1952. *The Language of Morals* (Oxford: Clarendon Press).

—— 1963. *Freedom and Reason* (Oxford: Clarendon Press).

—— 1975. 'Rawls' Theory of Justice', in Norman Daniels, ed., *Reading Rawls* (Oxford: Blackwell), 81–107.

—— 1981. *Moral Thinking* (Oxford: Clarendon Press).

—— 1984. 'Rights, Utility, and Universalization', in R. G. Frey, ed., *Utility and Rights* (Minneapolis: University of Minnesota Press), 106–20.

—— 1996. 'Foudationalism and Coherentism in Ethics', in Walter Sinnott-

Armstrong and Mark Timmons, eds., *Moral Knowledge?* (New York: Oxford University Press), 190–9.

—— 1998. *Objective Prescriptions* (Oxford: Clarendon Press).

Harman, Gilbert. 1975. 'Moral Relativism Defended', *Philosophical Review* 84: 3–22.

—— 1977. *The Nature of Morality* (New York: Oxford University Press).

—— 1978. 'Morality as Politics', *Midwest Studies in Philosophy* 3: 109–21.

Harrison, J. 1952/3. 'Utilitarianism, Universalisation, and Our Duty to be Just', *Proceedings of the Aristotelian Society* 53: 105–34.

Harrod, R. F. 1936. 'Utilitarianism Revised', *Mind* 45: 137–56.

Harsanyi, John. 1953. 'Cardinal Utility in Welfare Economics and in the Theory of Risk-Taking', *Journal of Political Economy* 61: 434–5.

—— 1955. 'Cardinal Welfare, Individualistic Ethics, and Interpersonal Comparisons of Utility', *Journal of Political Economy* 63: 309–21.

—— 1976. *Essays on Ethics, Social Behaviour and Scientific Explanation* (Dordrecht: Reidel).

—— 1977. 'Rule Utilitarianism and Decision Theory', *Erkenntnis* 11: 25–53.

—— 1982. 'Morality and the Theory of Rational Behaviour', in A. Sen and B. Williams, eds., *Utilitarianism and Beyond* (Cambridge: Cambridge University Press), 39–62.

—— 1993. 'Expectation Effects, Individual Utilities, and Rational Desires', in Hooker 1993b: 115–26.

Hart, H. L. A. 1955. 'Are There Any Natural Rights?', *Philosophical Review* 64: 175–91.

—— 1961. *The Concept of Law* (Oxford: Clarendon Press).

Haslett, D. W. 1987. *Equal Consideration: A Theory of Moral Justification* (Newark, Del.: University of Delaware Press).

—— 1994. *Capitalism With Morality* (Oxford: Clarendon Press).

—— 2000. 'Values, Obligations, and Saving Lives', in B. Hooker, E. Mason, and D. E. Miller, eds., 2000: 71–104.

Hill, Thomas E., Jr. 1971. 'Kant on Imperfect Duty and Supererogation', *Kant-Studien* 72: 55–76.

—— 1987. 'The Importance of Autonomy', in Eva Kittay and D. Meyers, eds., *Women and Moral Theory* (Totowa, N.J.: Rowman & Allanheld), 129–38. Repr. in Hill's *Autonomy and Self-Respect* (New York: Cambridge University Press, 1991), 43–51.

Hobbes, T. 1651. *Leviathan*.

Hodgson, D. H. 1967. *Consequences of Utilitarianism: A Study in Normative Ethics and Legal Theory* (Oxford: Clarendon Press).

Holley, David M. 1997. 'Breaking the Rules When Others Do', *Journal for Applied Philosophy* 14: 159–68.

Holmgren, Margaret. 1987. 'Wide Reflective Equilibrium and Objective Moral Truth', *Metaphilosophy* 18: 108–25.

Holmgren, Margaret. 1989. 'The Wide and Narrow of Reflective Equilibrium', *Canadian Journal of Philosophy* 19: 43–60.

Hooker, Brad. 1990. 'Rule-Consequentialism', *Mind* 99: 67–77.

—— 1991a. 'Rule-Consequentialism and Demandingness: Reply to Carson', *Mind* 100: 269–76.

—— 1991b. 'Brink, Kagan, Utilitarianism and Self-Sacrifice', *Utilitas* 3: 263–73.

—— 1993a. 'Political Philosophy', in L. McHenry and F. Adams, eds., *Reflections on Philosophy* (New York: St. Martin's Press), 92–110.

—— ed. 1993b. *Rationality, Rules, and Utility: New Essays on the Moral Philosophy of Richard Brandt* (Boulder, Colo.: Westview Press).

—— 1994a. 'Is Rule-Consequentialism a Rubber Duck?', *Analysis* 54: 62–7.

—— 1994c. 'Compromising with Convention', *American Philosophical Quarterly* 31: 311–17.

—— 1995. 'Rule-Consequentialism, Incoherence, Fairness', *Proceedings of the Aristotelian Society* 95: 19–35.

—— 1996a. 'Does Being Virtuous Constitute a Benefit to the Agent?' in Roger Crisp, ed., *How Should One Live? New Essays on Virtue Theory* (Oxford: Clarendon Press), 141–55.

—— 1996b. 'Ross-Style Pluralism versus Rule-Consequentialism', *Mind* 105: 531–52.

—— 1997. 'Rule-Utilitarianism and Euthanasia', in Hugh LaFollette, ed., *Ethics in Practice: An Anthology* (Oxford: Blackwell), 42–52.

—— 1998a. 'Rule-Consequentialism and Obligations to the Needy', *Pacific Philosophical Quarterly* 79: 19–33.

—— 1998b. 'Self-Interest, Ethics, and the Profit Motive', in C. Cowton and R. Crisp, eds., *Business Ethics: Perspectives on the Practice of Theory.* (Oxford: Oxford University Press), 27–41.

—— 1999a. 'Sacrificing for the Good of Strangers—Repeatedly' (a critical discussion of Unger 1996), *Philosophy and Phenomenological Research* 59: 177–81.

—— 1999b. 'Reciprocity and Unselfish Friendship', *Cogito* 13: 11–14.

—— 2000a. 'Rule-Consequentialism', in Hugh LaFollette, ed., *Blackwell Guide to Ethical Theory* (Cambridge, Mass.: Blackwell), 183–204.

—— 2000b. 'Moral Particularism—Wrong and Bad', in Hooker and Little, eds., 2000.

—— 2000c. 'Reflective Equilibrium and Rule Consequentialism', in Hooker, Mason, and Miller, eds., 2000: 222–38

—— 2000d. 'Impartiality, Predictability, and Indirect Consequentialism', in Crisp and Hooker, ed., 2000: 129–42.

—— 2001. 'Intuitions and Moral Theorizing', in Philip Stratton-Lake, ed., *Moral Intuitionism* (Oxford: Clarendon Press).

—— and Little, Margaret Olivia, eds. 2000. *Moral Particularism* (Oxford: Clarendon Press).

—— Mason, Elinor, and Miller, Dale E., eds. 2000. *Morality, Rules, and Consequences* (Edinburgh: Edinburgh University Press).

Horton, Keith. 1999. 'The Limits of Human Nature', *Philosophical Quarterly* 49: 452–70.

Hospers, John. 1972. *Human Conduct, Problems of Ethics* (New York: Harcourt Brace Jovanovich).

Howard-Snyder, Frances. 1993. 'Rule Consequentialism is a Rubber Duck', *American Philosophical Quarterly* 30: 271–8.

—— 1997. 'The Rejection of Objective Consequentialism', *Utilitas* 9: 241–8.

Hume, David. 1740. *A Treatise of Human Nature*, ed. L. A. Selby-Bigge, 2nd edn. revised P. H. Nidditch (Oxford: Oxford University Press, 1981).

—— 1741–2. *Essays Moral, Political and Literary* (Oxford University Press, 1963).

—— 1751. *Enquiry Concerning the Principles of Morals*, ed. L. A. Selby-Bigge, 3rd edn. revised P. H. Nidditch (Oxford: Oxford University Press, 1983).

Hurka, Thomas. 1993. *Perfectionism* (New York: Oxford University Press).

—— 2000. *Virtue, Vice, and Value* (New York: Oxford University Press).

Hursthouse, Rosalind. 1999. *On Virtue Ethics* (Oxford: Clarendon Press).

Ihara, Craig. 1981. 'Towards a Rule-Utilitarian Theory of Supererogation', *Philosophical Research Archives* 7: 1418–46.

Jackson, Frank. 1991. 'Decision-Theoretic Consequentialism and the Nearest and Dearest Objection', *Ethics* 101: 461–82.

—— 1998. *From Metaphysics to Ethics: A Defence of Conceptual Analysis* (Oxford: Clarendon Press).

James, William. 1897. 'The Moral Philosopher and the Moral Life', in his *The Will To Believe* (New York: Longmans Green; repr. New York: Dover, 1956), 184–215.

Johnson, Conrad. 1989. 'Character Traits and Objectively Right Action', *Social Theory and Practice* 15: 67–88.

—— 1991. *Moral Legislation* (New York: Cambridge University Press).

Johnson, Oliver. 1959. *Rightness and Goodness* (The Hague: Martinus Nijhoff).

Joseph, H. 1931. *Some Problems in Ethics* (Oxford: Clarendon Press).

Kagan, Shelly. 1989. *The Limits of Morality* (Oxford: Clarendon Press).

—— 1991. 'Replies to My Critics', *Philosophy and Phenomenological Research* 51: 924–5.

—— 1998. *Normative Ethics* (Boulder, Colo.: Westview Press).

—— 1999. 'Equality and Desert', in Pojman and McLeod, eds., 1999: 298–314.

—— 2000. 'Evaluative Focal Points', in Hooker, Mason, and Miller, eds., 2000: 134–55.

200   *References*

Kant, I. 1785. *Foundations of the Metaphysics of Morals.*
——— 1775–80. 'Why we have No Obligations to Animals', in his *Lectures on Ethics*, transl. Louis Infield (London: Methuen, 1930). Repr. in James Rachels, ed., *The Right Thing To Do: Basic Readings in Moral Philosophy* (New York: Random House, 1989), 209–11.
Kavka, Gregory. 1978. 'Some Paradoxes of Deterrence', *Journal of Philosophy* 75: 285–302.
——— 1986. *Hobbesian Moral and Political Theory* (Princeton: Princeton University Press).
——— 1993. 'The Problem of Group Egoism', in B. Hooker, ed., *Rationality, Rules, and Utility* (Boulder, Colo.: Westview Press), 149–63.
Kelly, P. J. 1990. *Utilitarianism and Distributive Justice: Bentham and the Civil Law* (Oxford: Clarendon Press).
Korsgaard, Christine. 1986. 'The Right to Lie: Kant on Dealing with Evil', *Philosophy and Public Affairs* 15: 325–49.
Kumar, Rahul. 1995. 'Consensualism in Principle', D.Phil. thesis, Oxford University.
Kymlicka, Will. 1990. *Contemporary Political Philosophy* (Oxford: Clarendon Press).
LaFollette, Hugh. 1996. *Personal Relationships* (Oxford: Blackwell).
Langton, Rae. 1994. 'Maria von Herbert's Challenge to Kant', in P. Singer, ed., *Ethics* (Oxford: Oxford University Press), 281–94.
Law, Iain. 1999. 'Rule-Consequentialism's Dilemma', *Ethical Theory and Moral Practice* 2: 263–76.
Le Guin, Ursala. 1980. 'The Ones who Walk Away from Omelas', in *The Wind's Twelve Quarters*, vol. ii (St. Albans: Granada), 112–20.
Lehrer, Keith. 1973. *Knowledge* (Oxford: Clarendon Press).
Lucas, George R., Jr. 1990. 'African Famine: New Economic and Ethical Perspectives', *Journal of Philosophy* 87: 629–41.
Lyons, David. 1965. *Forms and Limits of Utilitarianism* (Oxford: Clarendon Press).
——— 2000. 'The Moral Opacity of Utilitarianism', in Hooker, Mason, and Miller, eds., 2000: 105–20.
Mabbott, J. D. 1956. 'Interpretations of Mill's "Utilitarianism"', *Philosophical Quarterly* 6: 115–20.
McClennen, Edward. 1997. 'Pragmatic Rationality and Rules', *Philosophy and Public Affairs* 26: 210–58.
MacIntosh, Duncan. 1990. 'Ideal Moral Codes', *Southern Journal of Philosophy* 28: 389–408.
MacIntyre, Alasdair 1981. *After Virtue* (Notre Dame, Ind.: University of Notre Dame Press).
Mackie, J. L. 1973. 'The Disutility of Act-Utilitarianism', *Philosophical Quarterly* 23: 289–300. Repr. in Mackie 1985c: 91–104.

—— 1977. *Ethics: Inventing Right and Wrong* (Harmondsworth: Penguin).

—— 1978. 'The Law of the Jungle: Moral Alternatives and the Principles of Evolution', *Philosophy* 53: 455–64. Repr. in Mackie 1985c: 120–31.

—— 1982a. 'Co-operation, Competition, and Moral Philosophy', in A. M. Colman, ed., *Cooperation and Competition in Humans and Animals* (Wokingham: Van Nostrand Reinhold). Repr. in Mackie 1985c: 152–69.

—— 1982b. 'Morality and the Retributive Emotions', in Timonthy Stroup, ed., *Edward Westermarck: Essays on his Life and Works* (Helsinki: Acta Philosophica Fennica). Repr. in Mackie 1985c: 206–19.

—— 1985a. 'The Three Stages of Universalization', in Mackie 1985c: 170–83.

—— 1985b. 'Norms and Dilemma', in Mackie 1985c: 234–41.

—— 1985c. *Persons and Values: Selected Papers*, vol. ii, ed. Joan and Penelope Mackie (Oxford: Clarendon Press).

McNaughton, David. 1988. *Moral Vision* (Oxford: Blackwell).

—— 1996. 'An Unconnected Heap of Duties?' *Philosophical Quarterly* 46: 433–47.

—— and Rawling, Piers. 1991. 'Agent-Relativity and the Doing–Happening Distinction', *Philosophical Studies* 63: 167–85.

—— —— 1998. 'On Defending Deontology', *Ratio* 11: 37–54.

—— —— 2000. 'Unprincipled Ethics', in Hooker and Little, eds., 2000.

Mason, Elinor. 1998. 'A Can an Indirect Consequentialist be a Real Friend?' *Ethics* 108: 386–93.

Mill, J. S. 1859. *On Liberty*.

—— 1861. *Utilitarianism*.

Miller, Dale E. 2000. 'Hooker's Use and Abuse of Reflective Equilibrium', in Hooker, Mason, and Miller, eds., 2000: 156–78.

Miller, Richard. 1992. *Moral Differences* (Princeton: Princeton University Press).

Montague, Phillip. 2000. 'Why Rule Consequentialism is Not Superior to Ross-Style Pluralism', in Hooker, Mason, and Miller, eds., 2000: 203–11.

Moore, G. E. 1903. *Principia Ethica* (Cambridge: Cambridge University Press).

Mulgan, Tim. 1994a. 'Satisficing Consequentialism', *Ratio* 6: 121–34.

—— 1994b. 'Rule Consequentialism and Famine', *Analysis* 54: 187–92.

—— 1996. 'One False Virtue of Rule Consequentialism and One New Vice', *Pacific Philosophical Quarterly* 77: 362–73.

—— 2000. 'Ruling Out Rule Consequentialism', in Hooker, Mason, and Miller, eds., 2000: 212–21.

Murphy, Liam. 1993. 'The Demands of Beneficence', *Philosophy and Public Affairs* 22: 267–92.

—— 1997. 'A Relatively Plausible Principle of Benevolence: A Reply to Mulgan', *Philosophy and Public Affairs* 26: 80–6.

Nagel, Thomas. 1972. *The Possibility of Altruism* (Princeton: Princeton University Press).

—— 1979. 'Fragmentation of Value', in his *Mortal Questions* (Cambridge: Cambridge University Press), 128–41.

—— 1986. *The View from Nowhere* (New York: Oxford University Press).

—— 1991. *Equality and Partiality* (New York: Oxford University Press).

—— 1995. 'Personal Rights and Public Space', *Philosophy and Public Affairs* 24: 381–9.

—— 1997. *The Last Word* (New York: Oxford University Press).

Nelson, Mark. 1991. 'Intuitionism and Subjectivism', *Metaphilosophy* 22: 115–21.

Nowell-Smith, P. 1954. *Ethics* (London: Penguin).

Nozick, Robert. 1974. *Anarchy, State, and Utopia* (Oxford: Blackwell).

—— 1981. *Philosophical Explanations* (Oxford: Clarendon Press).

—— 1989. *The Examined Life* (New York: Simon & Schuster).

O'Neill, Onora. 1986. *Faces of Hunger* (London: Allen & Unwin).

Overvold, Mark. 1980. 'Self-Interest and the Concept of Self-Sacrifice', *Canadian Journal of Philosophy* 10: 105–18.

—— 1982. 'Self-Interest and Getting What you Want', in H. B. Miller and W. H. Williams, eds., *The Limits of Utilitarianism* (Minneapolis: University of Minnesota Press), 186–94.

Parfit, Derek. 1984. *Reasons and Persons* (Oxford: Clarendon Press).

—— 1997. 'Equality and Priority', *Ratio* 10: 202–21.

Pettit, Philip. 1987. 'Universalisability without Utilitarianism', *Mind* 96: 74–82.

—— 1991. 'Consequentialism', in Peter Singer, ed., *Companion to Ethics* (Oxford: Blackwell), 230–40.

—— 1994. 'Consequentialism and Moral Psychology', *International Journal of Philosophical Studies* 2: 1–17.

—— 1997. 'The Consequentialist Perspective', in M. Baron, P. Pettit, and M. Slote, *Three Methods of Ethics* (Malden, Mass.: Blackwell), 92–174.

—— and Brennan, G. 1986. 'Restrictive Consequentialism', *Australasian Journal of Philosophy* 64: 438–55.

Plato. *Protagoras*.

—— *The Republic*.

Pojman, Louis, and McLeod, Owen, eds. 1999. *What Do We Deserve?* (New York: Oxford University Press).

Powers, Madison. 1993. 'Contractualist Impartiality and Personal Commitments', *American Philosophical Quarterly* 30: 63–71.

—— 2000. 'Rule Consequentialism and the Value of Friendship', in Hooker, Mason, and Miller, eds., 2000: 239–54.

Price, Richard. 1787. *A Review of the Principal Questions of Morals*. Repr. in Raphael 1969: vol. ii, paras. 655–762, pp. 131–98.

Prichard, H. A. 1912. 'Does Moral Philosophy Rest on a Mistake?' *Mind* 21: 21–37.

Pufendorf, Samuel. 1672. *De Jure Naturae et Gentium*, transl. C. H. Oldfather and W. A. Oldfather as *The Law of Nature and of Nations* (Oxford: Clarendon Press, 1934).

Quinn, Warren. 1993. *Morality and Action* (New York: Cambridge University Press).

Rachels, James. 1993. *The Elements of Moral Philosophy*, 2nd edn. (New York: McGraw-Hill).

Railton, Peter. 1984. 'Alienation, Consequentialism, and the Demands of Morality', *Philosophy and Public Affairs* 13: 174–31.

Rakowski, Eric. 1991. *Equal Justice* (Oxford: Clarendon Press).

—— 1993. 'Taking and Saving Lives', *Columbia Law Review* 93: 1063–1156.

Raphael, D. D., ed. 1969. *The British Moralists* (Oxford: Clarendon Press).

—— 1994. *Moral Philosophy*, 2nd. edn. (Oxford: Oxford University Press).

Rawls, John. 1951. 'Outline for a Decision Procedure in Ethics', *Philosophical Review* 60: 177–97.

—— 1955. 'Two Concepts of Rules', *Philosophical Review* 64: 3–32.

—— 1958. 'Justice as Fairness', *Philosophical Review* 67: 164–94.

—— 1971. *A Theory of Justice* (Cambridge, Mass.: Harvard University Press).

—— 1974/5. 'The Independence of Moral Theory', *Proceedings and Addresses of the American Philosophical Association* 48: 5–22.

—— 1980. 'Kantian Constructivism in Moral Theory', *Journal of Philosophy* 77: 515–72.

Rescher, Nicholas. 1966. *Distributive Justice* (Indianapolis: Bobbs-Merrill).

Regan, Donald. 1980. *Utilitarianism and Co-operation* (Oxford: Clarendon Press).

—— 1997. 'Value, Comparability, and Choice', in R. Chang, ed., *Incommensurability, Incomparability, and Practical Reason* (Cambridge, Mass.: Harvard University Press), 129–50.

Reibetanz, Sophia. 1998. 'Contractualism and Aggregation', *Ethics* 108: 296–311.

Reid, Thomas. 1788. *Essays on the Active Powers of Man*. Repr. in Raphael, ed., 1969: vol. ii, 265–310.

Riley, Jonathan. 1998. 'Mill on Justice', in D. Boucher and P. Kelly, eds., *Social Justice: From Hume to Walzer* (London: Routledge), 45–66.

—— 2000. 'Defending Rule Utilitarianism', in Hooker, Mason, and Miller, eds., 2000: 40–70.

Rosen, Fred. 1998. 'Individual Sacrifice and the Greatest Happiness: Bentham on Utility and Rights', *Utilitas* 10: 129–43.

Ross, W. D. 1930. *The Right and the Good* (Oxford: Clarendon Press).

—— 1939. *Foundations of Ethics* (Oxford: Clarendon Press).

204   *References*

Sayre-McCord, Geoffrey. 1986. 'Coherence and Models for Moral Theorizing', *Pacific Philosophical Quarterly* 18: 170–90.

—— 1996. 'Coherentist Epistemology and Moral Theory', in W. Sinnott-Armstrong and M. Timmons, eds., *Moral Knowledge?* (New York: Oxford University Press), 137–59.

Scanlon, T. M. 1978. 'Rights, Goals, and Fairness', in S. Hampshire, ed., *Public and Private Morality* (Cambridge: Cambridge University Press, 1978), 93–111.

—— 1982. 'Contractualism and Utilitarianism', in A. Sen and B. Williams, eds., *Utilitarianism and Beyond* (Cambridge: Cambridge University Press), 103–28.

—— 1992. 'The Aims and Authority of Moral Theory', *Oxford Journal of Legal Studies* 12: 288–303.

—— 1993. 'Value, Desire, and Quality of Life', in M. Nussbaum and A. Sen, eds., *The Quality of Life* (Oxford: Clarendon Press), 185–200.

—— 1998. *What We Owe Each Other* (Cambridge, Mass.: Harvard University Press).

Scarre, Geoffrey. 1996. *Utilitarianism* (London: Routledge).

Schaller, Walter. 1990. 'Are Virtues No More than Dispositions to Obey Moral Rules?', *Philosophia* 20: 195–207.

Schauer, Frederick. 1991. *Playing By the Rules: A Philosophical Examination of Rule-Based Decision-Making in Law and in Life* (Oxford: Clarendon Press).

Scheffler, S. 1982. *The Rejection of Consequentialism* (Oxford: Clarendon Press).

—— 1985. 'Agent-Centred Restrictions, Rationality, and the Virtues', *Mind* 94: 409–19.

—— 1986. 'Morality's Demands and their Limits', *Journal of Philosophy* 83: 531–7.

—— 1989. 'Deontology and the Agent', *Ethics* 100: 67–76. Repr. in Scheffler 1994: 152–66.

—— 1992. *Human Morality* (New York: Oxford University Press).

—— 1994: *The Rejection of Consequentialism*, rev. edn. (Oxford: Clarendon Press).

Schneewind, Jeremy. 1990. 'The Misfortunes of Virtue', *Ethics* 101: 42–63.

Sellars, Wilfred. 1973. 'Givenness and Explanatory Coherence', *Journal of Philosophy* 70: 612–82.

Sen, Amartya. 1973. *On Economic Inequality* (Oxford: Clarendon Press).

—— 1982. 'Rights and Agency', *Philosophy and Public Affairs* 11: 3–38.

—— 1994. 'Population: Delusion and Reality', *New York Review of Books*, September 22.

—— and Williams, B. 1982. 'Introduction', in Sen and Williams, eds.,

Utilitarianism and Beyond (Cambridge: Cambridge University Press, 1982).

Sencerz, Stefan. 1986. 'Moral Intuitions and Justification in Ethics', *Philosophical Studies* 50: 77–95.

Shafer-Landau, Russ. 1997. 'Moral Rules', *Ethics* 107: 584–611.

Shaw, William. 1993. 'Welfare, Equality, and Distribution: Brandt from the Left', in Hooker, ed., 1993b: 165–87.

—— 1999. *Contemporary Ethics: Taking Account of Utilitarianism* (Malden, Mass.: Blackwell).

Sidgwick, Henry. 1907. *Methods of Ethics*, 7th edn. (London: Macmillan).

Singer, Brent. 1988. 'An Extension of Rawls's Theory of Justice to Environmental Ethics', *Environmental Ethics* 10: 217–32.

Singer, Marcus, 1955. 'Generalization in Ethics', *Mind* 64: 361–75.

—— 1961. *Generalization in Ethics* (New York: Alfred Knopf).

Singer, Peter. 1972a. 'Famine, Affluence and Morality', *Philosophy and Public Affairs* 1: 229–43.

—— 1972b. 'Is Act-Utilitarianism Self-Defeating?' *Philosophical Review* 81: 94–104.

—— 1993. *Practical Ethics*, 2nd edn. (Cambridge: Cambridge University Press).

Skorupski, John. 1992. 'Value and Distribution', in M. Hollis and W. Vossenkuhl, eds., *Moralische, Entscheidung and rationale Wahl* (Munich: R. Oldenbourg).

—— 1995. 'Agent-Neutrality, Consequentialism, Utilitarianism . . . A Terminological Note', *Utilitas* 7: 49–54.

—— 1996. 'Ethics', in N. Bunnin and E. P. Tsui-James, eds., *The Blackwell Companion to Philosophy* (Oxford: Blackwell), 198–228.

Slote, Michael. 1984. 'Satisficing Consequentialism', *Proceedings of the Aristotelian Society* suppl. vol. 58: 139–63.

—— 1985. *Common-Sense Morality and Consequentialism* (London: Routledge & Kegan Paul).

—— 1989. *Beyond Optimizing* (Cambridge, Mass.: Harvard University Press).

—— 1992. *From Morality to Virtue* (New York: Oxford University Press).

Smart, J. J. C. 1956. 'Extreme and Restricted Utilitarianism', *Philosophical Quarterly* 6: 344–54.

—— 1973. 'Outline of a System of Utilitarian Ethics', in J. J. C. Smart and Bernard Williams, *Utilitarianism: For and Against* (Cambridge: Cambridge University Press), 3–74.

Sorensen, Roy. 1988. Blindspots (Oxford: Clarendon Press).

—— 1996. 'Unknowable Obligations', *Utilitas* 7: 247–71.

—— Forthcoming. 'Vagueness Has No Function in Law.'

Stevenson, C. L. 1944. *Ethics and Language* (New Haven, Conn.: Yale University Press).

Stout, A. K. 1954. 'But Suppose Everyone Did the Same', *Australasian Journal of Philosophy* 32: 1–29.

Strang, Colin. 1960. 'What if Everyone Did That?', *Durham University Journal* 23: 5–10.

Stratton-Lake, Philip. 1997. 'Can Hooker's Rule-Consequentialist Principle Justify Ross's Prima Facie Duties?', *Mind* 106: 151–8.

Strawson, P. F. 1961. 'Social Morality and Individual Ideal', *Philosophy* 36: 1–17.

Sturgeon, Nicholas. 1986. 'What Difference does it Make whether Moral Realism is True?', *Southern Journal of Philosophy* 24, Supplement, 115–41.

Sumner, L. W. 1987. *The Moral Foundations of Rights* (Oxford: Clarendon Press).

—— 1996. *Welfare, Happiness, and Ethics* (Oxford: Clarendon Press).

—— 2000. 'Something In Between', in Crisp and Hooker, eds., 2000: 1–19.

Svavarsdóttir, Sigrún. 1999. Review of Griffin 1996, *Mind* 108: 165–70.

Temkin, Larry. 1993. *Inequality* (New York: Oxford University Press).

Thomas, Alan. 2000. 'Consequentialism and the Subversion of Pluralism', in Hooker, Mason, and Miller, eds., 2000: 179–202.

Thomson, Judith Jarvis. 1990. *The Realm of Rights* (Cambridge, Mass.: Harvard University Press).

Timmons, Mark. 1999. *Morality Without Foundations: A Defense of Moral Contextualism* (New York: Oxford University Press).

Toulmin, Stephen 1950. *An Examination of the Place of Reason in Ethics* (Cambridge: Cambridge University Press).

Trianosky, Gregory. 1976. 'Rule-Utilitarianism and the Slippery Slope', *Journal of Philosophy* 75: 414–24.

—— 1988. 'Rightly Ordered Appetites: How to Live Morally and Live Well', *American Philosophical Quarterly* 25: 1–12.

—— 1990. 'What is Virtue Ethics All About?' *American Philosophical Quarterly* 27: 335–44.

Ullmann-Margalit, E. 1977. *The Emergence of Norms* (Oxford: Clarendon Press).

Unger, Peter. 1996. *Living High and Letting Die: Our Illusion of Innocence* (New York: Oxford University Press).

Urmson, J. O. 1953. 'The Interpretation of the Moral Philosophy of J. S. Mill', *Philosophical Quarterly*, 3: 33–9.

—— 1975. 'A Defence of Intuitionism', *Proceedings of the Aristotelian Society* 75: 144–52.

Vallentyne, Peter. 1991a. 'The Problem of Unauthorized Welfare', *Noûs* 25: 295–321.

—— ed. 1991b. *Contractarianism and Rational Choice* (New York: Cambridge University Press).

Van der Maas, P. J. *et al.* 1991. 'Euthanasia and Other Medical Decisions Regarding End of Life', *Lancet* 338: 669–74.

VanDeveer, Donald. 1979. 'Of Beasts, Persons, and the Original Position', *Monist* 62: 368–77.

Warnock, G. J. 1971. *The Object of Morality* (London: Methuen).

Williamson, Timothy. 1994. *Vagueness* (London: Routledge).

Williams, Bernard. 1972. *Morality: An Introduction to Ethics* (New York: Harper & Row).

—— 1973. 'A Critique of Utilitarianism', in J. J. C. Smart and B. Williams, *Utilitarianism: For and Against* (Cambridge: Cambridge University Press), 77–150

—— 1979. 'Conflicts of Value', in Alan Ryan, ed., *The Idea of Freedom: Essays in Honour of Isaiah Berlin* (Oxford: Oxford University Press). Repr. in Williams 1981: 221–32.

—— 1981. *Moral Luck* (Cambridge: Cambridge University Press)

—— 1982. 'The Point of View of the Universe: Sidgwick and the Ambitions of Ethics', *The Cambridge Review*, 7 May. Repr. in Williams 1995: 153–71.

—— 1985. *Ethics and the Limits of Philosophy* (Cambridge, Mass.: Harvard University Press).

—— 1988. 'What Does Intuitionism Imply?', in Jonathan Dancy, J. Moravcsik, and C. C. W. Taylor, eds., *Human Agency: Language, Duty, Value* (Stanford, Calif.: Stanford University Press), 189–98. Repr. in Williams 1995: 182–91.

—— 1995. *Making Sense of Humanity and Other Essays* (Cambridge: Cambridge University Press).

Witt, L. A. 1984. 'Acceptance and the Problem of Slippery-Slope Insensitivity in Rule-Utilitarianism', *Dialogue* 23: 649–59.

Wolf, Susan. 1982. 'Moral Saints', *Journal of Philosophy* 79: 419–39. Repr. in R. Crisp and M. Slote, eds., *Virtue Ethics* (Oxford: Oxford University Press, 1997), 80–98.

—— 1997. 'Happiness and Meaning: Two Aspects of the Good Life', *Social Philosophy and Policy* 14: 207–25.

Wood, Alan. 1958. *Bertrand Russell: The Passionate Skeptic* (New York: Simon & Schuster).

World Bank. 1990. *World Development Report 1990* (New York: Oxford University Press).

INDEX